Watching Baseball,
Seeing Philosophy

Watching Baseball, Seeing Philosophy

The Great Thinkers at Play on the Diamond

RAYMOND ANGELO BELLIOTTI

McFarland & Company, Inc., Publishers
Jefferson, North Carolina, and London

LIBRARY OF CONGRESS CATALOGUING-IN-PUBLICATION DATA

Belliotti, Raymond Angelo, 1948–
    Watching baseball, seeing philosophy : the great thinkers
at play on the diamond / Raymond Angelo Belliotti.
        p.   cm.
    Includes bibliographical references and index.

    ISBN 978-0-7864-3303-2
    softcover : 50# alkaline paper ∞

    1. Baseball — Philosophy.   2. Baseball players.
3. Philosophers.   I. Title.
GV862.5.B425   2008
796.35701 — dc22   2007051485

British Library cataloguing data are available

Cover images ©2008 Shutterstock

Manufactured in the United States of America

*McFarland & Company, Inc., Publishers
    Box 611, Jefferson, North Carolina 28640
    www.mcfarlandpub.com*

For Marcia, Angelo, and Vittoria

Tutto vince chi ha vinto le proprie passioni

Acknowledgments

I owe debts of gratitude to Joanne Foeller for her exceptional word processing, editing, and indexing skills, and unvarying good cheer; to the *Journal of Social Philosophy*, Rodopi Editions, and Rowman & Littlefield for permission to adapt my previously published work; to the basketball and baseball players whom I have been privileged to coach; to the men too numerous to mention with whom I have coached, but in the past few years, Tony Bongiovanni, Bruce Chapman, Chuck Graves, Dick Kern, and Paul Lombardo; to my father, Angelo Belliotti, an excellent athlete who always reminded me that academics come first; and to my family — Marcia, Angelo, and Vittoria — for everything.

Table of Contents

Preface

Why am I here? What is my destiny? How should I live my life? The questions most fundamental to human existence vivified the activity of philosophy in the earliest recorded times. Prior to the rise and triumph of organized religions, societies turned to philosophers for guidance on such critical topics.

The answers to the most fundamental questions of life are contestable and revisable. Part of the human condition is that the answers we most desperately seek cannot be discovered once and forever, incontestable and pristine. We are fated to search continually, never embracing certitudes or securing glad tidings. Yet search we must because to evade the process is to relinquish a crucial dimension of our humanity.

Sports have been called a natural religion in America. The rituals, allegiances, struggles, and symbolisms energize our spirits and animate our secular faith. A few years ago, I was struck by how the lives and careers of baseball players illustrated or challenged the classical wisdom of Western philosophy.

The intensity and single-mindedness of Ted Williams breathed life into the ancient myth of Sisyphus invoked so cleverly by Albert Camus.

Billy Martin's maniacal competitiveness on the baseball field conjured comparisons to Niccolò Machiavelli's transformation of politics into a zero-sum contest.

Satchel Paige's homespun philosophy and cunning adaptation to his hostile environment summoned forth the Stoic wisdom of Marcus Aurelius.

The many facets of Joe DiMaggio's persona cried out for resolution in light of Friedrich Nietzsche's doctrine of perspectivism.

The unsurpassed calm and management skills of Joe Torre were reminiscent of Aristotle's theories of friendship and personal relations.

The social impact of Jackie Robinson unknowingly followed the script for nonviolent revolution penned by Antonio Gramsci.

The rise, fall, and redemption of Mickey Mantle demonstrated aspects of faith, reason, and human response crafted by St. Thomas Aquinas centuries earlier.

The superstitions of players such as John Franco involved connections between truth, belief, action, and performance that guided much of the work of William James.

And Jose Canseco's unsqueamish use of performance-enhancing drugs raised moral questions that once confronted Immanuel Kant.

Bringing philosophical reasoning to bear on matters of practical concern to everyday people is less difficult than academic philosophers might first suppose. The task is easier when the lives and careers of celebrated sports figures so neatly dovetail with major themes in the discipline. The careers of nine baseball players and the words of nine philosophers can help teach us how to lead robustly meaningful, valuable lives. Such is the genesis of this book.

First Inning

Ted Williams and Albert Camus

"Like a feather caught in a vortex, Williams ran around the square of bases at the center of our beseeching screaming. He ran as he always ran out home runs — hurriedly, unsmiling, head down, as if our praise were a storm of rain to get out of. He didn't tip his cap. Though we thumped, wept, and chanted 'We want Ted' for minutes after he hid in the dugout, he did not come back. Our noise for some seconds passed beyond excitement into a kind of immense open anguish, a wailing, a cry to be saved. But immortality is nontransferable. The papers said that the other players, and even the umpires on the field, begged him to come out and acknowledge us in some way, but he refused. Gods do not answer letters."

— John Updike (describing the final at bat of Ted Williams)[1]

The dream of becoming the best hitter in baseball history drove Ted Williams (1918–2002). Albert Camus (1913–1960), after declaring the world and human life inherently meaningless, was inspired to celebrate the fragile meaning and purpose he thought human beings could create and enjoy. Williams was a human exemplar of Camus's prescribed images of meaning and purpose.

"I am Ted bleeping Williams, the best bleeping hitter who ever lived."

Ted Williams churned with ambition. Raised in an unsupportive family environment by his alcoholic Scotch-Irish father and his indifferent Mexican-Basque mother, young Ted was unloved, unwanted, and frightened. His mother was deeply devoted to the causes of the Salvation Army and seemed to care more for the abstract needy in distant lands than she did for her own sons. His father owned a photographic shop, at least when he was not drinking excessively or out of work. Ted's younger brother, Danny, was a small-time thief who was well acquainted with local jails. After Ted became wealthy and famous, his mother would often ask him for money. Having provided well for his mother at this point in their lives, Ted knew that the money was earmarked for Danny's latest difficulty.

His mother was an enabler of her younger son's weaknesses and an exploiter of her older son's success. His parents divorced after Ted's rookie season in the majors.

Ted turned the profound insecurities that stalked him into allies. Blessed with athletic talent, he pursued his dream of becoming the greatest hitter in major league history with avaricious single-mindedness. Ted reached the major leagues in 1939 with the Boston Red Sox and crushed baseballs for over 19 seasons. During his career, Williams totaled 521 home runs, batted .344, with an on base percentage of .482 and a slugging percentage of .634. He is widely regarded as the best hitter of his era.

Williams accomplished his prodigious feats even though he lost almost five full seasons to military service during World War II and the Korean War. Ted was not a deeply reflective person except for the few projects in which he invested massive emotional energy. Hitting a baseball, of course, was his first passion. Trained as a Marine fighter pilot, Williams was so skillful that for a time he served as John Glenn's wingman. Ted flew over three dozen combat missions, earning several air medals. Somewhat out of necessity, flying under pressure become his second passion. After he retired, he settled in Islamorada and became an avid, uncommonly knowledgeable fisherman. Specializing in bonefish, tarpon, and salmon, Williams was eventually recognized as one of the greatest anglers of his time.

> [Williams] wasn't a nice guy. He was an impossibly high-wide-and-handsome, out-sized, obstreperous major-league *overload* of a man who dominated dugouts and made grand any ground he played on — because his great warrior heart could fill ten ballparks.[2]

Albert Camus and Cosmic Meaninglessness

Camus revived the ancient myth of Sisyphus. Condemned by the gods to push a huge rock to the top of a hill from which it fell down the other side, to be pushed again to the top from which it fell again, and so on forever, Sisyphus was doomed to futile, pointless, unrewarded labor. His immortality was part of his punishment. His consciousness of the futility of his project was his tragedy.

Sisyphus's life supposedly represents the human condition: repetitious, meaningless, pointless toil that adds up to nothing in the end. The myth portrays the eternal human struggle and indestructible human spirit. Although Sisyphus is not mortal, that deepens and does not redeem the absurdity of his life. Some might think that while human life bears more variety than Sisyphus's life, the matter is only one of degree.

Some humans take solace in producing and raising children, but that can be viewed as more of the same: adding zeros to zeros. Unlike Sisyphus, we are mortal and our children — the next generation — assume our burdens when we expire.

Camus argues that human beings desperately crave inherent value, meaning, and a rational cosmos, but discover only a neutral, meaningless, indifferent universe. We cry out for understanding and for answers to our most fundamental questions, but the universe is silent. The enormous gap between these human needs and an unresponsive universe is the crux of absurdity. Once we recognize the absence of a master plan and the absurdity of our existence, we underscore our own insignificance, our alienation, and lack of ultimate hope. In the end, our acts are futile. The absurd is not a philosophical concept, but a lived experience. Centuries earlier, Marcus Aurelius had turned to Stoicism as an antidote to the possibility of cosmic meaninglessness. Marcus insisted that faith in (the unprovable) meaning and purpose built into the world was necessary for vibrant living. Camus would deride Marcus Aurelius's choice as an inauthentic, psychological crutch. Instead, Camus concluded that we cannot transcend or destroy the absurd, but we can forge and manifest our characters by our response to it.[3] Absurdity involves ridiculous incongruity. Extreme irrationality, a striking disharmony or discrepancy between states of affairs, and unrealistic pretension typically constitute the absurd. According to Camus, three responses to the absurd are available. First, we can seek the false consolations of psychological crutches. The most common crutch is religious commitment which desperately tries to eliminate the absurd by fabricating a possibility for attaining our deepest cravings. Inherent value, meaning, and a rational cosmos may not be available to us in this lifetime, but leading our life in prescribed ways will earn redemption and ultimate fulfillment in an afterlife. Alternatively, we could take the approach of Marcus Aurelius: personal immortality is unavailable to us but we nevertheless play a role in the progress of an inherently purposive universe. If we lack the faith or imagination required for religious commitment, another kind of psychological crutch centers on denying our yearnings for inherent value, meaning, and a rational cosmos. If we do not desire this lofty trinity, then the benign indifference of the universe is untroubling. Both psychological-crutch strategies allow us to pretend that human life is not absurd. Camus regards these mechanisms of denial as inauthentic, weak, and unworthy of us. They seek flight in fantasy as a distraction from robust confrontation with our fate.

Second, we can always commit suicide. But Camus views ultimate despair as cowardly. Peering into the profound void and feeling the hot breath of nothingness, we cravenly evade our fate by ending our lives. While suicide may be rational under the direst conditions — when we can no longer benefit from or contribute to our most cherished projects, interests, relationships, and commitments — under ordinary circumstances it bears no honor.

Third, Camus understands that most human beings continue to act on their preferences, values, and concerns despite a sense of cosmic meaninglessness, an awareness that no preordained or built-in meaning or value permeates our universe. Camus's preferred authentic response requires awareness of the absurd, living life in the face of our fate, affirming life through rebellion, maximizing life's intensity, and dying unreconciled.

Williams and His Critics

To call his personality large or compelling is too weak. Ted Williams did not speak, he bellowed. Ted Williams did not argue, he pontificated. Ted Williams did not excel, he dominated. Ted Williams did not pepper his discourse with profanity, he seasoned his profanity with discourse. The insecurities of his youth made every disagreement a major contest, every slight an unforgiveable insult. His intelligence was belligerent, his will was uncompromising, his passion for excellence in those areas of his concern was boundless. Although impatient, uncomfortable, and anxious in normal circumstances, Williams was controlled, poised, and startlingly effective in perilous situations. More than anything else, Williams was never wrong — at least in his own mind — about those matters that interested him most.

> You had to accommodate him, because he could not accommodate you ... he had never bent to fashion.... Here was a man who had always been true to himself.... There were critics everywhere. He always fought back. He fought back when he was in the right, and he fought back when he was in the wrong, on the theory that he was never wrong.... Everything became an issue of personal honor and integrity.... He was so easily wounded, yet he could also just as easily wound other people without realizing it.... Every slight seemed so permanent with him.[4]

During his playing career, Williams often exploded at his perceived critics. He often gave the finger to annoying fans, sometimes spat in their direction, and was invariably dismissive of or abusive to sportswriters, whom he derided as "knights of the keyboard."

His basic offense against the fans has been to wish they weren't there. Seeking a perfectionist's vacuum, he has quixotically desired to sever the game from the round of paid spectatorship and publicity that supports it. Hence his refusal to tip his cap to the crowd or turn the other cheek to newsmen.[5]

Despite his stunning batting statistics, his detractors concentrated on Williams's imperfections: he had a poor throwing arm, fielded carelessly, lacked foot speed, and was an undistinguished base runner.

More pointedly, they attacked his batting philosophy and clutch performance. Williams refused to expand the strike zone and offer at pitches that were balls even if he was at bat with runners in scoring position. He reasoned that once batters began swinging at pitches outside the strike zone, this approach would become habitual, or at least more common, and pitchers would gain a general advantage. To swing at a pitch outside the strike zone was to court disaster for one's overall hitting strategy. Williams did not attain a career .482 on base percentage by swinging at bad pitches. His methods led to hundreds of bases on balls. Also, pitchers knew he would not offer at tosses outside the strike zone and were often forced to hurl more pitches over the middle of home plate, Ted's hot zone for batting success. From Williams's perspective, swinging only at pitches in the strike zone was by far the best strategy for long-term batting success. Nitpickers insisted, though, that Williams's approach selfishly put the sanctity of his batting statistics ahead of team goals. By contrast, the great Joe DiMaggio's teams won and he often expanded his strike zone with runners in scoring position. Maybe his batting average was a tad lower than Ted's at the end of the year, but Joe, unlike Ted, seemed to drive in the big runs in clutch situations.

In the ten biggest games of his life, his detractors continued, Ted Williams came up small. In his only World Series, against the St. Louis Cardinals in 1946, he hit only .200 with 1 RBI and no extra base hits in 7 games. The Red Sox lost. In the 1948 playoff game against the Cleveland Indians to decide the American League pennant, Williams managed only one single in four trips to the plate and also made an error in the outfield. The Red Sox lost. In 1949, the Red Sox traveled to New York with a one game lead in the pennant race with two games to play. Needing to win only one of the two games to claim the American League championship, the Red Sox blew a four run lead in the first contest, losing 5–4. Williams went 1 for 3 with no RBI. Going into the final game tied with the Yankees, the Red Sox lost 5–3 and blew the pennant. Williams went 0 for 2 and in the outfield misplayed a ball that should have been a double into a triple. The misplay led to a Yankees run in the first inning. In those ten crucial contests, Williams hit a cumulative .206 (7 for 34) with no extra base hits and only one measly RBI. His slugging percentage was also a dainty .206.

In nineteen seasons, some of which found him surrounded by extraordinary teammates such as Rudy York, Bobby Doerr, Dominic DiMaggio, Johnny Pesky, Vern Stephens, Billy Goodman, Mel Parnell, Ellis Kinder, Tex Hughson, and Boo Ferriss, Ted's Red Sox participated in only one World Series. The Red Sox fell short by one game in 1948 and 1949, and were four games in arrears in 1950. The team was just good enough to lose with and Ted Williams was the vortex of controversy.

Camus and Fragile, Human Meaning

Sisyphus embodies the existential hero. He relentlessly confronts his fate, refuses to yield, rejects psychological crutches, embraces no doomed hopes for release, and creates a fragile meaning through endless rebellion and luxuriating in the immediacy of life. Camus imagines Sisyphus "happy" as the "struggle itself toward the heights is enough to fill a man's heart."[6] Camus oscillates, then, between two responses Sisyphus might embrace to wrench conditional meaning from his absurd context.

Sisyphus as Cool Hand Luke. Paul Newman played the lead role in the 1960s film *Cool Hand Luke*. Luke is a victim of the brutality and sadistic discipline of his chain-gang wardens, but also of the indirect cruelty arising from the idolization of his fellow prisoners. He treats his jailors with defiance, endures their abuse, escapes only to be recaught, wins the admiration of his fellow prisoners, struggles mightily to maintain his pride and will, but is eventually hunted down and killed. This movie fits well much of Camus's description of one of Sisyphus's possibilities for constructing meaning.

Camus advises Sisyphus to meet the gods of the myth with scorn and rebellion. He must condemn the gods for condemning him. Fueled by resentment and bravado, Sisyphus refuses to bend or to beg for relief. He cannot live within an overbearing cosmic perspective from which his life is insignificant, so Sisyphus revels in his hardness and endurance. He creates virtues out of contempt, pride, and strength. Like a stubborn army recruit sentenced to continually dig and fill the same hole in turn, Sisyphus's victory is in his refusal to seek the consolations of ordinary human beings. He will not admit defeat or yield. He will not ask his tormentors, whom he regards with disdain, for mercy: they can control his body but cannot influence his mind. Sisyphus lays a patina of defiance on extraordinary mental toughness. His attitude is a monument to the human spirit: authenticity leavened by determination.

Sisyphus turns the gods' sentence into a test. He resolves not to yield to the futility and boredom that would crush ordinary spirits. He will show the gods that he will not be defeated. He will take the punishment and come back for more. Through his defiance, Sisyphus will prove to himself and the gods that his is not a common spirit. He will forge an eternal project from what is an inherently futile, meaningless, mundane task.

The image invokes mixed blessings. Some of us will admire Sisyphus's heroism and defiance as he distances himself from typical human reactions. He has proved himself superior to his peers and has denied the gods the added satisfaction of watching him writhe in misery. Oriana Fallaci, in her memorable novel, *A Man*, captures well the allure of the rebellious spirit:

> The true hero never surrenders, he is distinguished from the others not by the great initial exploit or the pride with which he faces tortures and death but by the constancy with which he repeats himself, the patience with which he suffers and reacts, the pride with which he hides his sufferings and flings them back in the face of the one who has ordered them. Not resigning himself is his secret, not considering himself a victim, not showing others his sadness or despair.[7]

Other people, though, will not embrace Sisyphus's self-styled martyrdom. Fueled by resentment, utterly detached from commitment beyond rebellion, intolerant of lesser responses, and keenly aware of his punishment, Sisyphus may embody a destructive romanticism.

Robert Solomon, for example, is deeply ambivalent about Camus's embrace of rebellion and scorn as an antidote to an inherently meaningless universe:

> There is something both beautiful and pathetic in [Camus's] quasi-rational, emphatically existential attitude. Shaking that puny fist at God or the gods is so poignantly human, so pointless, and at the same time meaningful. Of course, such behavior makes no conceivable difference to anything, except in our own attitudes.... But what is beautiful and revealing about [Camus and other like-minded existentialists] is precisely their refusal either to dismiss [the philosophical question about the meaning of life] or to despair at the answer. They provoke an irresolvable tension ... between our passionate commitments and our awareness that, nevertheless, our lives are ultimately not in our hands.[8]

Is Sisyphus a robust battler or is he a fugitive from life? Does the martyrdom of Sisyphus bear victory or does it confer additional power on the gods' decree?

Sisyphus is and his project does all of these. Critics might insist that to assume this perspective is to reject life. But others will rejoin that we should never embrace the oppressor. And if the universe lacks inherent value and meaning then life is an oppressor. All that remains is the refusal to yield.

Sisyphus as Flowmeister. Camus offers Sisyphus another possibility: to bask in the immediacy of his life, to engage in the process of living to the fullest extent, to immerse himself in the textures of experience. Sisyphus should avert his gaze from questions of what he is accomplishing by hurling himself into his task with gusto. He must pay close attention to the rock as it travels and to the textures of his journey. By luxuriating in the process of life and by living in the present, to the extent possible, Sisyphus makes the rock his own. He is so thoroughly engaged in his task that the meaning of his life is single-minded engagement. From this perspective, Sisyphus is too busy and too fascinated with the wonders surrounding his journey to focus on contempt for the gods: "Each atom of that stone, each mineral flake of that nightfilled mountain, in itself forms a world."[9]

Ken Ravizza and Tom Hanson capture well the image of Sisyphus as Flowmeister:

> The gods watched Sisyphus take a different approach each time he pushed the rock up the hill. The first time he got a feel for what the rock and hill were like. The next time he went as fast as he could, the third time he tried to see how gracefully he could push the rock, and the fourth time he tried to see how slowly he could push it. Each time he had a different purpose in mind. Because he had a purpose, Sisyphus stayed focused on his task and pushed the rock with intensity. He actually enjoyed the challenge of coming up with different ways to push the rock and took pride in that ability.[10]

Here Sisyphus ignores his punishment. No longer fueled by resentment nor preoccupied with scorn of the gods, Sisyphus basks continually in the wonder of the moment. This image softens the condemnation of the gods by ignoring it. The gods' victory is diminished by its irrelevance to Sisyphus's life. Sisyphus appreciates his life and finds joy, even meaning. He rejects bitterness, refuses to view his world cynically, and chooses engagement.

Psychologist Mihaly Csikszentmihalyi describes these periods of total engagement: "the state in which people are so involved in an activity that nothing else seems to matter; the experience itself is so enjoyable that people will do it even at great cost, for the sheer sake of doing it."[11] The wisest way to animate our lives, then, is to increase the amount and type of flow experiences. The way to nourish our maximally affirmative attitude toward life and to realize unalienated labor is through increasing our experiences of flow.

Although flow experiences are immeasurably valuable for their own sake, they also bear great instrumental value. Such experiences not only express our creativity in salutary ways, but are also for our greatest existential projects: making a worthy self, leading a life worth examining, and constructing a valuable narrative.

> [Every flow experience] provided a sense of discovery, a creative feeling of transporting the person into a new reality. It pushed the person to higher levels of performance, and led to previously undreamed-of states of consciousness. In short, it transformed the self by making it more complex ... in the long run optimal expe-

riences add up to a sense of mastery — or perhaps better, a sense of participation in determining the content of life.[12]

Existential philosophers, such as Søren Kierkegaard, Jean-Paul Sartre, and Martin Heidegger, argued that social obsequiousness and abject conformity are the greatest obstacles to leading an authentic life. By subconsciously trying to renounce much of our freedom and fixing our characters through the perceptions of others, we renege on the task of authentic self-creation. We fail to recognize our total freedom, avoid making self-conscious choices upon which we act, and flee from taking responsibility for the person we are becoming. Flow experiences invigorate our robust sense of freedom by focusing on gratifications stemming from our own creative powers: "If a person learns to enjoy and find meaning in the ongoing stream of experience, in the process of living itself, the burden of social controls automatically falls from one's shoulders."[13]

Existentialists who believe that the cosmos is inherently meaningless, that no preordained value or meaning is built into the world, claim that our attitudes and creative powers can construct meaning and value. Much like we can create meaning and value upon a blank canvas through our creative endeavors, we can endow the universe. But the benign indifference of the cosmos is initially frustrating. We yearn for a connection to enduring value, an ultimate culmination for our lives, and a rational and just universe. The universe cannot answer our entreaties. We cannot take solace in societal conventions or popular opinions because such standards pander to mediocrity. Flow experiences distance us from the crowd and revitalize our sense of freedom and autonomy.

> To overcome the anxieties and depressions of contemporary life, individuals must become independent of the social environment to the degree that they no longer respond exclusively in terms of its rewards and punishments. To achieve such autonomy, a person has to learn to provide rewards to herself. She has to develop the ability to find enjoyment and purpose regardless of external circumstances.[14]

Flow experiences that foster enjoyment have eight dimensions: a project we think we have a possibility of completing; that demands our focus; is defined by specific goals and furnishes immediate feedback; requires profound involvement that pushes aside our mundane anxieties and frustrations; affords us a sense of control over our activities; temporarily allows us to transcend our self-absorption but later energizes our sense of self; and permits us to lose track of time as we are unaware of the pace at which moments pass by. Flow experiences are so enjoyable that we are willing to expend great effort, much time, and forego numerous other opportunities to pursue them. They are the best antidote to boredom and repel the hot breath of nothingness.

The justification of climbing is climbing, like the justification of poetry is writing; you don't conquer anything except things in yourself.... The purpose of the flow is to keep on flowing, not looking for a peak or utopia but staying in the flow.... In normal life, we keep interrupting what we do with doubts and questions.... But in flow there is no need to reflect, because the action carries us forward as if by magic ... people become so involved in what they are doing that the activity becomes spontaneous ... they stop being aware of themselves as separate from the actions they are performing.[15]

Athletics often speak of being in the zone, a condition in which they perform to their highest capability with no apparent increase in effort: "a mental state so focused and intense that it evokes a semiconscious-like euphoria that facilitates peak performances."[16] Their concentration, loss of self-awareness, and oneness with their activity constitute the experience of flow.

When we get out of our own way, and channel the tremendous mental power that we all have, allowing our personality, physical skills, and hard work to take over, it's an incredible experience that we never forget.... It almost feels effortless, and to achieve it takes a combination of physical and mental skills.[17]

Activities that fulfill the main strategies for happiness positively transform the self. This is one reason why identifying happiness and pleasure is unsuccessful. Numerous pleasures fail to positively transform the self. Many Americans gain pleasure by passively viewing *Desperate Housewives* and pounding down burgers at fast food franchises. Few people are positively transformed and re-created by doing so.

Pleasure is an important component of the quality of life, but by itself it does not bring happiness ... [many pleasures] do not produce psychological growth. They do not add complexity to the self. Pleasure helps to maintain order, but by itself cannot create new order in consciousness.... Enjoyment is characterized by forward movement: by a sense of novelty, of accomplishment ... we can experience pleasure without any investment of psychic energy, whereas enjoyment happens only as a result of unusual investments of attention.... Complexity requires investing psychic energy in goals that are new, that are relatively challenging.[18]

To throw yourself into the task, to be so deeply engaged that time is irrelevant, to enjoy an activity for its own sake and not merely its outcome is a metaphor for baseball itself. Unlike other sports, baseball is not ruled by the clock, only the number of innings and outs. At its best, baseball seduces players and fans into losing track of time. The process becomes paramount. The daunting metaphysical question — "To what does it all add up?" — is brushed aside. In the grand scheme of things, from a cosmic vantage point, it matters not which team wins today or emerges as league champion. But for engaged participants and fervent fans this is where they have staked their lives for periods of greater or lesser durations. Baseball becomes important only because we deem it so. We invest our energies, efforts, commitments, and convictions on what is inherently only a contrived game. We mark time and correlate history, at least in the United States, by the development of the "national pastime." While playing the game, if we become flowmeisters, process overtakes outcome. And we will become better performers. The zen of baseball is that less is more: focusing less on the result will increase the probability of victory.

The best experiences of flow, though, are episodic and unique. We cannot live our entire lives as flowmeisters even if we want to. The temporary loss of a sense of self, total immersion in the project at hand, and suspension of our awareness of time energize our spirits. At their best, flow experiences add complexity and nuance to our selves. The risk, however, is dehumanization through inadequate reflection. Bracketing the cosmic perspective, without a robust sense of past and future, and oblivious to other possibilities, Sisyphus as perpetually engaged flowmeister could become less human. Perhaps Sisyphus would be relatively happy, innocently contented, or simply too engaged to assess his condition. He, nevertheless, risks dehumanization as his givenness destroys his transcendence. Sisyphus works busily in his chains, but does not recognize how he remakes his context.

An important message lies at the heart of the image. Human beings too often project into the future while immersed in the everydayness and routines of life. We ignore the textures of the immediacy of life as we busily fulfill our daily schedules and fantasize about a better future. In the meantime much that is valuable in life seeps through our fingers. Sisyphus's obsession with the moment threatens his humanity, but maybe he has little choice given his fate. We have more freedom of focus. Even if total immersion in the flowmeister image is dehumanizing, a dose of it is healthy given the structure of our lives.

In sum, neither the unrepentant rebel nor the thoroughly engaged flowmeister is a fully adequate response to the supposed absurdity of the human condition. Both images, though, reflect different virtues that are crucial to constructing a robustly meaningful life. Instead of choosing one image over the other, we are better advised to combine aspects of each.

Williams in Perspective

The criticisms of Ted Williams are overblown. Taking ten games out of a career of almost 1300 and using them to define a player is unfair. Countless superstars have performed below expectations in one World Series or another. (For example, Mickey Mantle hit .120 in the 1962 World Series, Willie Mays checked in with .182 in the 1951 series, Babe Ruth managed a .118 average in 1922, Joe DiMaggio limped in with .111 in 1949, and Duke Snider hit .143 in 1949.) Moreover, Williams was instrumental in several

Red Sox pennant runs. In 1948, the Red Sox won three straight to force the playoff with the Indians. Ted Williams batted .750 in those games and wangled several bases on balls. In 1949, the Red Sox gained the league lead by winning nine in a row. Williams won four of those games with home runs. The evidence that Ted Williams did not hit in the clutch is flimsy and unpersuasive.

Williams, though, was not a complete baseball player. His arm was weak, his foot speed deficient, his fielding uninspiring. He was not particularly concerned about these imperfections. Perhaps he should have been. But Williams had wanted only one thing: To be considered the best hitter who ever lived. He came so close to achieving that goal that any general manager in history would have ecstatically welcomed him to his ball club.

Although he refused to widen his strike zone, even with runners in scoring position, to argue with his results is folly. Williams's philosophy of batting is difficult to refute. Baseball is a game of habits, good and bad. To go against a carefully cultivated, fruitful routine may well be the first step to undermining general success. Sure, DiMaggio did this, but was Jolting Joe a better all-around hitter than Ted? Not likely.

The Red Sox fell short — when they were in a position to contend — because the Yankees and Indians had superior pitching. Granted, the Red Sox also were inferior defensively (and Williams contributed to this), but pitching was the crucial difference. Even at their best, the Red Sox could not match the Yankees' hurlers Vic Raschi, Allie Reynolds, Ed Lopat, and later, Whitey Ford. Nor did they match up with the Indians' Bob Feller, Bob Lemon, Early Wynn, and Mike Garcia.

If Williams's critics were unjustifiably harsh, his apologists were occasionally indefensibly outraged by perceived slights. For example, Ted's fans to this day rant about his second place finish in the balloting for the Most Valuable Player (MVP) award in 1947. Williams that year won the batting Triple Crown, leading the American League in batting average, home runs, and runs batted in. He was unquestionably the greatest offensive player in the majors that year. The MVP award was voted on by the members of a 24-man panel who ranked their favorites through ten spots. DiMaggio beat Williams by a single point. A Boston sportswriter, Mel Webb, allegedly left Williams completely off the ballot. Webb was one of the "knights of the keyboard" with whom Williams had a long-running feud. Thus, Williams's supporters concluded that Ted had been robbed of the MVP trophy by a disgruntled, unscrupulous, vengeful panelist. Other than Webb, no member of the panel ranked Williams below seventh.

What Williams's fans overlook, however, is that three writers left DiMaggio off their ballots. Was Joe D the victim of conniving sportswriters? Also, the Yankees won the pennant, leaving the Red Sox in the distance by 14 games. The MVP vote in 1947 was close only because the Yankees vote was split between DiMaggio (8 first place votes), Joe Page (7 first place votes), and George McQuinn (3 first place votes). Only three of the twenty-four voters placed Williams first. Although Williams had by far the better offensive year, DiMaggio's team won, he played the more important defensive position (center field) gracefully, was a far superior base runner, and played half his games in a worse hitter's stadium than did Williams. The MVP award is not automatically given to the player who had the best offensive statistics in a league, but, often, to the player on the pennant winner who contributed the most to team success. That Ted Williams was denied the MVP award in 1947 because of the chicanery of a resentful sportswriter is far from clear.

In 1941, though, all fair-minded sports fans applauded Ted Williams's integrity on the final day of the season. He entered the final-day doubleheader batting .39955. If he chose not to play that day he would have been the first player to bat .400 in eleven years. Although advised to sit out by his manager, Ted refused to allow round-up-to-the-nearest-tenth mathematics to confer honor. He played in both games, smashed six hits in eight official trips to the plate, finishing the season at .406. No one has hit .400 in the major leagues since. In 1960, John Updike captured the drama of Ted's final major league at bat superbly. At the age of 41, Williams finished his career to a rousing ovation which he, true to character, refused to acknowledge.

His record as a husband and father was disappointing. When his first wife was giving birth to his first child, Williams was in Florida fishing. Upon hearing this news, fans in Boston were irate at his insensitivity. Predictably, Ted Williams was unrepentant: "To hell with them."[19] He was married and divorced three times. He had other relationships with women that failed. Ted's perfectionist, unforgiving, overly aggressive, uncompromising nature made him an unlikely candidate for deep intimacy that required mutual vulnerability and reciprocity. An apathetic father throughout the formative years of his three children, Williams took a stab at parenthood during the last few years of his life. He gave a parcel of land he owned to his elder daughter, who for years had been a lightning rod for Williams's unsurpassed rage, for a home. He tried to get closer to his younger daughter, who had come by her fierce independence honestly. His only son, John Henry, assumed control of Ted's life. Regarded by several of Ted's friends as a money grabbing opportunist, John Henry was enamored of the burgeoning memorabilia industry and determined to wrench every dollar from his father's celebrity.

> [John Henry] meant to turn Ted's signature, and Ted, into an industry. Even as his father had a second stroke, and then a third, John Henry kept Ted signing—bats, balls, shirts, caps.... They would do it for hours at a time until the man was so tired

he couldn't write anymore. [John Henry] pushed and pushed his dad.... Even when John Henry would erupt in rage *at Ted* ... the old man tended to blame himself ... even as the boy offended Ted's admirers, and dismissed the workers who took care of Ted's health and home ... even after John Henry's businesses fell apart in lawsuits, bad loans, bankruptcy.... Ted looked for reasons to admire the kid ... he was in love with the idea of loving his son.[20]

Life had come full circle. The scared, unloved, unwanted child was now an exploited, famous father who enabled his own son's capriciousness and greed. When Ted Williams died, John Henry had the corpse cryogenically frozen. According to Ted's elder daughter, John Henry aspired to sell Ted's genes for future cloning.

Ted Williams and Sisyphus

No baseball player ever combined Camus's two images of Sisyphus better than Ted bleeping Williams, the best bleeping hitter who ever lived. As *Cool Hand Luke*, Williams brimmed with grace under pressure — whether at bat, on a combat mission, or hauling in the big fish. Unrepentant, uncompromising, warring against the insecurities of his youth, desperate to succeed on his own terms, burning with energy, confronting external forces larger than himself, Ted Williams was Sisyphus-in-Rebellion. He was often his own worst enemy as he pridefully brandished his patina of defiance. Doomed to fail — for even he succeeded only around 34 percent of the time, the skills of all players recede, and human beings are born to suffer and die — Ted Williams, nevertheless, forged a life of robust meaning from those projects that earned his attention.

From a cosmic perspective, striving to become the best hitter who ever lived is insignificant. Baseball, itself, viewed from a cosmic perspective, is trivial: a bunch of players in silly uniforms and duck-bill caps flinging a ball, while other players similarly adorned and armed with round sticks of wood (or aluminum) try to smack the hurled projectile. All for the privilege of running around a 360-foot diamond and returning from whence they began. The ultimate reward is called scoring a run with the team having the greater number of runs being declared the winner of the travesty.

Here, though, is where Ted Williams was Sisyphus-as-Flowmeister. From a personal perspective, baseball can become important, even all-consuming. Riveted by a project that animated his life and energized by intense experiences through which he defined himself, Williams was deeply engaged in the moment, at least when he was at the plate staring down a big league pitcher. Questions such as "To what does it all amount?" evaporated from consciousness. The cosmic perspective faded away. The wonder of the moment, temporarily, permitted respite from rage and defiance. The engagement, animation, and self-definition *became* the meaning of life. The unalienated labor of trying to sting a baseball fueled Ted Williams's maximally affirmative attitude toward life. We must imagine Ted, Camus, and Sisyphus laughing.

Billy Martin and Niccolò Machiavelli

"Some people have a chip on their shoulder. Billy has a whole lumberyard."
— Jim Murray, sports columnist

"Billy Martin is not an intellectual, but there is a cunningness to him that is something to behold."
— Reggie Jackson

"Nobody is better than you. Never take no shit from nobody."
— Jenny Salvini Pisani Martin Downey,
Billy Martin's mother

"Billy could hear somebody giving him the finger."
— Mickey Mantle

"I wouldn't beg for water if my heart was on fire."
— Billy Martin

Niccolò Machiavelli (1469–1527) understood the world as a zero-sum, competitive battleground for *virtù*. He strategized political life in order to win this contest for his own group. Billy Martin (1928–1989), as good a game manager as there ever was, understood baseball and, probably, life in the same way. Both men inadequately recognized the value of cooperation. Their brands of tribalism, nevertheless, inspired many.

Billy Martin and the Combative Life

We cannot understand Billy Martin without saying a little about his mother. Jenny Salvini was a diminutive, confrontational woman who threw fists, chairs or whatever else was handy and did not bother to ask questions later. Born to struggling Italian immigrants in West Berkeley, California, Jenny grew up fast and hard. At age sixteen, she was given in marriage — I mean that literally — to one of her mother's boarders, Donato Pisani. They were married for three years and had a son, Frank. Neither spouse was happy and they eventually divorced. Both may have been unfaithful. At some point, Jenny met and fell in love with smooth-talking, guitar-strumming Alfred Manuel Martin. They married. Of Portuguese descent, Martin had a roving eye. Jenny gave him a wristwatch, but later noticed Alfred was not wearing it. Upon learning from a meddling friend that Martin had given it to a fifteen year old high school girl, Jenny did what her hardscrabble code demanded. She found the girl, reclaimed the watch, then beat the frightened teenager to a pulp. Jenny returned home, gathered Alfred's clothes, stomped them, threw them in a suitcase, and hurled them onto the lawn. When Alfred arrived home from work, Jenny took a hand mirror and systematically destroyed every window of the car. She informed Alfred that they were through. She was three months pregnant at the time with Billy (who was named Alfred Manuel Martin, Jr.). During their separation but prior to their divorce, Jenny discovered from her network of officious cronies that Alfred had a woman in his room. What else was Jenny to do? She proceeded to the love nest and beat the stuffing out of both Alfred and his paramour. Policemen eventually intervened. Jenny and Alfred divorced. Alfred beat feet to Hawaii.

Jenny soon met and married a gentle Irishman, Jack Downey, who served as stepfather to her two sons. Their union produced three more children, two girls and a boy. Jack worked a series of blue-collar jobs during the Depression. Although not materially comfortable, the Downeys were no worse off than their neighbors. Jack Downey was too even-keeled to have significant influence over Billy, who was his mother's son. The "Billy" derived from his mother's cooing of "bellissimo" and "bellino" when she saw him.

But beautiful Billy was not. To call his nose generous, his ears expansive, and his teeth uneven is to be charitable. Plus, he was small. Billy learned life's paramount lessons from his ferocious mother:

> Rule #1: Life is struggle.
> Rule #2: Most people are out to get you. Trust few, if any, people.
> Rule #3: Nobody is better than you.
> Rule #4: Do not bother to respect any authority outside the family.
> Rule #5: Never take shit from nobody.
> Rule #6: Every insult must be avenged.
> Rule #7: To earn respect you have to use your fists.
> Rule #8: Fight to win ... at any cost

When Billy, already a promising athlete, attended junior high school in Berkeley he was exposed to the more fortunate sons and daughters of upper class parents. The invidious comparison fueled Billy's insecurity, outrage, hypersensitivity, and combativeness. If life was a zero-sum game then Billy Martin was going to ensure he got his innings. Whether competing on the baseball field or confronting a contrived enemy in one of his countless fist fights, only victory mattered: "Winning acted on him like a drug. If he won, he could bury for a short time his feelings of self-loathing while he basked in the satisfaction of victory. If he lost, those negative feelings would surface, and his frustration and anger would simmer."[1]

As Billy grew, the child was father to the man. Brashness shrouded his insecurity, aggression masked his self-destructiveness, belligerence covered his social awkwardness. He grasped greedily for a sense of belonging. For a baseball player no greater membership could be granted than to become a New York Yankee. They were baseball's best team; they were the victors in the major league zero-sum game. Winning conferred the external validation Billy desperately craved. Better still, the Yanks were the squad, at various times, of Ping Bodie, Tony Lazzeri, Frank Crosetti, Joe DiMaggio, and Phil Rizzuto. Although half Portuguese, Billy identified entirely with his mother's Italianism.

Niccolò Machiavelli and Human Character

The legacy of Machiavelli has, regrettably, been reduced to slogans extolling realistic statecraft, self-seeking opportunism, and amoralism. More accurately, Machiavelli imagined a crucial early stage of zealous nationalism founded on the values of the ancient Roman republic that paved the way for the modern nation-state.

His two most famous works, *The Prince* and *The Discourses Upon the First Decade of Titus Livius*, appear incompatible at first blush.[2] *The Prince* is dedicated to Lorenzo d'Medici and was written in part to regain political employment under the new regime. *The Prince* champions absolute monarchy while *The Discourses* fervently advocates republicanism. A deeper analysis, though, shows that *The Prince* is a manual for rejuvenation, and possibly unification, in an unsettled context. Once the monarch attains these goals, promotes the common good, and nurtures a strong national character, his power disperses. Once the conditions required for a sound republic are in place, the advice of *The Discourses* should prevail. Many supposed differences between *The Prince* and *The Discourses* can be reconciled once we understand that *The Prince* was written as a battle plan for one situation, the revitalization of a corrupt city-state, while *The Discourses* was a general account of Machiavelli's political philosophy and showed his appreciation for popular forms of government in those countries enjoying favorable conditions.

In Machiavelli's judgment, the five loose-knit regions of Italy were in a dire predicament in the early sixteenth century. They could either remain disunified and provide easy targets for invading barbarians, or they could follow the leadership of a strong man, rise above factional bickering, and unite for the greater good: either victimization or unification.

Like Plato, Machiavelli insisted that praiseworthy personal character required a nurturing social context. Glorious individuals emerge from strong states. Machiavelli uses the term *virtù* as shorthand for a host of admirable character traits: deserved pride, courage, vigor, intelligence, ambition, spirit, even genius. In individuals, the ability to provide strong, vigorous, decisive leadership and to instill victorious qualities in one's soldiers and fellow citizens are crucial. Machiavelli's examples are of generals who, through fortitude and insightfulness, emerged victorious in trying conditions. The ability to overcome adversity often is shown by people who gain, secure, extend, and preserve military and political power. The most important sense of *virtù* centers on energy of will, manliness, or the ability to prevent others from imposing their will.

Derived from the Latin root, *virtù* on a national level means the power to fashion events and peoples to one's own designs. Rome manifested such dominance in the ancient world and it is the lack of *virtù* which Machiavelli thought reduced the city-states of Italy in his day to the prey of French, Spanish, and Swiss invaders.

In *The Prince*, Machiavelli argues that the regionalized people of Florence, and Italians generally, were largely corrupt — they lacked *virtù*— so the monarch would sometimes be forced to use fraud and coercion to establish order and security, and invigorate citizens. Sounds peculiar, does it not? The cure for corruptness is fraud and coercion? What Machiavelli meant was that the prince, while governing, should not always abide by the standards of conventional private morality. If certain inherently evil practices had to be used, that should be thought of as evil well used because they flow from necessity: external forces, antecedent events, and compelling circumstances. Necessity will often compel the ruler to commit deeds that are correctly judged immoral when performed outside the political arena: miserliness, cruelty, deceit, and promise-breaking are often preferable, politically, to liberality, mercy, honesty, and promise-keeping. The purpose, though, of the prince's strategies is facilitating the common good of his nation, not his own narrow interests.

Billy in the Majors

Martin eventually caught the eye of Yankees scouts. More important, he curried the favor of Casey Stengel, one of his managers in the minor leagues, who became the leader of the Yankees in 1949. Despite his often carefully cultivated folksiness and garbled syntax, Stengel was at his core a hard drinking, brawling, give-no-quarter competitor. Casey loved Billy's cockiness, intensity, and zeal for fisticuffs. First arriving in the big leagues in 1950, Billy soon became know as "Stengel's bobo." Casey often used Martin as a bench jockey — a player not in the starting lineup whose job was to ride an opponent mercilessly throughout the game in order to impair the enemy's performance.

As soon as he arrived, Billy Martin acted as if he owned Yankee Stadium. Horror of horrors, he even poked fun at Joe DiMaggio! Shockingly, Joe enjoyed it and appreciated Martin's energy, ambition, commitment, and fiery personality. That Billy wore his Italianism on his sleeve did not hurt.

Billy was a fine defensive second baseman, with special skill at turning the double play. He and Rizzuto upended many an opponent's rally by acrobatically executing twin killings. As a hitter, Martin was a fine defensive second baseman. In eleven seasons, his career batting average was only .257 with an anemic on-base percentage of .300 and a weak slugging percentage of .369. In fact, despite his later reputation as a Yankees mainstay, Martin had only two years in pinstripes when he earned at least 400 at-bats in a season.

The reputation of Billy Martin as Yankees legend flowed from two sources. First, he was Billy the Battler. He fought with numerous opponents, including Jimmy Piersall, Clint Courtney, and Larry Doby, and became a fan favorite. Martin was the blue-collar Yankee. He had less talent than most of his peers, but no one exceeded his desire and competitive heart. Martin personified the Yankee quest for victory. Fans could relate to his ordinariness and celebrate his combativeness.

> He had something burning inside him the others didn't have. Billy hated to lose so badly that he played with an intensity and a dedication that anyone playing with him had to admire and anyone playing against him had to despise. For Billy to keep up, he had to work harder. He was more driven than others because he didn't have their ability.[3]

Second, Billy Martin had a unique talent during World Series contests to amplify his intensity, focus, and competitive cunning. Billy the fine defensive second basemen muscled up into Billy the Bomber. His clutch performances in the World Series, when Billy sidled into phone booths and donned his Super-Stick tights, vivified his fans and established his legend. His series performances came at the expense of the Brooklyn Dodgers. Billy would work himself into a froth and convince himself that he could show the world he was a better ballplayer than his counterpart on the Dodgers. And who was the Brooklyn second baseman? None other than Jack Roosevelt Robinson, Hall of Famer and destroyer of baseball's color barrier. If you think Barry Manilow is a superior musical stylist to Frank Sinatra, if you are convinced professional wrestling is on the level, if you insist that Roseanne Barr has always been better looking than Sophia Loren, you will also conclude that there was even a day in which Billy Martin was a better baseball player than Jackie Robinson. Well, maybe not.

But Billy Martin's overreaching mind and deranged will overcame reality, at least in October. During four World Series, Martin clearly outperformed the great Jackie Robinson. The Yankees won three of the four championship contests, and Billy had a higher batting average than Jackie in each of the four series. Here are their overall comparative batting statistics for the 1952, 1953, 1955, and 1956 World Series:

	G	AB	R	H	2B	3B	HR	RBI	BB	SO	BA	OBP	SLG[4]
Martin	27	99	14	33	2	3	5	19	5	15	.333	.371	.566
Robinson	26	94	17	22	4	1	2	7	15	8	.234	.339	.362

Martin was the MVP of the 1953 World Series, scorching Brooklyn pitching for a .500 batting average, seasoned by 12 hits, 8 runs batted in, and 2 homers. In the seventh and deciding game of the 1952 Series, Brooklyn was losing 4–2 in the seventh inning, but had the bases loaded and two outs. The batter popped relief pitcher Bob Kuzava's change-up to the first base side of the pitcher's mound. With two outs, the base runners were moving on contact. Normally, the first baseman would take charge and make the simple play, ending the inning. But Joe Collins, inexplicably, lost the ball in the sun. At the last moment, Billy Martin stormed in from second base. The wind blew the ball away from him, but Martin hustled in and caught the ball below knee level to save the game for the Yankees. Which Brooklyn batter hit the pop fly to the pitcher's mound? None other than Jackie Robinson.

During his years as a Yankee, Billy began a self-destructive pattern of behavior that intensified as he aged. He was a heavy drinker, insatiable pursuer of girls (the younger the better), indiscriminate brawler, and knee-jerk rebel. Subconsciously, Martin was convinced he did not deserve the glory and victory he so relentlessly pursued. Every time he appeared to have attained his greatest dreams, Billy the Kid would find a way to undermine his achievements.

His relations with Yankees general manager George Weiss were always strained. Weiss tolerated him only so long as no clearly superior alternative was available at second base. Weiss judged, correctly, that Martin was not that skilled a player and the general manager, unlike Stengel, did not enjoy the sideshow that Martin orchestrated. Weiss, preoccupied with pleasing his wealthier fans and recognizing that even Billy's most rabid supporters would not apply the adjective "class" to the second sacker, waited for an excuse to dump the obstreperous Martin. For his part, Martin accurately regarded Weiss as a tight-fisted, arrogant, emotionally frigid, self-serving bureaucrat.

In May 1957, a handful of Yankees went out to celebrate the birthdays of Yogi Berra and Billy. After dinner and a stop to see a show at the Waldorf-Astoria, they arrived at the Copacabana to view a performance by Sammy Davis, Jr. At some point, some of the Yankees players got into a verbal dispute with other customers, probably over a racial epithet hurled at Davis by one of the revelers at an adjoining table. Within an hour, the loudmouth who had insulted the performer was knocked cold in the men's room, suffering a broken nose and other head injuries. The most likely perpetrator was Yankees outfielder and ex–Marine Hank Bauer, whose face was once described as resembling a closed fist.

Lots of negative publicity ensued. Weiss was outraged by this affront to the Yankees image. Finally, he had his excuse to unload Billy Martin. Using the pretext that Martin was a bad influence on the team and a likely antagonist at the Copacabana, Weiss traded Billy to the hapless Kansas City Athletics. Billy's performance up to that point in 1957 made his dismissal all the easier: a career low .241 batting average, a pathetic .257 on base percentage, and an effete .324 slugging percentage.

Martin was devastated. The Yankees had artificially inflated his self-image and had validated his ticket to respectability. He spent his final four years as a major league player traveling from one dead end team to another: Kansas City Athletics, Detroit Tigers, Cleveland Indians, Cincinnati Redlegs, Minnesota Twins. At each stop, Martin entered with big talk and high expectations. Within a season or less, he had worn out his welcome through mediocre play, bellicose behavior, and off-the-field indiscretions.

Machiavelli and the Battle for Glory

Machiavelli, in *The Prince*, insists that the masses determine the rightness of actions by reference to their consequences. Machiavelli's highest value is the common good — the establishment of a powerful city-state, and possibly an Italian nation-state, that revitalizes the *virtù* of citizens — and all actions are judged in accordance with their effects on the common good. The relevant consequences are narrowly construed. They consist of the interests of only those who would be citizens of the prince's regime. In his calculus, Machiavelli is not concerned with the impact of actions on all human beings. Instead, he extols a tribal consequentialism — at least from the perspective of the masses — because he views the world as a competitive battleground for *virtù* and all nations as independent competitors. Machiavelli's numerous and varied diplomatic missions convinced him that an international brotherhood and sisterhood of nations was impossible.

The overall amount of *virtù* in the world remains constant while the amount in a particular country will vary.[5] One nation's success will come at the expense of one or more other nations. Nations that possess much *virtù* will disproportionately control world affairs. If one nation rises in power, which means its collective *virtù* increases, it will have done so by depriving other nations of like power, which means their collective *virtù* decreases. For this reason, these forces always will be in balance and the amount of *virtù* in the world remains constant. The struggle for international power, much like the American League pennant race, is a zero-sum game. Some will win which means others will lose. No permanent winners and losers, though, emerge. All advantages and all disadvantages are temporary. The game and the struggle go on, with all gains and all losses canceling out one another when taken as a whole.

Success, for the individual and the nation, consists of harmonizing *virtù* and *fortuna*. *Fortuna* connotes circumstances and external factors affecting the actions of princes and nations. But *fortuna* is not merely luck or fate. The man of *virtù* uses *fortuna* for his purposes when he can and tries to minimize her effects when *fortuna* is unfavorable.[6] He is not totally at her mercy in either case. *Fortuna* changes and the wise prince must be adaptable and sense the temper of the times.

Machiavelli was convinced that only an absolute monarch can transform a corrupt society. In his judgment, civic *virtù* in Italy had disintegrated and this made a popular republic impossible. *Virtù* could be spawned only through proper laws, training, and education. The corrupt, fragmented state cannot rehabilitate itself. Instead, an omnipotent lawgiver must mold it by crafting a pure social foundation directed toward the common good. The strong nation-state prevents foreign intrusions, helps citizens rise above selfish individualism, establishes communal bonds, increases the material and spiritual quality of life, and cultivates personal and national *virtù*.

Billy Ball and the Fast Life

After retiring as a player in 1961, Billy coached with Minnesota, then managed for a year in the minor leagues at Denver. In 1969, he was promoted and as Twins manager promptly won a divisional title. In sixteen seasons as a major league manager, from 1969 through 1988, Martin won five divisional titles with four franchises, two American League pennants, and one World Series. At all stops, Martin improved the teams he joined, sometimes strikingly. Soon thereafter, he would implode with self-destructive behavior. His deep conviction of unworthiness would surface with fist fights, alcoholism, mindless escapades with young girls, failed marriages, insurrection against authority, and self-undermining strategies.

> Martin proved what a powerful strategic tool paranoia is. He believed that everyone was against him. And so he spent every waking moment figuring out how imaginary enemies could be defeated in their nefarious plots. And sometimes he not only created strategies to defend against things that would have never been done against him, but realized that those attacks were in themselves novel and would then try those attacks that he had already dreamed up a defense for.[7]

During all his managerial stints, Billy was always a fan favorite. They admired his enthusiasm, fire, combative nature, refusal to lose. He was an ordinary blue-collar worker who conjured magical results. They did not have to live with him. They were not subject to his excesses.

He was fired, ostensibly for a fight with one of his players, after winning a dramatic divisional title in Minnesota. One year stint. He won a divisional title with the Detroit Tigers in 1972 in his second year. He was fired prior to finishing his third year, presumably for ordering his pitchers to throw at opposing batters in retaliation. Less than three year term. He finished that year with the Texas Rangers, took the team from last to second in 1974, but was fired during the following season. Two hundred seventy-nine game tour. Martin finally landed his dream job, manager of the Yankees, late in 1975. The next two seasons, he won American League pennants and a world championship. But soon after mid season in 1978, he collapsed with intractable disputes with Reggie Jackson and owner George Steinbrenner. The Yankees went on to win another world championship without him.

He was hired and fired again by Steinbrenner in 1979. Martin landed with the Oakland A's in 1980 and transformed them into divisional winners in 1981. He was canned at the end of 1982. He bounced back to manage the Yankees for all of 1983, most of 1985, and almost half of 1988, with firings spaced between.

Billy Martin was the greatest quick fix manager of all time. He would swagger into any team situation, no matter how bleak, energize the troops, and make them winners. He commanded respect, made players believe in themselves, circled the wagons, and demanded intensity. Most ballplayers responded eagerly, at least for a time. Most opponents wilted, at least a tad, under the pressure.

> Billy transformed baseball from a game to something akin to war. Playing against Billy took away a lot of fun and added an element of danger. At the same time he forced the opposition to play the game his way. Since few teams could match Billy in ruthlessness or managerial skill, at the end of the game, Billy usually ended up a winner.[8]

But just as surely as a team's sudden improvement under Martin was the certainty of Martin's self-destruction. Martin's teams reflected his personality, for better or worse, in the shorter and longer runs.

> Martin creates an emotionally charged atmosphere. When you go into a clubhouse which is flat, stale, and lethargic and charge that clubhouse with emotion, that's great. But to live in an emotionally charged atmosphere over a period of years is quite another matter.... [Martin's] immaturity, his high-pressure tactics, and his mind games over time create so much resentment and hostility that he is a long-term detriment — indeed, he simply can't manage a baseball team for longer than a couple of years, or he will self-destruct.[9]

Aside from Martin's psychological frailties, one of his managerial strategies also contributed to his short tenures: he tended to overuse his starting pitchers at all of his stops, and too many of these hurlers suffered arm injuries within two or three years of Martin's arrival. Billy preferred hard throwers who threw strikes — bases on balls yielded by his teams typically decreased on Martin's watch — and he was one of the slowest hooks in the game. He expected his starting pitchers to work out of their own jams. The result was an inordinately high number of innings borne by a relatively small number of pitchers. For Billy, the future *was* now and he managed for the season at hand. In fairness, several of the pitchers who suffered injuries shortly after being overused by Martin refused to blame Billy. He trusted them and they continued to believe in him.[10]

While at Oakland, his brand of baseball was dubbed *Billy Ball*: it used more frequently and artfully strategies such as the hit and run, double steal, theft of home, squeeze play, sacrifice bunt, and straight steal. Fans and opposing teams expected the unexpected from Billy. In truth, trick plays and special strategies played only a small role in his success. The same year that the *Billy Ball* mantra was invented, his Oakland team led the majors in home runs.

Martin's success, aside from immediately energizing any clubhouse he entered, flowed from his keen eye for talent, his ability to command respect, his acute knowledge of the nuances of baseball, his intuitive feel for game situations, his unwavering confidence that spilled over to his players, his ability to spot a player's weakness and instruct the player on how to minimize it, his knack for identifying power pitchers and convincing them to throw strikes, his intense desire to win, his intolerance of sloppiness, and his unshakeable faith in his ability to command any situation.

> More successfully than any other manager, Martin has been able to make an entire collection of athletic young bodies into an expression of his own will. Like everything else Martin does, this is the short-term strategy, for each of the players in truth has his own will, his own desires and goals and ambitions, and while he may allow those to go into remission for awhile, they will return to the fore within a few years.... Successful long-term teams ... are built on a successful merging of

individual wills into group strength, not on the obliteration of anything that opposes the manager's master plan. But tomorrow may be a dream or a nightmare or it may never be. If you want to win *today*, Billy Martin is the best manager there is.[11]

On Christmas Day in 1989, Martin was killed in a one-vehicle accident in front of his home near Binghamton, New York. Ensnared, yet again, in a counter-productive marriage, anticipating another call to resume the managerial reins of the Yankees, intoxicated well beyond legal limits, Martin drove his pickup truck into a ditch in front of the gates of his home. If he had stepped on the brakes, the truck would have stopped and Martin would have survived. Instead, Billy, determined to leave the ditch at all costs, stepped on the gas. The vehicle accelerated and ran straight into a headwall made of fieldstone. Billy Martin's unvarying aggression, so often the ballast of his fan appeal and the animator of his baseball success, was the architect of his demise. As we all must, he lost his final zero-sum contest.

Machiavelli and the Passionate Republic

In *The Discourses*, Machiavelli praises republicanism. Citizens no longer can be used as mere means to advance the common good. He recognizes constraints on what can be done to individuals, a form of rights that transform the tribal consequentialism of *The Prince* into a more acceptable public morality. The only thing that underwrote the prince and his actions was the supreme importance of revitalizing a corrupt, weak citizenry. Once this goal is attained and the nation solidified, the prince's power should be spread more widely and a republican government inaugurated. *Virtù* is, then, best secured through republicanism. A Machiavellian republic has a system of checks and balances much like those that existed among the counsels, senate, and plebeians in the ancient Roman republic. Machiavelli also thought republics were best placed to compete in the international political and military arenas. Territorial expansion was necessary in the worldly contest for power and *virtù*.

He distinguished human nature from national character. Human nature is mainly self-interested, fearful, and acts out of need. Loyalty flows only from self interest and identification with the other, whether a friend, family member, or ruler. Human nature bears a deep, insatiable *ambizione* (ambition) for political glory and security, and is dominated by *animo* (passion) not reason. Natural scarcity — of resources, honors, successes, glories — fuels *ambizione*. The world is replete with conflicts as human beings cannot acquire all they desire. National character, though, can be altered by new habits, laws, and education. This requires a wider identity. We need to go beyond the self and establish communal bonds. We need a vital city-state or nation-state for salutary personal and collective transformation. National character, like national *virtù*, is variable among and within different states at different times, while human nature, like the overall amount of *virtù* in the world, is invariable.

Unlike most Greco-Roman philosophers who championed peace, internal harmony, and social tranquility as the highest values, Machiavelli insisted that human beings burned with *ambizione* and *animo*. A timid soul lacks value. We aspire, instead, to vitality, boldness, and forceful action in political and military arenas. We seek greatness, not serenity. Whereas Plato extolled the benefits of contemplation, moral virtue, and spiritual health through a balanced soul; and Marx gushed over unalienated, creative labor as the locus of human fulfillment; Machiavelli, prefiguring Nietzsche, venerates passion, conflict, and vibrant personal energy.

For Machiavelli, the importance of Rome as an example largely flows from the extent and duration of its power, that Rome could have influenced so many peoples for so long a time makes it the supreme case of *virtù*. Through his study of ancient Rome, Machiavelli found support for his instinctive personal values: passion for competition, zest for honor, yearning for community, and distrust of other states.

> The Romans recognized no difference between moral excellence and reputation, having the same word, *honestas*, for both.... Praise was what every citizen most desired.... To place personal honor above the interests of the entire community was the behavior of a barbarian ... citizens were schooled to temper their competitive instincts for the common good ... in their relations with other states, however, no such inhibitions cramped them.[12]

Machiavelli also found ballast for his convictions that the quest for *virtù* was a zero-sum competition that could be taught through proper laws, family values, and military and political contests.

> Ruthless competition was regarded as the basis of all civic virtue.... Hardness was a Roman ideal. The steel required to hunt out glory or endure disaster was a defining mark of a citizen. It was instilled in him from the moment of his birth.... To raise heirs successfully, to instill in them due pride in their bloodline and hankering after glory, these were achievements worthy of a man.... "Gain cannot be made without loss to someone else." So every Roman took for granted.[13]

Undeniably, Machiavelli was not merely an opportunist seeking an increase in his personal fortunes. He was a patriot deeply concerned with the fate of his disunified city and country. He cried out:

> The sea has parted, a cloud has shown the way, a stone has poured forth water, manna has rained down from the sky; all things have conspired to show your [Lorenzo d'Medici's] greatness.... This opportunity, therefore, must not be allowed to pass, so that Italy after so long a time may find her redeemer. I cannot describe with how much love, with what thirst for revenge, with what resolute loyalty, with

what tenderness, with what tears he would be received in all those provinces which have endured these foreign hordes. What gates would be closed to him? Whose envy would oppose him? What Italian would withhold his allegiance? This barbarian domination stinks in everyone's nostrils. Let your illustrious house take up this task, then, with that boldness and with that hope which is reserved to just enterprises, so that this nation may be ennobled under your banner.[14]

Machiavelli derives his political conclusions from observations about human nature and historical examples, mostly drawn from the Roman republic. Despite his reputation, Machiavelli is far from objective. He selects his examples carefully, choosing only those that support his foregone convictions. He is not above falsifying historical accounts if doing so supports his conclusions better than the actual accounts. Why would a supposed detached political scientist use such unreliable and disreputable methods?

Despite his reputation as the founder of cool, calculating, dispassionate statecraft, Machiavelli was a romantic. Disgusted by the rancid disgrace of being dominated by barbarians, while at the same time observing the skills and courage of individual Italians in duels and competitions involving only a few, Machiavelli placed his trust in the ascent of one great man to wreak vengeance and to initiate future Italian triumphs. Following the tradition of Plato and Aristotle, he was convinced that once this superman emerged, the masses would be spiritually transformed, *virtù* would flourish, and the state would prosper. His treatises are not the labors of an objective scientist, but rather the poems, aspirations, and implorations of a lover. His emotions, passion, and anguish permeate his writings. They frequently cloud his thinking, they sometimes animate his insights, they always starkly reveal the source of the blood in his veins. In short, the strengths and weaknesses of Niccolò Machiavelli flow from his relentless patriotism.

Martin, Machiavelli and Baseball

For Machiavelli, Europe in the late 15th and early 16th centuries *was* a zero-sum situation. Whether one *wanted* this to be the case was irrelevant. His primary concern was how to act effectively in that context. To act effectively meant to maximize the prospects of victory — judged in terms of increased aggregate *virtù*—for his nation.

Machiavelli overplays the role and distorts the nature of competition in human fulfillment. He participates in a grand philosophical tradition in doing so. Thinkers too numerous to catalog have overemphasized one aspect of human personality, have taken it to define our nature, and concluded its attainment constitutes our fulfillment. For example, Plato celebrated peace and harmony, Marx glorified unalienated labor, and Nietzsche honored relentless striving for the few capable of bearing it. The quest, though, to identify one part of our nature and showcase it as definitive of *who we are* is unfaithful to human complexity.

Machiavelli took competition, played out on battlefields and diplomatic maneuvers, as the essence of human fulfillment. The natural fact of scarcity fueled the *ambizione* and *animo* at the center of human nature. Less clear is whether ambition and passion are inherently part of human nature or whether they emerge because of natural scarcity. If we can imagine a world of material abundance — much as Marx did with the blossoming of communist economics — would human beings still be relentless competitors? My suspicion is that Machiavelli would answer, "Yes, they would." For our imagined material abundance would not eliminate the scarcity of honor, success, glory, and *virtù*. Material scarcity exacerbates but does not generate *ambizione* and *animo*.

From a Machiavellian standpoint, baseball is a tamer quest for *virtù*. Winners, losers, zero-sum logic prevail ... or so it seems. Billy Martin would agree with Machiavelli about both baseball and, more important, life. Martin was convinced at a young age by his mother's instruction and his experiences that everything important was a zero-sum event. Winning those events brought more than temporary victory. Winning, as Machiavelli so clearly understood, increased one's *virtù*. For Martin, *virtù* implied a sense of belonging, external validation, social recognition, and abundant proof that nobody was better than he was. Conventional morality, for sure, should not be a restriction on attaining *that*.

Although athletic competition is ripe with zero-sum calculations, I am not convinced the Machiavellian-Martin perspective fully captures other possibilities within sports. For example, glorious defeat can increase one's *virtù* in a way that tepid victory or ignoble defeat cannot. Unlike war or combative diplomatic negotiations, both sides can be winners in a sense in sport even if one side is declared the official loser. Bear with me here, I am not resorting to Stengelese.[15]

Consider the famous "Thrilla in Manilla": Muhammad Ali defeated Joe Frazier but both fighters enhanced their reputations immeasurably from the contest. Ali did not steal Frazier's *virtù* in triumph. Instead, overall *virtù* did not remain the same after a redistribution. *Virtù* increased. Had Ali defeated just another bum of the month, he would not have enhanced his *virtù* in any meaningful way. Worthy opponents are needed to establish one's own greatness. And sometimes more glory and honor are won in valiant defeat than in lop-sided victory. We might make the same case about war, say Davy Crockett at the Alamo or those who die heroically for a grand cause. Machiavelli might point out that Davy and dead heroes remain dead. Their posthumous reputations are enhanced. But Machiavelli is more likely to agree with actor George C. Scott's opening lines in the movie *Patton*: "No soldier ever won a war by dying for his country. Better to make the other poor, dumb SOB die for his country" (paraphrased).

The mantra of amateur road racing, especially marathoning, for years was, "everyone can be a winner." To the extent participants fulfilled their personal goals — and at least in principle everyone could as long as the goal was not zero-sum, such as to finish first in the race — everyone could, in Machiavellian terms, attain more *virtù*. So, too, with baseball. When I coached, I would often tell my teams that finishing with a perfect record would be easy: just play a bunch of 10-year-old neophytes over and over. Finishing with a record of complete failure is also easy: just play a major league team over and over. (The hapless Kansas City Royals and Pittsburgh Pirates notwithstanding.)

Phil Jackson, when he was coaching the Chicago Bulls against their staunchest rival, the Detroit Pistons, provided an antidote to the excesses of Machiavellian zero-sum competition:

> I used something I'd learned from the Lakota of the Dakotas. They had a mortal enemy in the Crow, but they honored them because they were wonderful warriors and to fight against the Crow demanded bravery, cunning, and teamwork. I borrowed that theme. The conflict brought about the best of both tribes. So rather than getting angry and frustrated in a contest with a physically stronger team like the Pistons, and failing out in futility, we resorted to meeting them with focused willpower, resilience, and teamwork. We honored the Pistons ability to compete and it worked in our favor.[16]

Competition in baseball can increase, decrease, or not affect a participant's *virtù*. Much depends on the quality of competition, the energy expended in the process, the values promoted by the effort. Baseball, though, is rarely just a game, if by that we mean a mere form of leisure — a way of killing time. We can fool around with bats, balls, and fielders' mitts. We can kill time, but that is not baseball at its best. Winning athletic contests, though, is no guarantee that the victor's *virtù* has thereby increased. *Virtù* has an irreducible internal dimension. Winning has transformative effects on the victor and on the loser. The way we are changed by our participation in sports becomes crucial. Did baseball victories make Billy Martin a better person in the more valuable aspects of human life? Not likely. Perhaps without baseball his prospects would have been dimmer — say, 15 to life in a federal penitentiary — but his triumphs in zero-sum athletic contests were not enough to sustain strong personal character. Results, in sports or life generally, can never be assessed in isolation from the process values that created them.

THIRD INNING

Satchel Paige and Marcus Aurelius

"When I was seven, hustling baggage at a railroad depot in Mobile, I rigged up ropes around my shoulders and waist, and I carried a satchel in each hand and one under each arm. I carried so many satchels that all you could see were satchels. You couldn't see no Leroy Paige."

— Leroy "Satchel" Paige[1]

Satchel Paige (circa 1906–1982) led a life supposedly informed by a host of homilies (for example, "Don't look back, something may be gaining on you"). As an African American in a generally hostile social environment, Paige adopted ways of acting that moderated pain. The Greek and Roman Stoics, such as Marcus Aurelius (121–180), did much the same centuries earlier. These ways of life were mixed bundles of endurances, satisfactions, sufferings, and triumphs.

The Legend of Satchel Paige

"World's Greatest Pitcher, Leroy 'Satchel' Paige, Guaranteed to Strike Out the First Nine Men or Your Money Back." So advertised management when the legendary Satchel Paige was scheduled to hurl.

Paige was born in 1906 or 1908 or 1903 or in the 13th century, depending on who was speaking and for what purpose.[2] In his prime, he was a string bean of around 180 pounds, who stood just over 6 feet 3 inches. Denied entry into the major leagues by the color barrier, Paige played for over twenty years in the Negro Leagues with numerous teams including the Birmingham Black Barons, Nashville Elite Giants, New Orleans Black Pelicans, Kansas City

Monarchs, and Pittsburgh Crawfords. During that period, he also barnstormed in the United States, Mexico, and Cuba with makeshift squads.

Born into poverty, without benefit of formal education, and transversing a racist world with strict color lines, Paige created a fluid image that traded on tall tales, mystery, and an ingratiating personality. He was friendly to almost everyone, but intimate with only a handful.

He was without argument one of the greatest pitchers in history. Paige often competed against major leaguers in exhibition games. He struck out Rogers Hornsby five times in one game, Charley Gehringer three times in another, Jimmy Foxx three times in a third. Hornsby, Gehringer, and Foxx are not only Hall of Famers, but also are among the best three or four ballplayers to ever play at their respective positions. Some witnesses claimed the greatest game ever pitched was between Paige and 30-game winner Dizzy Dean in 1934. Dean held the Paige All Stars to one run over 13 innings, striking out 15. Paige shut out the Dean All Stars and fanned 17. After the contest, Dizzy, who led the St. Louis Cardinals to the 1934 world championship and who won 102 games over a four-year span, insisted that Satchel Paige was the best pitcher on the planet:

> If me and Satch had been together at St. Louis, we would've clinched the pennant by July and gone fishing from then until it was time to come back for the World Series. He was, without any doubt, the greatest pitcher I've ever seen. And I've been looking in the mirror for a long, long time.[3]

Bob Feller, one of the greatest and fastest pitchers in major league history, locked up with Paige on several occasions for exhibition all-star games. He agreed with Dean: "The prewar Paige was the best I ever saw. And I'm judging him on the way he overpowered or outwitted some of the best big league hitters of the day."[4]

To call Paige colorful or a showman understates reality. Although uneducated, he was blessed with a sharp wit, a storyteller's charm, and a keen understanding of self-promotion. One of his tricks, later copied by great softball pitchers, was to call in his infield and outfield, and have them simulate playing poker while he was effortlessly striking out opposing batsmen.

Satchel threw from several different arm angles — overhand, sidearm, and underhand or submarine style — and gave his pitches unusual names. His mesmerizing change-up was the *two-hump blooper*. His inside and high submarine straightball was *the barber*. His typical fastball was *Little Tom*. His special fastball was *Long Tom*. When he stopped in mid throw before delivering and following through, he was tossing his *hesitation pitch*. But do not take this glossary as definitive. The names changed to fit the audience and Paige's sense of the dramatic (*bat dodger, hurry-up ball, midnight creeper, four-day rider, ball bee ball, jump ball, trouble ball*).

Aside from the colorful nomenclature of his repertoire, Paige's success was due mainly to his exceptional velocity and uncanny control. Witnesses claimed that even at an advanced age he could throw strikes over a gum wrapper.

But Satchel Paige was more than a great baseball pitcher. His charisma and invariably friendly manner translated into social stardom:

> The celebrities who crowded around him and socialized with him included Wallace Beery, Billie Holiday, Jelly Roll Morton, Dizzy Dean, Louis Armstrong, Orson Welles, Cab Calloway, and Latin dictators Rafael Trujillo and Fulgencio Batista. He'd sung with Al Hibbler and Louis Prima; got in the ring and did quick exhibitions with Joe Louis, Sugar Ray Robinson, and John Henry Lewis; danced with Bojangles, who was also best man at his marriage; played basketball with Meadowlark Lemon and Goose Tatum of the Harlem Globetrotters; made a movie with Robert Mitchum and Julie London; and even worked a few nights on stage in two or three of the big touring medicine shows.[5]

The Humanity of Marcus Aurelius

Marcus Aurelius embodied the ideal of the philosopher-king. He reigned as Roman emperor from 161 until his death. Although not a stunning original thinker, Marcus exemplified and refined Stoicism. As a ruler, Marcus Aurelius was moderate, just, and effective during troubled times. The fabled *Pax Romana* was breaking down. Marcus struggled with internal discord — aggravated by natural disasters such as famines and plagues — and external threats from Germanic tribes in the north and Parthians in the east. But Marcus persevered and improved social conditions for the disadvantaged, slaves, and criminals. He also fiercely persecuted Christians, particularly in Gaul, because he viewed them as superstitious immoralists whose values jeopardized the principles underlying Roman greatness.

The family life of Marcus Aurelius was troubled. His wife, Faustina, was rumored to be an instigator of a conspiracy against Marcus, while his son, Commodus — who was widely thought to be the product of Faustina's adulterous affair with a gladiator — was anxiously eyeing the throne. One school of thought is that Marcus was poisoned by a medical doctor in the employ of Commodus. Once Commodus assumed power at Marcus's death, his reign exhibited excesses of corruption, sadism, cruelty, and debauchery similar to those that devoured the terms of Nero and Caligula.

In *The Decline and Fall of the Roman Empire*, historian Edward Gibbon described Marcus Aurelius's life:

> His life was the noblest commentary on the precepts of Zeno [founder of Stoicism]. He was severe to himself, indulgent to the imperfections of others, just and

beneficent to all mankind. He regretted that Avidius Cassius, who excited a rebellion in Syria, had disappointed him, by a voluntary death, of the pleasure of converting an enemy into a friend; and he justified the sincerity of that sentiment, by moderating the zeal of the senate against the adherents of the traitor. War he detested ... but when the necessity of a just defence called upon him to take up arms, he readily exposed his person to eight winter campaigns on the frozen banks of the Danube, the severity of which was at last fatal to the weakness of his constitution. His memory was revered by a grateful posterity, and above a century after his death, many persons preserved the image of Marcus, among those of their household gods.[6]

The gods of the Greco-Roman world did not provide clear rules of behavior for everyday life. Human beings living during those periods observed natural phenomena and their own personal qualities. Lacking a refined science to provide explanations, they mythologized their observations into a pantheon of deities — fertility, love, pestilence, famine, thunder, rain, power, anger, and the like, were all represented. Stories were conjured that accounted for the occurrence of, say, famine — the governing deity in this area must have been offended by human conduct. Elaborate ceremonies intended to please the gods were established, as well as rituals of atonement after the gods had been offended and had retaliated. Beyond the felt need to curry favor with the gods and avoid divine retribution, few specific principles of behavior followed. Philosophy was the discipline that filled this void and tried to answer the fundamental questions of human existence: What is the good life? Why am I here? What, if anything, is my destiny? How should I live my life?

For around five centuries, philosophical schools of thought such as Stoicism, Epicureanism, Cynicism, and Socratic-Platonism, among others, competed for advocates and disciples. Romans were generally tolerant of foreign deities and religious practices. But Christianity, as viewed by Marcus Aurelius and many others, was founded on passiveness and, at best, muted allegiance to the state. These values were unsuited to the continued vitality of the Roman Empire. Conventional Roman wisdom insisted that veneration of the state was required of all good citizens. Christianity, influenced strongly by Platonism, adamantly contended that this world is a pale imitation of a higher reality. Where, as here, foreign religious practices were inconsistent with the values of Roman greatness, tolerance was misplaced. Accordingly, Gibbon's commentary to the contrary notwithstanding — Marcus Aurelius was "beneficent to all mankind" — the emperor expressed no qualms about his persecution of Christians.

Marcus Aurelius composed his *Meditations* during the time he was repelling an insurrection in the Danube. The work consists of reflections, aphorisms, and principles by which good people should live their lives. A historically influential text, the *Meditations* crystallize Marcus's refinement of the

Stoic tradition. At the crux of Stoicism are commitments to inner harmony and the single-minded pursuit of virtue.

> If we take this position firmly, expecting nothing and avoiding nothing, but instead remaining content simply that we have conducted ourselves in accordance with what we know to be right, and with truthfulness with our fellow man, then this is the path to a happy life, and there is no man or god who can prevent us from following it.[7]

Satchel in the Bigs

One year after Jackie Robinson broke the color barrier in the major leagues, Satchel Paige was signed by Bill Veeck, the P.T. Barnum of baseball, to pitch for the Cleveland Indians. Probably somewhere between 40 and 42 years of age, Paige pitched a complete game shutout in his first major league starting assignment. On August 20, 1948, before 78,382, the largest crowd at that point to witness a night game, he shut out the Chicago White Sox on three hits. Overall, he won 6 and lost 1 with a splendid earned run average of 2.48. He started 7 games and relieved in 14, striking out 45 batters in 72 innings. He helped pitch the Indians to the 1948 world championship.

In 1951 he followed Veeck to the St. Louis Browns, completing his major league career in 1953. Well, not exactly. In 1965, another baseball maverick, Charles O. Finley, enlisted Paige to make an appearance for the Kansas City Athletics. At an age probably between 57 and 59, Paige hurled three shutout innings.

The confusion surrounding his age and background, the lack or unevenness of record-keeping, his natural charm and ability to weave a yarn, and his unique athletic abilities conspired to establish and amplify the aura of Satchel Paige. He is credited with having described Negro League star Cool Papa Bell as "so fast he could turn out the light and jump into bed before the room got dark." He pondered the question of the effects of aging and concluded, "Age is a question of mind over matter. If you don't mind, it doesn't matter." Asked about the sharpness of his control, he replied, "I could nip frosting off a cake with my fastball."

A few years after Paige entered the majors, an eager reporter began to regale the master storyteller about the exploits of Joe DiMaggio, Stan Musial, and up and coming Mickey Mantle. Satchel countered with a tale featuring Josh Gibson, the greatest long-ball hitter in Negro League history:

> We were playing the Homestead Grays in the city of Pittsburgh. Josh comes up in the last of the ninth with a man on and us a run behind. Well, he hit one. The Grays waited around and waited around, but finally the umpire rules it ain't com-

ing down. So we win. The next day we were disputing the Grays in Philadelphia when here comes a ball out of the sky right in the glove of the Grays' centerfielder. The umpire made the only possible call: "You're out, Gibson ... yesterday, in Pittsburgh."[8]

Stoic Doctrines

Stoics were monotheists and adhered to natural law, a universal code. Everything happens as it must happen, according to fate. The world-soul or God or Nature directs everything for the best. Happiness flows from reasonableness, from understanding the natural law, and from judging and acting compatibly with natural law. Although external events are fated, our attitudes toward and judgments about those events are in our control.

Stoics took happiness to be freedom from passion and the realization of inner peace. We should be indifferent to joy and grief, and flexible when facing life's changes. Virtue and right attitude are enough for happiness. By living according to nature, elevating reason over the passions, nurturing good habits, freeing ourselves from the desire to change the unalterable, and being indifferent to pleasure and pain, we can achieve inner harmony. The cardinal virtues are meditation, courage, self-control, and justice. Distinguishing things within our control from things beyond our control is paramount. Our judgments, attitudes, and evaluations are the only things solely under our control. By controlling these we can attain right will and virtue. The usual litany of desirables — love, honor, wealth, good health, worldly success, avoiding maltreatment from others, the well-being of friends and relatives, congenial family life, personal freedom — depend too much on external circumstances beyond our control, including the actions of others. Once we accept the slings, arrows, and seductions of life without rebellion or discontent, we are in control of our lives and happiness is attainable.

Epictetus, who greatly influenced Marcus Aurelius, captured the gist of Stoicism:

> Some things are under our control, while others are not under our control. Under our control are conception, choice, desire, aversion, and in a word, everything that is our own doing; not under our control are our body, our property, reputation, office and, in a word, everything that is not our own doing. Furthermore, the things under our control are by nature free, unhindered, and unimpeded; while the things not under our control are weak, servile, subject to hindrance, and not our own ... if it has to do with some one of the things not under your control, have ready to hand the answer, "It is nothing to me."[9]

In sum, Stoics regarded pleasure, along with sorrow, desire, and fear, as an evil. We must be indifferent to both pain and pleasure if passion is to be purged. Stoics advocated social engagement. They recognized a brotherhood and sisterhood of human beings, and denied the currency of class distinctions and social hierarchies. We have a duty to promote a world that mirrors the rationality embedded in the universe. Stoics thought marriage and family facilitated inner peace. Stoics were monotheists who believed in one supreme, universal deity as creator and sustainer of the universe. They accepted the Roman deities as media for the worship of God. Stoics believed our fate to be determined by the mechanistic laws governing all natural phenomena.

The Stoics defined happiness as inner tranquility. Their recipe for attaining happiness included minimizing desire, controlling our own judgments and attitudes, and acting in accord with natural law. Stoics explained how and why following this recipe makes us happy by analyzing human desire and our relationship to the world. Stoicism invented the happiness quotient: divide what you have by what you want; the higher the figure, the happier you will be. The best recipe for happiness is limiting what you want. The happiness quotient is still unveiled breathlessly, without attribution to the Stoics, in popular self-help books today: divide your satisfactions by your desires; the higher the figure the greater the happiness; limiting your desires is the surest road to success.

The happiness quotient is unsuccessful. It fails to distinguish the satisfaction of worthy from unworthy desires. If hundreds of our unworthy but relatively few of our worthy desires are satisfied we will still be unhappy regardless of a high average on the happiness quotient. If we correct this problem by stipulating that only worthy desires are candidates for the quotient, other difficulties appear. The happiness quotient would still fail to distinguish the intensity of our desires. We want some things much more than we want other things. Even if most of our weaker desires are fulfilled, we will be unsatisfied if some of our stronger desires remain unsatisfied. The happiness quotient also does not distinguish between needs and wants. If most of our wants are satisfied but a few of our needs are unfilled, we will have a high score on the quotient but an unhappy life. The happiness quotient also makes no mention of how our desires are satisfied. If our desires are satisfied through simulated instead of real accomplishments, a worthy happiness cannot result.

Let us brush these objections aside. I will now play my trump criticism: even if all of our desires are satisfied and we achieve a perfect score on the happiness quotient, we will still be unhappy. This is true even if we stipulate that all our satisfied desires are worthy. We would still be unhappy because our life would be inhuman. We would have nothing further to strive for, no unsatisfied projects to address, no future toward which to aspire. We would be saturated sponges of desire. Unless we could quickly devise new desires, immediately driving our happiness quotient down, boredom and anomie would result. Accordingly, the happiness quotient requires considerable refinement.

The broader critique of Stoicism is by now a cliche. While Stoicism can bring consolation to those struggling under harsh conditions, its expectations are too low for general use. The expansive richness and creativity of human experience are sacrificed on the altar of accommodation. Although it does not insist on passivity, Stoicism inclines in that direction.

Can we, should we, be indifferent to poverty, disease, natural disasters, suffering, and evil in the universe? Imagine going home today for lunch. Under the first scenario, you are met by a loved one, engage in a wonderful social interaction (fill in your own details, make them as satisfying as you can), and return to work with maximum fulfillment. Under the second scenario, you discover your loved one has been brutally murdered (fill in your own details, make them as gruesome and upsetting as you can). How can a person be indifferent as to which of these scenarios occurs? Or in his reactions to these two scenarios? If someone were indifferent we would stigmatize him as psychologically impaired. To be indifferent is to relinquish what we value most.

Stoics draw a distinction between preferences and goods. They would understand that we would prefer one scenario, the loving lunch, over the other, the brutal murder. They would deny that one scenario is better than the other. They would understand that we would prefer a gourmet Italian dinner to hunger. They would deny that the Italian dinner is better than hunger. Nothing is inherently good or evil. Human beings label events as such. Eliminate the labels and we remove needless anxiety and suffering. Stoics can thereby account for our preferences — we are not antecedently or posteriorly indifferent to numerous events — but retain their view that outcomes are inherently neutral. By focusing on the inherent neutrality of events, Stoics aspire to mute our reactions and judgments to them.

Why, though, would we prefer one scenario over another? Because we take the preferred scenario to be better than the other or to be good in itself, because we value one scenario over another. Stoics have a heavy burden that goes unaddressed: to account for why we prefer X over Y without referring to our values. Some preferences have their genesis in mere personal tastes or whims. Other preferences exist only because a value judgment, a labeling, has occurred. The Stoic bow to common sense, which acknowledges that we do prefer some events over others, is purchased at a stiff price: a spectacularly unpersuasive view of the relationship between preferences and goods. We prefer the loving lunch to the brutal murder because we judge, accurately, that the loving lunch is a good while the brutal murder is monumental evil.

The Stoics were wrong. Grieving, sorrow, and suffering are not inherently evil. Human beings are by nature valuing creatures. We cannot be stonily indifferent and retain our humanity. To value something is to make it an object of concern. We cannot coherently value everything. We partially construct who we are through what we value. If we remain indifferent to the loss of what we value we call into question the intensity of our commitment, we hedge our bet. Because our evaluations, convictions, and actions define our lives, we cannot be indifferent to our defeats, disappointments, and losses. We stake our being on and experience life most directly through our values. Grief, sorrow, and suffering are appropriate responses to the tragedies of life. The Stoics were correct in thinking that sorrow and suffering are too often exaggerated, that they can impinge on a worthwhile life, that we can obsess inappropriately on our losses. To remain indifferent to everything not fully under our control, however, is unwarranted. We should not cry over spilled milk. We should cry over spilled blood.

Outlooks, such as Stoicism, that appeal to fate have trouble accounting for robust action. If I aspire to change the world I am focusing on things outside my control and trying to alter fate. I have judged the status quo deficient and taken steps to change it. If that aspiration and the results attendant to my actions are themselves fated then my judgments about external events — how I evaluated the state of the world prior to my actions — are not under my control. I was fated to a negative view of the world and the motivation to try to change it. Rendering my freedom and control over my own judgments and actions, the pervasive direction of the world-soul, and vigorous social action compatible is no simple chore.

Even if we eliminate the presence of the world-soul and natural law, are my judgments and attitudes about events totally within my control? They are probably more in my control than most social and natural conditions in the world. But many influences, my socialization in a broad sense, contribute to my outlook. That my conscious judgments and evaluations arise fully from my freedom is far from obvious.

The presence of natural laws that are both descriptive and prescriptive complicates matters. Following the natural law, which binds all human beings in all places at all times, is reasonable, proper, and enhances prospects for happiness. According to Stoicism, such laws are antecedently external to those things within our control, but we should not be indifferent to them. We should understand and abide by them because they are good. Although outside our control, they provide the ground for our action. If so, then good and evil are more than labels that human beings wrongly attach to events. Events and actions that violate the prescriptions of natural law are evil as such. To regard such events and actions indifferently would itself not be in accord with natural law. Again, we see that fundamental Stoical doctrines do not coalesce easily.

Stoicism's kernel of insight — do not dwell on misfortune, put suffering behind you, do not become intoxicated with unimportant pursuits or frivolous desires — is obscured by its demand that nothing else matters that much. Even on its own terms it fails to distinguish earned tranquility from simulated tranquility. If Bob is peaceful because he has been hypnotized into thinking his life is other than what it is, or because he has been drugged, then his tranquility does not translate into a worthy happiness. Instead, it is merely a simulated, unearned state of mind. Bob has been tricked into thinking his unsatisfying life is satisfying. Worthwhile happiness must be earned, not merely induced. Stoicism, though, wisely points out that happiness is not simply achieving a set of external conditions, not just flourishing. Happiness requires some fit between a person's expectations and results, as well as an extended internal peace.

Part of the greatness of Marcus Aurelius is that he sensed weaknesses in Stoic doctrine and tried to refine it. For example, he understood well the Stoic conviction that if one chooses not to value anything in life — other than the agency one has over his own judgments and attitudes — then one cannot lose anything of value. But Marcus concluded this conviction signals a retreat, even a withdrawal, from the world. He anticipated, then, a modern criticism of Stoic rectitude. For Marcus Aurelius, worldly engagement entailed that we must risk disappointment in the results of our projects and sorrow at the loss of those people whom we cherished.

He also adjusted Epictetus's division of phenomena into things fully under our control and everything else. Instead of siding with the inflexible Stoic orthodoxy that a person's will is sufficient for making morally correct choices, Marcus Aurelius concluded that the will must be helped by things not under its control. In such matters, human will "needs the help of the gods and fortune."[10] Marcus, then, ends up with three categories of phenomena: those fully under the control of a person's will, those outside the control of human will, and those partially under and partially outside the control of human will.

We might be tempted to tweak Stoic doctrine under Marcus Aurelius's advisement. Perhaps we should be concerned with something *to the extent* it is under our control. We should attend to events in proportion to how much control we have over them. Still, the doctrine is unsatisfying. A single person has little control over world peace, reclamations from natural disasters, and the prevention of major wars, yet such events are reasonable foci of our attention. Maybe we need to add a dimension: we should be concerned with something to the extent it is under our control and in proportion to its effects on the common good. This addition to Stoic doctrine would allow us to attend to major world and national events even though individuals have meager control over them. But Marcus Aurelius would still think the doctrine is insufficient. He would be correct. Sometimes, for example, we should invest significant emotion in events over which we have no control and which do not seriously harm the common good. The loss of people whom we cherished and the destruction of our dearest projects are two such cases. Even if those losses do not measurably detract from the common good and even if we have no control over them, sorrow is appropriate. Marcus Aurelius intuited that suffering, contrary to orthodox Stoicism, is not an evil as such. Our struggles with suffering are a crucial part of creating worthy selves.

The possibility of cosmic meaninglessness, the lack of any inherent order and purpose in our world, repelled Marcus Aurelius. He prefigured the existential tension of the 20th century: human beings have a compelling need to understand reality in meaningful and purposive ways, but the cosmos seems indifferent to our yearnings. Marcus responds through faith — belief, conviction, and action in the face of radical uncertainty. Again adjusting Stoic orthodoxy and refusing to accept cosmic meaninglessness because doing so devalued human intellect and reason, he places his faith in a type of pantheism. The divine is the universe and all things, including human beings.

> All things are implicated with one another, and the bond is holy; and there is hardly anything unconnected with any other things. For things have been coordinated, and they combine to make up the same universe. For there is one universe made up of all things, and one god who pervades all things, and one substance, and one law, and one reason.[11]

The eternal journey of the divine is assumed to be worthy and grand, although ineffable. Anticipating Hegel,[12] Marcus Aurelius locates the meaning of human life in its role in advancing the divine goal. The divine, for Marcus, is not an independent being or substance, but rather the process of glorious cosmic evolution toward more valuable ends.

> Constantly regard the universe as one living being, having one substance and one soul; and observe how all things have reference to one perception, the perception of this one living being; and how all things act with one movement; and how all things are the cooperating causes of all things which exist; observe too the continuous spinning of the thread and the contexture of the web.[13]

As a faith, Marcus Aurelius understood that his world view could not be independently and rationally proved. His faith, though, spawned a practical advantage: it vivified engagement with the world and nourished healthy human relations. A worthwhile human life must be purposive. The highest human purpose is contribution to society. The most valuable human skills are scarce and make the greatest positive impact on the common good.

Marcus Aurelius, unsurprisingly, advised us to accept our mortality and view death as transmutation and not as an end. Part of our gratitude for our lives required that we perceive our deaths as necessary for the cosmic cycle. He does not champion personal immortality. Instead, our souls persist after death only to reenter the cosmos and the flow of nature.

> You have existed as a part. You shall disappear in that which produced you; or rather, you shall be received back into its seminal principle by transmutation.... Pass then through this little space of time conformably to nature, and end your journey in content, just as an olive falls off when ripe, blessing nature who produced it, and thanking the tree on which it grew.... Every part of me will be reduced by change into some part of the universe, and that again will change into another part of the universe, and so on for ever. And by consequence of such a change I too exist, and those who begot me, and so on forever in the other direction.[14]

He was convinced that regardless of whether we live short lives or long lives, our loss upon death is equal. Marcus Aurelius reasoned that a person cannot lose more than he possessed — a person must first possess something for that something to be taken away. We do not possess our future for it is yet to come and we cannot possess it until it becomes present. We do not possess our past for it is mere recollection. Although we may glean honor or dishonor from the past, we do not possess it. At any span of life, then, people possess only the present. Thus, whether we live long or short lives, we lose only the present.

Within this suspicious argument lay a few kernels of wisdom. We should not assume an entitlement to the future. As the cliché reminds us, tomorrow is not promised to anyone. Also, we should not hold onto the past in self-defeating ways. Savoring the past should not prevent us from engaging in the present.

On the whole, though, the argument is stunningly unpersuasive. Even if we agree that all deaths involve only the loss of the present it hardly follows that loss upon death is equal. Not all presents are equally valuable under Marcus Aurelius's own criteria because not all lives are equally worthwhile and purposive. Those lives that greatly energize the common good through virtuous use of scarce, positive human skills are more worthwhile than lives that do not. Even if we agree that the death of two people who exemplify those two sorts of lives involve only the loss of their respective presents it does not follow that the losses are equal. One loss is of a present that, on Marcus's own criteria, vibrates with worth and meaning, while the other loss is of a present that does not.

Moreover, although the future is never guaranteed, probabilities come into play. If I am 20 years old, in good health, and reasonably prudent my life expectancy — the probability of my future — is greater than if I am 80 years old, suffering from numerous diseases, and reckless to boot. To die under such circumstances at 20 is, other things being equal, a greater loss than to die at 80.

Much the same can be said about the respective quality of different presents independently of their contribution to the common good. The presents of two lives can vary dramatically in terms of suffering and enjoyment even if their contributions to the common good are equal. Thus, the respective losses upon death may well not be equal.

Marcus Aurelius's view of the past is also incomplete. While it is true that obsessing about the past can often hinder engagement in the present, it is equally true that reflecting on the past can facilitate successful engagement in the present. The past is not irrelevant to us. Our past choices, actions, and relationships help form the people we are becoming. We do, in a sense, possess the past, or it possesses us.

His reflections on the passage of time and temporality were generally interesting but unpersuasive. For example, Marcus Aurelius rejected a common view during his time that attaining enduring fame is a worthy goal for the good life. He argued that to pursue the adulteration of future generations was just as irrational as resenting that our forebearers do not lavish honor upon us. This position is probably consistent with his focus on the present and it underscores the unreliability of banking on the reactions of generations yet unborn — for those responses are not fully under our control. But his reliance on a supposed symmetry between the distant past and future is misplaced. Our distant forebearers cannot lavish anything upon us because their deaths precede our births; they have no record upon which to evaluate our lives. Such is not the case with those who immediately succeed us. While the biographies of most of us fade quite quickly from memories and history, a few human beings do achieve enduring fame or ignominy. While Marcus Aurelius is correct to point out that pursuing enduring fame is not typically a wise goal, resting that conclusion on a supposed symmetry between the distant past and future is unsound.

While I resist the particular expectations Stoicism urges and question whether extended peace, however attained, is enough for everyone, Stoicism contains admirable lessons. We often cause ourselves needless suffering by our unnecessary, self-undermining reactions to events outside our control. We bear primary responsibility for our attitudes, judgments, and evaluations. We should not whine, we are accountable for what we can control, we should suck it up. Our overall well-being depends largely on our character. Stripped of its more extravagant ideas, Stoicism also provides the foundation of the proper mental approach to baseball. Determine the extent to which outcomes and events are under your control. Focus on and take responsibility for the things within your control. Let go of most outcomes and events outside of your control. And remember that you cannot alter the past, but you can maximize possibilities for a fulfilling present and immediate future.

Paige, Aurelius, and Rules for Living

In 1953, a national magazine posted six rules for *How To Stay Young* under the signature of Leroy Satchel Paige.[15] Remarkably, Marcus Aurelius could relate to those rules.

Avoid fried meats which angry up the blood.

We certainly know now that fried foods are ill-advised for a healthy diet. Was Satchel Paige ahead of his time? Did his dietary regimen play a major role in his athletic longevity? Not likely. He later described one of his favorite meals on the road:

> Heat up a frying pan and toss in a little grease ... cut up some onions real fine and toss them and stir them around till they were brown ... put in hamburger, maybe two pounds ... ground chuck, that's got a little fat in it. Lean meat won't do it ... add a big can of Campbell's Pork & Beans and a number two can of Del Monte tomatoes. Hamburger and beans ... I can close my eyes right now and I can taste it.[16]

Few meals, one would think, could "angry up the blood" more thoroughly. Why the inconsistency? The quickest explanation is that Satchel Paige never knelt before the altar of logic. In Satchel's church, consistency was a distant also-ran in a race up the aisle against entertainment and self-promotion. The deeper explanation is that the six rules for staying young were simply concocted by an author with an eye to selling magazines. Paige claimed as much years later:

> [The media] even make up words that I was saying. And rules I had to live by. Hell, they even had me on some crazy-assed diet. Said I didn't eat fried foods because it "angrifies" the blood. What in the hell kind of word is "angrify"?... I eat fried eggs. And I eat fried bacon. And I eat fried ham and fried sausage and fried everything.[17]

Note, though, that "angrifies" does not appear in the original magazine account, although the phrase "angry up" does. The original story, though, appears with Paige's signature. My best guess is that the rules for living were, indeed, contrived by the story's author, but that Satchel Paige, not supposing the rules would take on a life of their own, signed off on them and cooperated in the accompanying story in return for payment.

Paige's deeper point suggests that the white press intentionally caricatured him as a comic figure, which may have impinged on his greatness and made him less socially threatening. (In fairness, the press did the same to numerous white ballplayers including Dizzy Dean, Babe Herman, Yogi Berra, and even Babe Ruth.)

He was, of course, correct in part. The media played up his fables, and foibles, embellished his already colorful language, and freely attributed actions and sayings to him that seemed consistent with what he might have done and said. Some of these attributions may well have struck Paige and others as demeaning, either at the time they were made or in retrospect. Painting him as child-like, naïve, and comical in a subservient way, the media distorted the dignity of the man for their own purposes. Paige was, then, exploited in that sense.

But those who cultivate a shuck and jive routine in order to cope with a hostile world can expect to suffer at times for doing so. Satchel Paige conjured and exploited an image that amplified the considerable fame he won on baseball diamonds. He played the clown, even the fool, when he judged it advantageous to his ends. Anyone freely participating in *Mr. Bones and Mr. Interlocutor* minstrel shows, for example, is hard pressed to complain about social caricature.[18]

Satchel Paige was not a social reformer. He instinctively embraced a partial Stoicism: don't be concerned with those events not under your control. He rejected, though, the call to emotional indifference. Paige sought pleasure, early and often. He lived an exciting, worthwhile, robustly meaningful life. We must regret, though, that he was born into a world where some men, such as he, of great innate intelligence and enormous athletic gifts were denied full opportunities to forge their personalities and develop their talents. All that only because of the color of their skin.

Marcus Aurelius was familiar with the ancient Pythagorean practice of vegetarianism. The Pythagoreans believed in the transmigration of the soul upon death. If a human being died with an impure soul, that soul was reborn within the body of another human being or animal to continue its quest for internal harmony. To eat an animal was, possibly, to eat the new body of dearly departed Uncle Stavos. The Pythagoreans also advised against eating beans. The flatulence often induced during digestion was evidence that eating beans "angries up" the soul. From this perspective, Satchel Paige's hamburger and beans recipe would send the soul into major trauma.

The Pythagorean practice rested on a strict dualism between the soul (or mind or psyche) as the life-giving force that defines human identity and the body (mere substance or material) that dulls the soul's sensibilities and thereby serves as a temporary tomb or prison. Only the disembodied, pure soul is free and enjoying its full capabilities. Marcus Aurelius shared the basic Pythagorean dualism but did not subscribe to transmigration and personal immortality. Adopting a pantheistic approach, Marcus accepted transmutation. Upon our deaths, the life force of our souls reenters the cosmos and becomes, again, part of the universe. Although he ate sparsely, we lack evidence that Marcus Aurelius avoided fried foods (or beans).

If your stomach disputes you, lie down and pacify it with cool thoughts.

Keep the juices flowing by jangling around gently as you move.

The second and third rules of Satchel Paige's supposed secrets of successful living concern physical movements and their psychic effects. After pounding down generous helpings of hamburger and beans, Satchel's stomach undoubtedly disputed him often. Lying down, resting, and reflecting in positive ways are wise antidotes. Certainly, Stoics such as Marcus Aurelius recommend contemplation regardless of the condition of your stomach. The art of contemplation distinguishes human beings from beasts and allows us to take control over the process of self-making. If our stomachs are pacified along the way, so much the better.

The advice to "jangle around gently" is more obscure. If a person is moving, he or she is already in motion. Should we jangle around *in contrast to* quick, herky-jerky gyrations? Or should we jangle around *in addition to* the movement that comes naturally once we are in motion? Or is jangling around a code phrase meaning stretching exercises or actions preliminary to more vigorous activity? In any case, Roman military gear made jangling around difficult, if not impossible. So Marcus Aurelius is unlikely to have anticipated Paige's advice.

Go very light on the vices, such as carrying on in society. The social ramble ain't restful.

Paige's fourth rule is right out of the Stoic handbook. The social ramble — other than military and political activities, and friendships and intimate relationships that facilitate the common good — is proscribed by Marcus Aurelius. The presence of this rule, though, provides strong evidence that the secrets of living were not authored by Satchel Paige. He was well known for thoroughly immersing himself in the social ramble. Fast cars, faster women, and suitable spirits were his constant companions as he savored a free-spending, unregimented life. (Or might Satchel have authored this rule to squeeze some irony into the magazine article?)

Avoid running at all times.

In Paige's day conventional training wisdom included a hefty schedule of running for pitchers. Proper leg strength was thought to be a requirement for strong drive off the pitching rubber and for maximizing lower body power. Johnny Sain, a renowned pitching coach, was probably the first to question this conventional wisdom in the 1960s. Is Paige making a serious point about the training of pitchers, one that anticipates Johnny Sain's view? Or is Paige here merely endorsing the indolent life? Or is he, again, citing his preference for jangling gently over more vigorous activity? Or is this rule thrown in for purposes of humor or irony? Hard to say, but Marcus Aurelius could not agree with any of these possibilities. As a military and political man, he could not subscribe to indolence. Nor did Marcus ever suggest a preference for jangling gently when more vigorous activity was available. Neither humor nor irony adorns Marcus's prose. Although it is speculation, my guess would be that Marcus Aurelius, if a baseball manager, would not hire Johnny Sain as his pitching coach. Leo Mazzone, maybe.

Don't look back. Something might be gaining on you.

Here Satchel Paige and Marcus Aurelius, again, join company. Marcus emphasizes, always, the present as all that a person possesses. We cannot alter the past, the future is only anticipation, the present should rivet our attention. Satchel mirrors that approach in rule six. His reason for doing so is less clear. Is it trying to outrun, oops, outjangle an aggrieved pursuer? Is it trying to forget his past victimization?

Neither Paige nor Aurelius is at his best with temporality. Reflecting on the past, savoring memories, learning from our mistakes, and analyzing our triumphs are only a few ways in which looking back can be fruitful.

Obsessing about the past, surely, is time misplaced and ill used. Irrationally trying to alter the past bears no currency. Wailing over spilled milk is unwise. But these distortions should not lead us to conclude that looking back as such is imprudent.

Joe DiMaggio and Friedrich Nietzsche

"Hey, Willie Mays is great. Mickey Mantle can hit a ball over a building. But you never saw DiMaggio, kid. You never saw the real thing."

— Bob Costas's father to his son.

"Sometimes a fellow gets a little tired of writing about DiMaggio; a fellow thinks 'there must be some other ball player in the world worth mentioning.' But there isn't really, not worth mentioning in the same breath with Joe DiMaggio."

— Columnist Red Smith

"There was never a day when I was as good as Joe DiMaggio at his best. Joe was the best, the very best I saw."

— Stan Musial, St. Louis Cardinals superstar and Hall-of-Famer

"DiMaggio is the best. He's the greatest team player I've ever seen."

— Connie Mack, legendary manager
of the Philadelphia Athletics

"I must have confidence, and I must be worthy of the Great DiMaggio, who does all things perfectly even with the pain of the bone spur in his heel."

— From Ernest Hemingway's
The Old Man and the Sea

Joe DiMaggio (1914–1999) was seen, among other things, as a hero of the ages by many people and as a bitter, ungenerous recluse by other people. Who was Joe DiMaggio? Friedrich Nietzsche (1844–1900) advanced perspectivism, a view that denied human beings had access to an objective world order and absolute truths. Nietzsche's perspectivism can help us understand the conflicting, multiple aspects of Joe DiMaggio, national icon.

Jolting Joe and Heroism

Joe DiMaggio, who played for the New York Yankees from 1936 through 1951, was the first five-tool baseball player in the major leagues. He could hit, hit for power, throw well, run fast, and field superbly. (Oscar Charleston, who terrorized the Negro League from 1915 to the late 1930s, was probably the first five-tool player in professional baseball.) DiMaggio also exuded class, style and skill. He not only achieved great results — 9 world championships, 10 American League pennants, in his 13 year playing career — he looked graceful, even elegant, in the process. Countless fans insisted that to understand the aesthetics of baseball a person needed to see DiMaggio go from first base to third base on a teammate's single.

Joe was the eighth of nine children born to Giuseppe and Rosalia Mercurio DiMaggio, natives of Isola delle Femmine, a rocky, isolated islet off the coast of Sicily. Settling in San Francisco, the DiMaggios continued their generational labors as fishermen. Giuseppe's boat was too small to venture far from shore in search of highly desired crabs and salmon, and the DiMaggios were poor even by the modest standards of their immigrant peers. Joe showed little aptitude for fishing and less for formal education. After graduating eighth grade, he left high school about as quickly as he had entered. But he was a natural athlete, who excelled first in tennis, then in baseball. The older DiMaggio sons, Mike and Tom, were drawn into the family business. The younger three boys, Vince, Joe, and Dom, all became major league ballplayers. In the 1940s, in fact, three of the four greatest defensive outfielders in the game were named DiMaggio. (The fourth was Terry Moore of the St. Louis Cardinals.)

Joseph Campbell once defined a hero as "someone who has found or done something beyond the normal range of experience or achievement. A hero is someone who has given his or her life to something bigger than oneself."[1]

The definition, though, is too broad. For example, every major league baseball player has done something beyond the normal range of experience and achievement. So has every lawyer, doctor, and holder of a Ph.D. Yet, we do not consider all such folks heroes. To give one's life to something bigger than oneself does not help much either. Taken literally, *not* to give one's life to something beyond the self is difficult. Almost every major project we undertake goes beyond the self. Taken loosely, the expression might mean that a hero sacrifices the self for the common good. But that seems too harsh a standard.

Instead of looking for a strict definition of hero, we are better advised to look at traits often attributed to those whom we dub heroes: exceptional courage or nobility or strength; someone who fights for a higher cause in service of the common good; someone celebrated for bold exploits; a person possessing and exercising abilities and character far greater than typical people; someone who has sacrificed his own narrow interests for a grand purpose; a person celebrated for extraordinary achievements in a particular field; someone who stands as an exemplar of human behavior.

DiMaggio was considered a hero in three primary ways. He showed nobility and strength in overcoming injuries to perform superbly as an athlete. He possessed and manifested baseball abilities far greater than almost all other players, thereby producing extraordinary achievements. He displayed character traits that could reasonably be seen as exemplary. Adoring fans project traits upon those they choose as heroes, traits that reflect the idealized images harbored by the public. DiMaggio conducted himself, on and off the field, in a way that allowed us to do this.

> There never was a guy like DiMaggio in baseball. The way people admired him, the way they admire him now. Everybody wanted to meet Joe, to touch him, to be around him.... Joe was a hero.... You can't manufacture a hero like that. It has to be there, the way he plays, the way he works, the way he is.[2]
> [What makes a hero?] In DiMaggio's case, it was the ability to give a sense of dignity and worth to the fantasies of thousands of kids on the weed-strewn lots of America.... That spark of class and dignity DiMaggio gave to simply doing his job was gleaned by [everyone] who ever watched DiMaggio on or off the field, watched him simply doing his job, without grandstanding, without arm-pumping exhibitions of narcissism.[3]
> Strictly a class guy.... He's affable, gracious, mannerly, and generous. And no artist ever approached his profession with more respect or greater dignity. To DiMaggio baseball is not just a game, just a way to make a fast buck, it's an important calling that demands the best a man can give. This goes a long way in explaining his pre-eminence.[4]
> He was the perfect Hemingway hero ... the man who exhibited grace under pressure, who withheld any emotion lest it soil the purer statements of his deeds. DiMaggio was that kind of hero; his grace and skill were always on display, his emotions always concealed. This stoic grace was not achieved without a terrible price: DiMaggio was a man wound tight.[5]

Baseball, though, is not war. DiMaggio's purpose — winning championships — often required him to sacrifice his interests for those of the team, but calling such a purpose grand is a stretch. Ted Williams was a hero in the fuller sense of someone who risked his life in a just military cause. Comparing DiMaggio's sacrifices to those of war heroes or patriots who relinquish much for the common good or individuals who devote their lives to service for the disadvantaged and disenfranchised is fatuous. Joe DiMaggio, nevertheless, was a hero in the lesser senses noted and as a famous embodiment of appealing values.

Nietzsche and Perspectivism

Nietzsche denies the existence of absolute, transcendent truths and affirms the need for perspectival interpretation.

> Everything the philosopher has declared about man is, however, at bottom no more than a testimony as to the man of a very limited period of time. Lack of historical sense is the family failing of all philosophers ... there are no eternal facts, just as there are no absolute truths.[6]

He understands that some propositions become embedded in language and common sense and earn the honorific title of truth, but he denies that our way of speaking about the world necessarily reflects an independent reality. Instead, our language and conventional understandings of truth mirror the needs, interests, and general psychology of different human types. Those understandings that flow from the masses reflect the leveling mindset of the herd. Although Nietzsche sharply disparages the mediocrity, banality, and muted will to power, as well as the attitudes of ressentiment and revenge, that typically accompany the judgments of the herd, he sometimes acknowledges the refinements to human possibilities that the herd has produced.

Nietzsche accepts unsqueamishly that our beliefs are false, at least when judged by the humanly-created standard of absolute truth. Instead of being preoccupied with transcendent standards of absoluteness and unconditionality, however, we should embrace this life fully by accepting the contingency and fallibility of the perspectives we advance.[7]

Perspectives are not merely particular sets of coherent beliefs.[8] Nietzsche accepts that there can be untrue beliefs in a perspective; indeed, he often asserts the need for falsity in life and within one's perspective. Moreover, one could adopt a perspective, even self-consciously, and not believe all the truths implied by it. Nietzsche also holds that statements can be true in certain perspectives but not in others, but he does not hold that our believing something establishes truth, even within a perspective. Embracing a perspective is related to coping and comprehending the world, to imposing order related to one's character, experiences, and powers. This process includes both social and individual dimensions: churches, cultures, states, communities, races, individuals, and so on all adopt and create perspectives.[9] Thus a particular person is influenced by numerous, often conflicting perspectives. Where there are loci of power, where there is life, perspectives are generated.[10]

The relationship of perspectives, reality, facts, and truth is at the heart of Nietzsche's philosophy. If Nietzsche is correct we have no bare facts — facts independent of our perspectival interpretations — to which we can appeal for foundational justification of our truth claims. Thus, there is no particular account that uniquely captures the complexities of physical reality or that unequivocally discovers a natural order in the universe. Indeed, Nietzsche's most strident rhetoric is directed against the prevalent philosophical view of his time that there are things-in-themselves which stand above space, time, and human notions of causality.

For Nietzsche, a thing-in-itself is an incoherent concept because all things must have properties and all properties are relational in the sense that they are effects of a thing on other things. Given such a view, the concept of an unrelated, pure entity which somehow exists independently of other entities is nonsense. He does not, however, subscribe to a crude idealism which accepts only a mind-dependent world. Instead, he embraces a Heraclitean world of inherently undifferentiated, chaotic flux. Rejecting an independent, objective world structure, Nietzsche takes the project of human life to be imposing order, interpretation, and evaluation on the world of Becoming and on our own characters. Through the structure of our language we reflect our conceptions of the world.

His view of the world underwrites Nietzsche's perspectivism. Because the world is inherently undifferentiated flux it lacks stable, independent metaphysical attributes which could objectively measure human evaluations. No particular perspective can rightfully claim to capture the world as it really is or to be the best possible rendering of the world because the world is inherently unstable and reality is nothing more than a name for the entire range of institutions, theories, and conventions human beings select and impose. Thus there are no bare facts, there are only interpretations.

> Against that positivism which stops before phenomena, saying "there are only facts," I should say: no, it is precisely facts that do not exist, only interpretations.[11]

As a result, the distinction between truth and error is much fuzzier than generally imagined. The human quest to impose order and meaning must be undertaken without metaphysical guarantees: no particular perspective can portray the world as it really is because undifferentiated flux resists further description — there are no fine details to describe.[12]

DiMaggio's Panache

His career batting records are admirable, but he leads in no statistical category. Like many of his contemporaries, DiMaggio lost three prime years in military service during World War II. DiMaggio entered the service at age 28 and left at 31. He was also uniquely hampered by the ballpark in which he played his home games. Yankee Stadium measured 461 feet in straightaway center field and 457 feet in left center, DiMaggio's power alley. (Today, major league ballparks rarely reach 380 feet in left center.) In Yankee Stadium, he played 880 career games, hitting .315 with 148 home runs and 720 runs batted in. On the road, DiMaggio played 856 games, batting .333 with 213 home runs and 817 runs batted in. (In neutral ballparks, DiMaggio had a higher batting average than Ted Williams, who hit a career .328 away from Fenway Park.) Bill James, baseball's premier statistician, concluded that no batter in major league history suffered as much from the dimensions of his home park as Joe DiMaggio. One of DiMaggio's most striking accomplishments was hitting 361 career home runs while striking out only 369 times. (By contrast, Mickey Mantle hit 536 homers but struck out 1,710 times. Reggie Jackson smacked 563 homers but struck out 2,597 times. Hank Greenberg stroked 331 homers and struck out 844 times.) During 7 seasons, Jolting Joe had fewer strikeouts than he had home runs. Putting aside the deadball era in baseball, when both homers and strike outs were rarer, he holds the record for that feat.

During the off season between the 1949 and 1950 campaigns, 85 percent of all major leaguers in a poll conducted by *The Sporting News* named DiMaggio as the player they most admired. Players of the New York Yankees named him the player they most admired in the history of baseball. In 1969, during baseball's centennial celebration, a poll of sportswriters tabbed DiMaggio as the greatest living ballplayer.

DiMaggio smoldered with pride and determination. Almost every player *tried* to win, most *wanted* deeply to win, but DiMaggio *had* to win. He *needed* to win to maintain his self-image and worth.

> No one played with more pride than The Great DiMaggio. Every game he strived to be the best player in the world. Perfection was his goal, and no one ever came closer. Once he was asked why he pushed himself so hard on the field [even in situations that seemed unimportant]. He replied, "I always think there might be someone out there in the stands who has never seen me play.[13]

DiMaggio measured himself by the success of his team. Unlike Ted Williams, who yearned to be the best hitter that ever lived, DiMaggio needed to be the greatest winner in baseball. Teammate Ed Lopat spoke of DiMaggio's only goal:

> If he went zero-for-four and we lost, he'd sit there in front of his locker for thirty, forty minutes and never move. He'd felt he'd let the club down. No man can carry a club by himself. But that's just the way he felt. He hadn't done the job that day. He'd let his teammates down.[14]
>
> [DiMaggio] wanted to be the man in whose hands the fate of the game would rest. He expected to deliver that game, every game, to his team. He expected to dominate, not by doing something right but by doing everything right. Here was the difference between Ted Williams and Joe DiMaggio: Ted wanted to be the

greatest hitter who ever lived.... Joe's ambition was more astonishing: he wanted to be perfect, not at something but everything.... And more amazing was how close he came.[15]

Outwardly, DiMaggio maintained a stoical face. "Dead Pan Joe" was his nickname in the minor leagues. The few people who thought they knew him well were probably mistaken. DiMaggio did not let the world look inside of him. He protected his privacy more fiercely than a junkyard dog guards his food and turf. A classic story of the inwardness of DiMaggio was recalled by a sportswriter who noticed Joe and his two San Francisco, Italian American, Yankees friends, Frank Crosetti and Tony Lazzeri, in the lobby of a St. Louis hotel. The three ballplayers sat in silence for almost 90 minutes. At that point, DiMaggio cleared his throat. Crosetti looked up and said, "What did you say?" Lazzeri responded, "Shut up. He didn't say nothing." The trio then resumed their silence.[16]

Inwardly, his determination was all-consuming. During his playing days, he smoked three packs of cigarettes a day, drank countless cups of coffee, and slept irregularly. Teammate Tommy Henrich described DiMaggio's intensity:

> More than any ballplayer, I never saw a guy bear down, day after day, pitch after pitch, supreme — oh, my golly — the pride he had. Playing like a pro, never dog it, never relaxed. I don't know how his body could stand it.[17]

His body, it turned out, could not stand it. DiMaggio developed ulcers while still in his twenties. He was afflicted with an ankle that was burned by a diathermy lamp; tooth, toenail, and adenoid ills; charley horses; a trick right shoulder and a bad elbow; bone spurs in both heels; pneumonia; and a bad back. DiMaggio's seemingly endless physical woes were the taxes he paid for the pressure he placed himself under and his relentless striving.

Still, the good impression and beautiful appearance — *la bella figura* — prevailed. Classy, elegant, graceful, dignified, effortless, regal, dependable, peerless, heroic, hungry, tough, relentless, nerves of steel, intense, solitary ... these were the adjectives most commonly used to describe Joe DiMaggio.

> This [DiMaggio] is the whole ball player, complete and great. There are no defects to discuss.... Winning sometimes with his presence alone, because the other people knew how good he was and choked up a little.... Remembering DiMaggio never lied to me.... Or broke his word.... Or hurt anyone to make himself a bigger man. You don't forget a guy like this.[18]

On the baseball field, nothing captured his hold on America better than his record 56-game hitting streak in 1941. A consecutive game hitting streak allows for no off days, no slumps, no excuses. The drama, energy, and pressure build proportionately to the length of the streak. Opposing players are aware of the streak and aspire to break it. Every plate appearance takes on added significance. Most strikingly, DiMaggio's streak defied probability in a way no other baseball achievement has. Stephen Jay Gould, renowned scientist, argues that DiMaggio's hitting steak is the "greatest accomplishment in the history of baseball, if not all modern sport."[19]

Nothing ever happened in baseball above and beyond the frequency predicted by coin-tossing models. The longest runs of wins or losses are as long as they should be, and occur about as often as they ought to ... [with one exception], one sequence so many standard deviations above the expected distribution that it should never have occurred at all: Joe DiMaggio's 56-game hitting streak in 1941.... DiMaggio's streak is the most extraordinary thing that ever happened in American sports ... a unique assault upon the otherwise unblemished record of Dame Probability.... [The streak] embodies the essence of the battle that truly defines our lives.... [DiMaggio] cheated death, at least for awhile.[20]

What Gould might not have known is that Joe DiMaggio, in his first full season as a professional ballplayer in 1933 with the San Francisco Seals, managed a 61-game hitting streak! (Also, after his 56-game hitting steak was broken in 1941, DiMaggio promptly went on a 17-game streak.)

Beyond the streak, DiMaggio's reputation, unlike that of Ted Williams, was of someone who always produced in the clutch.

Playing with a painful charley horse on one leg and a spur on the other, DiMaggio was scarcely able to run out his numerous base hits, but there wasn't a day when you wouldn't have preferred to have him on your side rather than Williams ... that indefinable something DiMaggio had and Williams didn't have when the chips were down.... Giuseppe was a champion.[21]

In 1949, already far beyond his peak, DiMaggio missed the first 65 games of the season with a bone spur injury in his heel. In late June, the Yankees visited Fenway Park for a crucial three-game series with the contending Red Sox. DiMaggio played his first games of the season. In the three contests, he smashed four home runs and drove in nine runs. The Yankees swept the series, erasing a six-run deficit in the second game as DiMaggio homered twice.

In 1939, well within his prime, DiMaggio was batting .409 late in the season. He suffered an eye infection in early September that affected his vision. Although the pennant was well in hand, manager Joe McCarthy kept DiMaggio in the lineup every game despite his debility. DiMaggio went 17 for 73 (.233) for the rest of the month, finishing the season at .381. But for the infection and his continued presence in the lineup, DiMaggio would probably have beaten Ted Williams to the magic .400 circle.

In 1951, DiMaggio's final season, he was performing well below expectations. Bob Feller, at that point still the greatest pitcher in the game, delivered what appeared to be the final insult. With two outs and a runner on second base, Rapid Robert intentionally walked up-and-coming star Yogi

Berra to face Joe DiMaggio. Feller was announcing to the world his lack of respect for the 1951 version of the Yankee Clipper. DiMaggio, the man who hated to be embarrassed, was slapped in the face by this *infamia*: "He was staring at nothing. His face was expressionless. You had to be a Dago-watcher to note the veins, like cords on his neck, and the ominous darkness around his eyes."[22] Feller quickly gained the edge, 1 ball 2 strikes, and fired his fabled fastball to end DiMaggio's agonies. Joe D, who had hit exceptionally well against Feller over their careers, had other aspirations. He crushed a frozen rope to the 457-foot sign in left center field. Cruising into third base with a stand-up triple, DiMaggio gave a barely perceptible nod of his head as the 70,000 fans who packed Yankee Stadium deliriously roared their approval. You don't tug on Superman's cape, you don't spit into the wind ... and you sure as hell don't try to show up Jolting Joe DiMaggio, even if he was on his last legs.

Former teammates, managers, and coaches almost unanimously recalled that DiMaggio never made a mental error or base-running gaff. Their memories exaggerate. Every baseball player who ever lived made at least a few. One of DiMaggio's occurred in 1939 during what may have been his greatest fielding play. On August 2, playing against the Detroit Tigers, Joe was patrolling center field when superstar Hank Greenberg strode to the plate with a teammate on first base. Hammering Hank cracked a long drive to the deepest recesses of Yankee Stadium. DiMaggio took off at once, heading for the 461-foot sign in center. The base runner headed for home and even lead-footed Greenberg harbored fantasies of an inside-the-park home run. DiMaggio glanced once at the ball and kept running. At the last possible instant, he looked again, extended his glove, and snagged the horsehide. He had traveled over 200 feet for the ball. The Tigers base runner was rounding third when Joe caught the ball. But DiMaggio had forgotten the number of outs and did not throw the ball into the relay man in time to execute what should have been an easy double play. Few remember the rare mental error. Many who witnessed the catch still recall it as the best defensive play they ever saw.

Perspectivism and Evaluation

Perspectivism highlights the role that human evaluations, interests, purposes, and goals play in the formation of truth. Moreover, perspectivism underscores the part historical struggle among interest groups plays in establishing the social conventions that become enshrined as common sense: there is no available Archimedean point, no all-encompassing master perspective, no available unsituated vantage point from which human beings can discern the truth.

Moreover, adopting particular perspectives is not a matter of immediate choice. At birth we find ourselves in one social setting, with a certain range of possibilities, with a circumscribed set of life prospects. We are socialized into certain world views, which often embody the seeds of their own destruction. Conversions to new perspectives require accepting new arrangements of life that resist simple commitments of will. Only great effort, revised self-images, and personal re-creation can animate such conversions.

None of this troubles Nietzsche because, if he is correct, things could hardly be otherwise. He is distressed, however, at the way perspectives often masquerade as more than what they are, how they arrogate to themselves the trappings of absolute truth, universal authority, and timeless necessity. When perspectival interpretations assume such imperial self-understandings they wrongfully renege on the contingency of life.

When we interpret from a perspective we select and simplify. Because Nietzsche claims there is no world-in-itself and no aperspectival rendering of reality, human selection and simplification underscore the partial nature of all perspectival interpretations. Once we renounce the pretension to transcendent truth, truth that stands above human interests and purposes, we can impose order and meaning on the world only through simplifications that are motivated by the needs and desires of particular peoples at particular times. Moreover, peoples will be (largely) unaware of the precise motivations that fuel their specific world visions. In sum, perspectival interpretations both reflect and constitute modes of life that promote particular types of people in specific historical contexts.

Perspectivism's self-conscious partiality has several dimensions: there is no final, fixed, best perspective simpliciter; different peoples embracing conflicting modes of life will impose different perspective understandings on their worlds; reinterpretation, reevaluation, and re-creation are not only possible but also salutary; we will be mostly unaware of the precise ways we have simplified the world and of the motivations and values that underwrote those simplifications; and the pretension to universal authority is dangerous illusion which can artificially limit human possibilities.

Perspectivism's partiality contrasts with absolutism or dogmatism — the view that certain truth claims pertain to all human beings in all contexts at all times; that at least some of these claims are discoverable by human reason; that once discovered and validated these claims are fixed and final, and can thus serve as epistemological foundations. Dogmatism of this sort is typically supported by a commitment to objective metaphysical structures such as Kantian things-in-themselves, Platonic forms, or the Judeo-Christian-Islamic Supreme Being.

Nietzsche, clearly and consistently, rejects all versions of dogmatism. When describing "philosophers of the future" he says:

Are these coming philosophers new friends of "truth"? That is probable enough, for all philosophers so far have loved their truths. But they will certainly not be dogmatists. It must offend their pride, also their taste, if their truth is supposed to be a truth for everyman — which has so far been the secret wish and hidden meaning of all dogmatic aspirations.[23]

Yet, in typically Nietzschean style, his rejection of dogmatism is not one-sided, but admits reversal and subtlety:

Without accepting the fictions of logic, without measuring reality against the purely invented world of the unconditional and self-identical, without a constant falsification of the world by means of numbers, man could not live — that renouncing false judgments would mean renouncing life and a denial of life. To recognize untruth as a condition of life — that certainly means resisting accustomed value feelings in a dangerous way; and a philosophy that risks this would by that token alone place itself beyond good and evil.[24]

Perhaps his message here is that our notions of objectivity and transcendence are themselves ingenious human creations that are in some sense necessary to life. But they are neither metaphysical facts nor aperspectival depictions of the world. Instead, they are one kind of human myth, one type of human interpretation and evaluation. Thus our notions of objectivity and transcendent truth are not pure foundations for absolutism; although they may present themselves in that fashion, at bottom they are no more than one interpretative schema among many. Nietzsche's clearest and most poetic denunciation of absolute truth is in "On Truth and Lie in an Extra-Moral Sense."

What, then, is truth? A mobile army of metaphors, metonyms, and anthropomorphisms — in short, a sum of human relations, which have been enhanced, transposed, and embellished poetically and rhetorically, and which after long use seem firm, canonical, and obligatory to a people: truths are illusions about which one has forgotten that this is what they are; metaphors which are worn out and without sensuous power; coins which have lost their pictures and now matter only as metal, no longer as coins ... to be truthful means ... the obligation to lie according to a fixed convention, to lie herd-like in a style obligatory for all.[25]

Nietzsche's views on truth and perspectivism connect with his views on life. The construction and application of concepts and (falsifying) language are part of the basic human activities: creation and evaluation. The structures of dogmatism — a transcendent world, things-in-themselves, objective truth that must be discovered, universal valuations, the quest for certainty — strike Nietzsche as limiting and suffocating. At bottom, human beings are creative artists (in a broad sense) who must impose meaning and order on their world of Becoming. Worse, the structures of dogmatism embody a no-saying attitude toward our world and a craven aspiration for a transcendent, pain-free, world. They thus constitute a denial of a favorite Nietzschean theme: reimagination and re-creation accompanied by conscious celebration of contingency and personal mortality. Moreover, dogmatism and absolutism wrongly assume that what is good for some is good for all. As such, dogmatism and absolutism falsely sanctify the conclusions of the herd — judgments which reflect the needs and desires of the masses of mediocrities — and deny the order of rank among human beings.

Healthy, strong human beings are not paralyzed by radical perspectivism, but rather rejoice in increased creative opportunities. The moment of nihilism — when all seems up for grabs because recognition of the lack of metaphysical foundations is widespread — prepares the way for delight in human artistic achievements as passion, reason, and experience create new values and modes of life. Indeed, creativity is largely unconscious and instinctual. The learned academician, scrupulously laboring on perfecting theoretical projects, is more likely to mirror current social and cultural contexts than to create subversively and to legislate new values and cultural practices.

But all this is put too simply. (In fact it is probably impossible not to oversimplify when outlining Nietzsche's work. But even this underscores broader Nietzschean themes: simplification and falsification invariably accompany the imposition of meaning and order on the world of Becoming; if perspectivism is persuasive then there are inevitably numerous conflicting ways to interpret Nietzsche's own work; thus powerful literary works create numerous interpretations and confusions.) Within each of us, multiple conflicting perspectives vie for supremacy. Nietzsche often talks of the inherent multiplicity of the self. Fundamental conflict is at the core of one's internal life and external relations. By highlighting that the self is not a natural unity, Nietzsche reminds us that we all embody internal battlegrounds where our conflicting drives fuel conflicting perspectival frameworks. To forge a unity out of inner conflict, to give style to one's character, to create out of oneself new values and perspectives are the missions of the philosophers of the future.

DiMaggio, Love, and Death

Always well-dressed and stylish off the field, a large part of DiMaggio's ongoing mystique and legend resulted from his marriages. Joe's first marriage was to actress Dorothy Arnold. The union produced a son, Joe Jr., but was fraught with career and lifestyle conflicts. Arnold enjoyed the nightlife and social whirl, Joe was unrepentantly private. After their divorce, rumors of reconciliation periodically circulated until Arnold remarried. So whom does Joe marry next? One of the most emotionally fragile, psychologically insecure, beautiful, sexy, celebrated women in the country: screen goddess Marilyn Monroe.

At first blush, DiMaggio reveals himself to be a hopeless, deluded, love-struck *cafone*. He is a man thoroughly infused with old-world Sicilian values about a woman's role in the family. He seethes with jealously. He places profound value on not being embarrassed. No champion of radical individualism, he understands that the excesses of any family member intrude on the reputation of the others. To call him private and guarded is like labeling Shaquille O'Neal as sort of tall. And whom does he marry? One of the most neurotic, vulnerable women in the world. Marilyn Monroe was addicted to celebrity, publicity, and sex as the only ways to define her worth. What sort of romantic rube could think such a marriage would be successful? Especially given that DiMaggio's first marriage was to Marilyn Monroe–lite.

The story is richer. What first appears like a faintly ridiculous mismatch trading in self-parody makes sense on other levels. What did Marilyn need? Someone who was strong, reliable, a white knight, a redeemer; someone who knew actually who he was and what his place was in American society; someone who could protect her and embraced values that she lacked but to which she thought she should aspire. She needed a hero. She needed Joe DiMaggio. For his part, Joe needed someone who needed him for precisely those reasons. DiMaggio could underscore his self-perception by seeing himself through Marilyn's appreciative gaze. He could still exercise his highest values long after his playing days were over. He could still be Joe DiMaggio, after all.

Thousands of attractive, domesticated women with old-world values would have loved to marry Joe DiMaggio. But DiMaggio was drawn to beauty, celebrity, and flash, even if he wanted to keep it under wraps, all for himself. Overwhelming physical attraction and mutually-satisfying psychological needs, though, are typically insufficient for long-term, everyday living. Marilyn Monroe was not going to give up her career and the fame she desperately needed to become Joe DiMaggio's stay-at-home wife. Joe DiMaggio remained jealous, prideful, and proprietary over his wife's life. He despised the Hollywood scene — its fake familiarity, phony ingratiation, contrived exhibitionism, incessant chatter, smug superiority, flimsy virtues. Inevitable conflict raged between Joe and Marilyn, perhaps punctuated by occasional domestic violence.

Less than a year after their marriage, Marilyn was co-starring in *The Seven Year Itch*. In front of an estimated 1,500 onlookers on a New York street, the director shot a skirt-blowing scene over a subway grate. Monroe's dress was blown above her knees, often to her waist, at least 15 times, while photographers — some of whom were strategically positioned at street level — enjoyed the view. DiMaggio happened by and was enraged, "What the hell is going on here?" he spewed before he stormed off. The next day, Marilyn gushed about how much she enjoyed shooting the scene. Lots of attention, over a thousand admirers, shouts of approval ... oodles of the external validation that she craved. DiMaggio had been humiliated. His own wife playing the fool for the amusement of whom ... a bunch of *stranieri* seeking cheap thrills. The pandering, the exhibitionism, his wife turned into a human *scappatella*, all dignity renounced. And she tells the press she enjoyed it! Two weeks later Monroe filed for divorce. DiMaggio did not contest.

But their story continued for eight years. Every time Marilyn was in a tough spot, every time she needed a hero, she did not turn to some Hollywood *stronzo*. She called on her hero. She contacted DiMaggio. Although she remarried for a time — to playwright Arthur Miller — and was sexually involved with countless other men, when the pressure was on she turned only to DiMaggio. He invariably responded. When she sought release from an unsuccessful stay at the psychiatric division of New York Hospital, it was DiMaggio who bullied her release ("Release my wife or I will take apart this building, piece of wood by piece of wood." He ignored, of course, that they were divorced.). When she needed surgery to remedy a digestive tract illness, DiMaggio was there for support. At the end in 1962 — just before her suicide or murder because of sexual involvement with John and Bob Kennedy, depending on which story one chooses to believe — rumors of remarriage to DiMaggio were circulating. Marilyn had apparently kept a life-size poster of Jolting Joe in her closet, even while married to Miller.

DiMaggio assumed control of her funeral. He barred the degenerates from Hollywood, closed the ceremony to the public, and invited only family and a few reliable friends. Dignity would finally define Marilyn Monroe, at least in death. DiMaggio leaned over her casket and whispered, "I love you," twice. For over 20 years, he sent six long-stemmed roses to her crypt three times a week. Not even the Grim Reaper could suffocate Eros, at least not Jolting Joe's version.

The romance of star-crossed lovers, unable to live with or without one another, amplified the DiMaggio legend. The appeal of simple but elusive values — eternal devotion, invariable reliability, the white knight prepared always to ride in during troubled times — stirred our fantasies and vivified our heroic impulses. Joe, Joe DiMaggio ... we want you on our side.

In retirement, he served as a pitchman for Mr. Coffee and Bowery Bank. Insisting always on dignified advertisements and worthy products, DiMaggio continued to polish his reputation and tend to his social legacy ("Where have you gone, Joe DiMaggio, a nation turns its lonely eyes to you."). Throughout the remainder of his life, the citadel of the inner man was steadfastly alert. No one really knew him: "He never felt the need to issue any public proclamations, or mercenary confessionals, to cheapen the awe of men who had seen him as children. It's enough to have been Joe DiMaggio."[26] In 1999, he died from the effects of lung cancer. Not even the Yankee Clipper could defeat death forever.

The Puzzles of Perspectivism

Some of Nietzsche's more strident passages on perspectivism suggest a virulent noncognitivism, an apparently outright rejection of the possibility of rationally discovering truth and value. He seems to conceive of reason as the mere instrument of deeper physiological forces which generate goals.[27] His insistence that the philosophers of the future must create new values that do not merely replicate existing arrangements and his emphasis on interpretation may suggest he implicitly endorses an abject relativism which cannot distinguish among competing perspectives.[28]

John Wilcox, however, points out that "some interpretations have merits that others lack ... they rise above the ordinary."[29] According to Nietzsche, interpretations and entire perspectives can be graded on the basis of their scientism, logical consistency, being supported by sensory evidence, subtleties, openness to revision, recognition of fallibilism, comprehensiveness, style, unity, honesty, and reflection of healthy and strong origins.[30] Satisfying such criteria counts in favor of interpretations. Thus Nietzsche's perspectivism is safe from charges of abject relativism and irrationalism. Wilcox describes Nietzschean truth as "this-worldly, fallible, hypothetical, perspectival, value-laden, historically developed and simplifying truth—which we might call, using Nietzschean hyperbole, 'erroneous' truth."[31]

Some commentators have claimed that Nietzsche adopts a pragmatic theory of truth: a proposition is true if it works or is useful and false if it does not.[32] But there is much textual evidence against this claim. In the context of considering the view that what makes people happy or virtuous is true, Nietzsche says:

> Happiness and virtue are no arguments. But people like to forget—even sober spirits—that making unhappy and evil are no counterarguments. Something might be true while being harmful and dangerous in the highest degree.[33]

Nietzsche underscores his conviction in the separability of effects and truths when he says: "[Those who say] it does not matter whether a thing is true, but only what effect it produces [manifest] an absolute lack of intellectual integrity."[34] He also makes clear that usefulness to life is no proof of truth.[35]

Nietzschean perspectivism, however, does confront a powerful puzzle: the paradox of self-reference. Nietzsche seems to hold that there is no uniquely correct interpretation of the world; that there is no uniquely correct interpretation of any particular thing; that there are only a variety of interpretations that are correct only from within their own perspectives, the frameworks that serve as the totality of reference points; and there is no such thing as a thing-in-itself. All these, and other, Nietzschean claims present themselves as "real truths," as insights that correct the mistakes of dominant culture, as clear improvements over the judgments of the herd, as healthy reminders of the rank among human types and the need to embrace wholeheartedly the flux that is the world and the contingency and conflict that define human existence.

The paradox of self-reference calls into question the status of Nietzsche's own assertions: to assert perspectivism — "all truth is perspectival" or "there is no absolute truth"— may undermine perspectivism because the assertion's claim to be true is unsettled by its own propositional content. To put the matter differently: If P ("all truth is perspectival") is itself a knowledge claim then P is either a case of perspectival knowing or a case of aperspectival knowing. If P is a case of perspectival knowing then it lacks unconditional power and the possibility of aperspectival knowledge remains. If P is a case of aperspectival knowing then P itself is true unconditionally and P undermines its own truth claim. In either case it appears that P cannot be asserted consistently.

There is some textual evidence suggesting Nietzsche was aware of the paradox of self-reference and chose to underscore the conditionality of his own interpretation that all interpretation was conditional. For example, he concludes a section of criticism with this sentence: "Supposing that this [Nietzsche's exposition] also is only interpretation — and you will be eager enough to make this objection?— well, so much the better."[36] Moreover, when describing philosophers of the future he adds: "'My judgment is my judgment': no one else is easily entitled to it — that is what such a philosopher of the future may perhaps say of himself."[37] Nietzsche also has Zarathustra say: "'This is my way; where is yours?'— thus I answered those who asked me 'the way.' For the way — that does not exist."[38] At times, Nietzsche also hints at the paradoxes that confront a seemingly unconditional denial of absolutism: "Every morality is ... a bit of tyranny against 'nature'; also against 'reason'; but this in itself is no objection, as long as we do not have some other morality which permits us to decree that every kind of tyranny and unreason is impermissible."[39]

Nietzsche further suggests the need for a new fusion of the objective and subjective dimensions of knowledge:

> To see differently in this way for once, to want to see differently, is no small discipline and preparation of the intellect for its future "objectivity"— the latter understood not as "contemplation without interest" (which is a nonsensical absurdity),

but as the ability to control one's Pro and Con and to dispose of them, so that one knows how to employ a variety of perspectives and affective interpretations in the service of knowledge.[40]

But such fragments are strikingly inconclusive and Walter Kaufmann is undoubtedly correct when he says, in the context of the self-referential puzzles of Nietzsche's conception of the will to power:

Nietzsche was not at his best with problems of this kind: he never worked out an entirely satisfactory theory of knowledge, and most of the relevant material remained in his notebooks and did not find its way into a more coherent presentation in his published works [41]

Accordingly, numerous questions linger: What, if anything, is Nietzsche's theory of truth? Can his perspectivism resist or overcome the paradox of self-reference? Is his literary work merely the mischief of a calculated ironist? Or must his style exemplify Nietzsche's broad themes, those about which he is most confident? Is Nietzsche merely a provocateur, laughing up his sleeve at the pedants of the future who will oversimplify his thought? Independently of Nietzsche's particular motives and intentions, can contemporary readers expropriate his rhetoric and ideas for their own purposes?

DiMaggio and the Dark Side

Our weaknesses are often nothing more than the exaggeration of our strengths. The person who is gregarious and witty can turn, quite easily, into an obnoxious show-off. The person who is celebrated for diligence and virtue can become a self-righteous, supercilious prig. Strong, silent types edge into indifference and cruelty.

Joe DiMaggio was a stunningly unsuccessful husband and father. Always better as a wooer and boyfriend than a husband, marriage pandered to Joe's worst qualities (or, alternately, seduced him into ratcheting up his best qualities until they morphed into horrors): his obsession with winning, his need to control reputation, his demand that life greet him only on his terms, his yearning for secrecy and silence; his relentless pursuit of *la bella figura*; his uncompromising distrust of *stranieri*; his subconscious rejection of intimacy.

His choice of marriage partners doomed long-term personal success. His first sub-par year, by DiMaggio standards, was 1942 when he and Dorothy Arnold were locked in ongoing conflict. Once he and Arnold divorced, Joe visited his son infrequently. Dad was of no help as son, Joe Jr., struggled unevenly to live up to the name. When the kid dropped out of Yale to join the Marines, Dad could only offer, "The Marines are a good thing." Eventually, the son married a single mother and adopted her two children. After divorcing his wife, Joe Jr., who was already deeply involved with alcohol and other drugs, had a serious auto accident that required a delicate brain operation. Surgery resulted in a major personality change. He became a homeless drug addict who died only a few months after his father. The two men were never reconciled.

DiMaggio's marriage and ongoing relationship with Marilyn Monroe, while consistent with some of their mutual needs and vulnerabilities, were at bottom self-destructive for both. A personal relationship cannot redeem anyone's self-worth or raging insecurities. Where one or both parties are looking to the other to bestow value where it otherwise is missing, the relationship is star-crossed.

When the sports memorabilia business began to boom, DiMaggio sensed both opportunity and confusion. Why would anyone pay for another person's signature? How could old sports products — junk, really — suddenly became more valuable than food and shelter? But Joe still had to win. He would ensure that his autograph cost more than those of any other living player. He would make sure no one else made a nickel by trading on his life. He would insist that he be introduced as the "Greatest Living Baseball Player" at all old-timer events and baseball ceremonies. He would count and squeeze every penny — he almost never picked up a tab. The money was, as the cliché championed, the only way he could now keep score. He didn't need it. Joe was materially well-off and had few ambitions that required high finances. But here was another game that he was thrown into by who he was. And he would damn well win. He almost always did.

His friends, more accurately described as acquaintances or cronies, knew that a single perceived betrayal, even a minor slight, would cut them off, possibly forever. If they revealed a confidence, DiMaggio would not act out against them, he would simply never speak with them again: "[His associates] knew that [DiMaggio] could be warm and loyal if they are sensitive to his wishes, but they must never be late for an appointment to meet him. One man, unable to find a parking place, arrived a half-hour late once and DiMaggio did not talk to him again for three months."[42]

DiMaggio never helped anyone know him for good reasons. He was uneducated formally, but never wanted to give up the psychological edge. The more others know you the more vulnerable you become, the more likely you are to be judged and used, to be played for a fool. Numerous *stranieri* were only too available and willing to ingratiate themselves for their own advantage. If he had any burning doubts about that, his relationship with Marilyn and the silliness of the memorabilia industry extinguished them: "No one else should ever know your business. Reputation is like currency, to be held in the fist: everybody else wants to take it from you.... It was a smart move by a smart man — canny, anyway. In latter years he cultivated the distance that set him apart from every other person of fame. He was revered for his mystery. We cheered him for never giving himself entirely to us."[43]

Ask as little as possible, say almost nothing, parry all intimate inquiries, be suspicious even of well-wishers, parcel out your trust more carefully than even your money — the DiMaggio code. Distinguished author Gay Talese, when asked to describe the Yankee Clipper, sometimes referred to him as "the creation of an island." Talese meant that Joe DiMaggio embodied the old world insularity, suspicion, paranoia, and superstition of Sicily. The native islet of DiMaggio's parents was strikingly parochial even by Sicilian standards. The description — coming from Talese, the son of mainland Italian immigrants — is redolent with the whiff of condescension from Northerner to Southerner. Much of the implied accusation, though, hits the mark.

The two DiMaggio brothers closest to Joe in age exuded different personalities. Vince was blessed with a voice so pleasing that for a time he toyed with the notion of traveling to Italy to study opera. He was effusive, engaging, and cheerful even after a bad day at the plate. Dominic, called the "Little Professor" because of his demeanor and eyeglasses, was not as outgoing as Vince but more introspective and scholarly. After an all-star career with the Red Sox he became a successful CEO and enjoyed numerous friendships. Of the three youngest boys of Giuseppe and Rosalia, only Joe was "the creation of an island."

If happiness is a predominantly positive state of mind then Joe DiMaggio was unhappy. He valued other things more highly. He lived a robustly meaningful, significant, important, valuable life.[44] He was one of sports' great winners. He was our hero. That would have to be enough.

DiMaggio and Nietzsche

From one perspective, Joe DiMaggio embodies the American Dream: son of immigrants who rises without formal education to national icon. From another perspective, DiMaggio exemplifies the American Tragedy: sad victim of his own hyper-competitiveness and amplified hunger for glory. From a third perspective, DiMaggio manifests the American Paradox: the greatest fame, material success, and highest societal honors cannot redeem a person's failed personal relationships. Numerous other shadings are available.

What is the truth? If Nietzsche is correct then all of these perspectives carry some merit, but none of them represents the objective truth. The closest we can come to objectivity in such an evaluation is to view our subject from as many plausible perspectives as possible. DiMaggio earns all these descriptions and more.

Nietzsche was always suspicious of an author's claim to impartiality. If Nietzsche's caution is warranted then I should belly up to the bar of truth and open up. I, too, am a creation of an island, the same one that produced Joe DiMaggio. I continue to struggle with many of the same suspicions, insularity, misplaced pride, and exaggerated competitiveness that characterized DiMaggio.

DiMaggio sprang forth during the Depression and his legend bloomed during World War II. At a period of great ethnic and racial rivalries, as Italians desperately tried to assimilate or make their way somehow in America, Joe DiMaggio was our manhood. The legendary Italian scientists, artists, musicians, seafarers, and statesmen bore zero currency on the street. But the Yankee Clipper surely did. He was not merely an Italian stalwart, he was an American hero. During unstable times, his reputation and appeal stood steadfast. He was etched into American art, music, and literature. The Laws of Probability ordain that the drama and energy of The Streak will never be equaled.

When I was an undergraduate, my class was assigned a term paper on the hero of our choice. After three seconds of deliberation, I chose DiMaggio. I poured my heart into that paper, which basically wrote itself. The esteemed professor returned the essay in a few weeks (most professors are unrepentant procrastinators) with only one comment: "Why did you choose this guy? Why not...?" He listed three or four writers, artists, and even a dancer! I felt sorry for this academic *mingherlino* (weakling). He had no keener concept than that of a turnip on what stirred young men's hearts. He did not even know there *was* a street, much less what was happening on it.

After his playing days, I followed and tried to polish the legend of DiMaggio. During old-timers games — the most insignificant events imaginable — I rooted hard for the Clipper to do it one more time. When he homered and the crowd resurrected its familiar delirium, the bedlam was not just for Joe but for all of us creations of his island.

They were cheering for my maternal grandparents, illiterate but hardworking with iron wills. They were cheering for my paternal grandparents, joyful and resolute during the hardest of times. They were cheering for my mother, with her eighth-grade education and fierce pride. They were cheering for my father, a man of virtue and responsibility. And they were even cheering for me, born in America but educated with the values of Sicily. Jolting Joe had redeemed our honor and pointed the way to our flourishing, whether he intended to or not. If Joe DiMaggio could rise to American stardom, with a glorious *la bella figura,* an immaculate reputation, the idol of every right-thinking American male, maybe there was hope for all of us ... all of us creations of the island.

FIFTH INNING

Joe Torre and Aristotle

"Torre gets the most out of every one of his players."
— Joe Girardi, former New York Yankee

"Winning is a by-product of living up to your highest standards, getting the most out of your natural talents, reaching down and rooting out your own drive, courage, and commitment."
— Joe Torre

"When we lost, I couldn't sleep at night. When we win, I can't sleep at night. But, when we win, you wake up feeling better."
— Joe Torre

"I will never have a heart attack. I give them."
— George Steinbrenner

"There is only a small difference between even the best and worst managers in terms of applied strategic decisions.... The manager's true influence on a team is revealed more by his ability to get the most out of his players than by his in-game decisions."
— James Click, sabermetrician

Aristotle (384–322 B.C.) was the earliest Westerner chronicler of the notion of friendship and its importance for the good life. Joe Torre (1940–), although not as clever a game manager as Billy Martin, is unequaled in dealing with players, opponents, umpires, and media. Together, Aristotle and Torre can help us understand how to extract maximum performances out of ourselves and in our relationships with others.

Joe Torre the Ballplayer

Joe Torre was the youngest of five children growing up in Brooklyn. His sisters, one of whom grew up to be a nun, lavished him with love. His older brothers were reliable, tough role models. Rocco became a beat policeman and solid family man. Frank was a professional ballplayer who played on the terrific Milwaukee Braves' teams of the late 1950s. When Joe was 17, he watched Frank stroke two home runs against the Yankees in the Braves' 1957 World Series victory.

Torre's home life was marred, however, by an abusive father, Joe Sr., a New York City detective. Joe Sr. raged against demons, real and imagined. He physically abused his wife, verbally abused his children, and cultivated an atmosphere of fear and turbulence. Unproductive yelling, threats, and verbal slurs ruled the Torre family roost. Once Frank was old enough, he orchestrated an end to the terror by negotiating Joe Sr.'s departure from the family home.

Joe was overweight as a youngster, probably using food as solace from his troubled relationship with his father, but a talented athlete. His aversion to his father's methods would profoundly influence his future view of proper human relations.

Torre made it to the majors with the Braves at age 19, hitting a pinch single in his first of two at bats at the tail end of the 1960 season. The next season, he finished second, behind future Hall-of-Famer Billy Williams, in the voting for National League Rookie of the Year. Torre was a semi-regular in 1961 and 1962, playing mostly catcher and filling in at first base. He quickly established himself as a strong hitter and passable backstop. By 1963, he was an everyday player and remained so for the next twelve years. For nine of those years, he made the all-star team. In 1964, he finished fifth in the Most Valuable Player voting and led National League catchers in fielding. That season he hit .321 with 20 homers and 109 RBI. In 1965, he hit 27 homers and won the catcher's Gold Glove, as well as smashing a home run in the all-star game. When the Braves moved to Atlanta in 1966, Torre responded with a career-high 36 homers supported by a .315 batting average and 101 RBI. Prior to the 1969 season, he was traded to the St. Louis Cardinals.

During his six year stint with the Cardinals, Torre played third base, first base, and caught. In 1971, everything came together for Joe Torre. He led the league in batting average (.363), RBI (137), total bases (352), and hits (230). He smacked 24 home runs, slugged .555, and compiled an on-base percentage of .421. He also led third basemen in putouts. You have probably already figured out that Joe Torre was voted National League Most Valuable Player in that year.

He had three more solid, if unspectacular, years with the Cardinals. Following the 1974 season, he was traded to the New York Mets as his career was winding down. On May 31, 1977, he replaced Joe Frazier as the Mets manager. Torre retired as a player within three weeks. His career statistics are

impressive, especially because during most of his active years playing conditions favored pitchers. Torre hit .297, slugged .452, with an on-base percentage of .365, earned 2,342 total hits, and 252 home runs. Although an all-star
for nine of his sixteen full seasons, Torre fell just short of being a Hall of Fame
caliber player.

Aristotle and Friendship

Aristotle distinguished three forms of friendship: those based on mutual
utility, on pleasure, and on moral goodness.[1] Friendships based on utility center on mutual advantage. Each of the parties gains from the association and
those gains are the grounds of the personal connection. Aristotle argued that
such friendships are too thin and sprout several flaws. First, these friendships
are ephemeral: the personal connection ends as soon as either party is no
longer useful to the other. Second, these friendships bear feeble relationships:
the parties typically spend relatively little time together and the time they do
spend is predicated on the ulterior motive of gain. Third, these friendships
do not automatically make the parties better human beings: material gains
and advances in status or occupational prestige may even impair our characters and loosen our link to moral virtue.

Friendships based on pleasure suffer similar defects. Pleasure is based on
changeable feelings and tastes. Once the preferences of one party change
significantly, the friendship ends. Affection evaporates as soon as one person
finds greater or different pleasure elsewhere. Such friendships, then, are always
hostage to trade-ups: If greater pleasure can be found with person X than
with person Y, and if maximizing my pleasure is the focus of my relationships, then my time is spent more wisely with X. My past connection and
mutually satisfying relationship with Y translate into no special consideration. Worse, friendships based on mutual pleasure typically center on accidental or contingent features of people — such as age, physical beauty, wit,
and charm — instead of essential features that make us who we are.

Aristotle's critiques of friendships based on utility and pleasure reveal
what he desires most in personal relationships: permanence, mutual concern
for the other as a person, moral improvement based on robust personal relations, and mutual affection flowing from the perceived value of the other. Only
friendships based on moral goodness embody these dimensions.

The deepest friendships, for Aristotle, occur between morally upright
people. A friend should desire the good for the other for the friend's sake and
not from expectation of personal advantage. Only people who are morally
good and similar in their goodness can attain genuine friendship. The par-

ties share affection for who the other is — in terms of content of character — not for accidental qualities (for example, physical appearance, status, material holdings). Such friendships will persist as long as both parties remain morally good, as long as each is worthy of genuine friendship. Because moral goodness, although not automatically permanent, is more enduring than mere utility and pleasure, these friendships are more likely to continue through time. Friendship centered on moral virtue nurtures a robust relationship between whole persons. For Aristotle, morally excellent people relate to a friend in a fashion similar to how they relate to themselves. A friend is a mirror in which to see oneself. We hold our friends in high esteem for their own sakes, not just for advantages or pleasures we may gain from the relationships. Through friendship we amplify moral virtue, we develop and extend our concern, we care beyond ourselves. Friends enlarge their shared idea of the good and pursue it through common projects that fortify community life. Friends influence and reinforce each other's zeal for moral rectitude.

Aristotle summarizes five dimensions of deep, complete friendship. If I am your friend:[2]

- I wish and do the good for you, for your sake.
- I wish that you live, for your sake.
- I spend time with you.
- I make choices similar to yours.
- I share your joys and sufferings.

For Aristotle, these five dimensions are akin to a virtuous person's self-perception. A good person wants to flourish, desires his survival, enjoys solitude at times, controls decisions, and finds joy and suffering where appropriate. Aristotle views friendship as flowing from self-love. My friend is at bottom another me, or a person quite close to another me.

Are Friends Similar?

At first blush, Aristotle appears to miss the mark. Aren't many worthy friendships generated by people who are radically different in temperament and personality? Don't friends often make strikingly different life choices without impairing their relationship? Are we truly seeking a twin in friendship? Or do we sometimes bond with others who exude qualities we lack?

My questions are all rhetorical. The answers seem to deal a lethal blow to Aristotle's depiction of genuine friendship. But Aristotle would remind us of the crucial role of moral virtue. The relevant focus of his five dimensions is the moral good. I am like my friend in that critical respect. We make similar *moral* choices and our relationship supports our growth in ways that make us seem more alike *in that pivotal way.* Surely, we still make numerous different life choices not in the moral sphere. You continue to gush over fried baloney and onion sandwiches, while I prefer pepper and eggs. You dress in basic black while I am adorned in Caravaggio red. You root for the Boston Red Sox while I cheer for the New York Yankees. You are extroverted and spontaneous, while I am introverted and reflective. You revel in urban life while I am drawn to small communities. Such choices and fashions of expression, for Aristotle, are trivial and flow from accidental features of who we are. Despite these differences and countless others, my friend and I stand together as seekers of the moral good, as pursuers of the righteous character that defines who we are.

Granted, Aristotle's depiction does not define what friendship must be. Nor does the inclusion of friendships of pleasure and utility complete that task. Friendships come in additional forms and emerge for different reasons than those sketched by Aristotle. He, though, would insist that the deepest, most genuine, most worthy friendships are those centered on sustaining and refining moral character. Self-love and affection for others should be linked to a correct perception of the moral good.

Genuine friendship of the highest quality, then, is uncommon for at least two reasons. First, relatively few people embody the requisite moral quality. Second, the enterprise of friendship requires considerable time, shared commitments, and joint activities. For Aristotle, friendship, like erotic love, is an inherently discriminatory notion. I cannot be a friend, in the deepest sense, to everyone even if I was so inclined and even if everyone was morally good. I would still not have enough time and I could not expend enough effort to pursue the common commitments and joint activities that genuine friendship demands.

Should Friends Trade Up?

Although Aristotle does not discuss the topic, this underscores why trading up is misplaced in genuine friendship. While I may perceive, accurately, that a stranger possesses a higher degree of moral virtue than my friend, my past connection and mutually satisfying relationship exudes currency. My friend and I are not *lontananza* (at a distance), but forge a shared identity. Our relationship, if profound enough, entails that my interests are not experienced as fully apart from my friend's interests and vice versa. Relationships, of course, vary in intensity and depth, but all genuine Aristotelian friendships share this element. Accordingly, I would not trade up easily because my current friend and I share a relationship that has valuable ramifications for who I am. I would recognize the transition costs — time, energy, uncertainty, changes to my self-image — of substituting the stranger for my current friend. I would also understand that even if the stranger bears more goodness than my friend, the stranger cannot exemplify that goodness in the same way as my friend. The moral virtue of my friend and that of the stranger will differ qualitatively in the particular ways they are manifested. Just as the stranger may be more physically beautiful than my friend, the stranger does not have more of *my friend's* beauty. The unique way my friend embodies and expresses beauty may be more appealing to me than the way the stranger expresses his admittedly greater physical beauty. Finally, the historical relationship friends have shared has special significance that should not be dismissed. Friends form a union or federation that is not defined merely by adding the interests of the parties together. In friendship, like in well-functioning marriages, the whole is greater than the sum of the parts. The bond or union or federation that friends nurture transforms the parties. The historical relationship that chronicles that development bears independent value in a way similar to the value produced by positive family relationships. Shared memories, gratitude, reciprocal self-making, and a sense of belonging make trading up in friendship problematic. Where trading up does seem to happen easily we can legitimately call into question whether a salutary, deep friendship was present.

I do not suggest that we should nurture only one friendship. Clearly, most of us have several friends of varying closeness and contact. We have even more acquaintances who provide a host of mutually beneficial interactions. Often, instead of facing a choice of trading up — dumping our current friend for another person — we can simply add to our list in a way that is precluded in romantic love. Still, practicalities limit the number of close friends with whom we can share deep relationships.

Even so, our choice of friends is limited by circumstances of geography, time, economics, culture, and the like. Our social context profoundly affects whom we meet and what activities we undertake. But the same can be said about our choices of spouse, career, and almost all else. Few of our most important choices are limitless.

Does Friendship Harm Personal Autonomy?

The joint identity principle I am urging will trouble some philosophers. They will screech that my standard of friendship is too high as it requires a loss of individual autonomy. Once we talk of extended or shared identity, we seem to infringe on an individual's freedom of choice and independence. My choices, projects, and actions are no longer *mine*, they are *ours*. Does this not demand concessions of the individual's will?

The short answer is, "Yes, but why the surprise?" Every intimate relationship has that consequence. Can we coherently conjure, say, romantic love where each spouse retains full, individual autonomy? Living together, sharing a life, pooling material resources, planning for the future require shared decision-making, reciprocity, and mutuality. To believe that full independence can be retained is fatuous. Granted, friendships come in more shadings and forms than Aristotle catalogued. But the deepest versions of friendship — the ones that are most transforming to our characters — are akin to loves. Why should we shrink back in horror when we find that our independence is no longer sacrosanct? A world of strangers may be a world of complete independence for individuals; a community of friends is not.

What Grounds Friendship?

We care about our friends, at least in part, because we perceive that they bear excellences or admirable qualities. We could be mistaken in that assessment, of course. Our evaluations are not infallible, our perceptions are not flawless. Once we realize our error, the incipient friendship may end. But the ground of our initial attraction is the value we think the other possesses.

A critic would rejoin, however, that making the perceived value of the other the ground of friendship is troubling. First, our real focus seems to be on that value, wherever it may reside, and not on a particular person. Human beings are not merely repositories of value, nor does value alone define who we are. We have other qualities — beyond our glorious value — that are neutral in terms of value or that are imperfections or disvalues. To focus only on the other's value is to befriend her only for a part of her personhood. Second, to ground friendship in only the other's current perceived value is to freeze the other in time. We all change, grow, and regress. To rivet a friendship in the current image of the other is to deny inevitable change. Again, such a friendship is not directed at a whole person but at certain value which we now think we have found in the other.

These criticisms are difficult, but not impossible, to answer. To establish a friendship of whole persons, our critic is correct: we must appreciate more than the current perceived value of each other. Each of us is a compendium of qualities, not all admirable, wrapped together by our unique way of embodying and expressing those qualities, seasoned by hosts of possibilities (potential qualities that we can develop into actualities). By considering the other person's qualities beyond their perceived value, we parry the charge that we are drawn only to value not-whole people. By attending to the other idealized possibilities, we block the charge that friendship wrongly freezes the other in the present. Friends affect each other's choices, actions, and personal development. They do not simply take the other as a fixed, permanent character.

Torre the Zen Master

With the Mets, Joe Torre was an undistinguished manager. His game strategy was predictable and uninspiring. Torre employed too many one-run strategies (sacrifice bunt attempts, stolen base attempts) and intentional walks to satisfy sabermetricians — the name given to those who steadfastly apply statistical and mathematical models to analyze optimum baseball methods, to evaluate past player performances, and predict future results: "Only six times in thirty-three years [1972–2004] has any manager used sacrifice attempts, stolen base attempts, and intentional walks to increase his team's win expectation over an entire season."[3]

His use of his bullpen was heavily criticized. Judged by Pythagorean winning percentages — a mathematical formula that, quite accurately, determines a team's overall record based on total runs scored and total runs allowed — Torre's Mets teams underperformed significantly during his three full seasons of managing. Attributing such failures entirely to poor managing is taking a leap, or at least a hop, of faith. But where a pattern exists, laying part of the blame on sub-par managing is not unreasonable. Overall, Torre managed the Mets to a 286–420 record during his five-year stay. Bill James, the father of sabermetrics, summed up the consensus:

> [Joe Torre] is articulate and polite, but that does not really explain how he was able to take over a team (the 1977 Mets) which was 45 games away from a season in which they had gone 86–76, manage them through consecutive seasons in which they finished 64–98, 66–96, 63–99, 67–95 and 41–62 and still emerge with his reputation untarnished. In New York, no less.... He never did establish a starting rotation.... He was indecisive, unreliable.... Maybe Torre's style just needs the right circumstances to be successful.... I'll believe it when I see a little more of it.[4]

Torre moved to Atlanta to manage the Braves in 1982. His team stormed out of the gate 13–0 and won a divisional title. Atlanta slipped to second in 1983, and after a third place finish in 1984, Torre was fired. The Braves slightly outperformed their Pythagorean projections during Torre's three seasons, and concluding that Joe was becoming a better manager is reasonable, if unverifiable.

After leaving the Braves, Joe turned to the first refuge of unemployed athletes: broadcasting, in his case for the California Angels. In August 1990, though, he returned to the major leagues' managerial ranks with the St. Louis Cardinals. He was fired forty-seven games into the 1995 season after compiling a 351–354 overall record as Cardinals skipper. In 1991, the highlight of his managing term in St. Louis, the club finished second in the National League East Division. The Cardinals slightly outperformed their Pythagorean projections during Torre's stint. Joe, it would appear, did a credible job with a mediocre squad.

In 1996, Joe Torre met his destiny. At the moment when he was convinced his managerial career had expired, Torre was presented the best and the worst possible job opportunity. The eccentric owner of the New York Yankees, George Steinbrenner, acting on the advice of crony Arthur Richman, offered Torre the managerial reins of the team with the most fabled history in sports. If you like hitting yourself over the head with a hammer because it feels so fine when you stop, you would like working for George Steinbrenner. If you thrill at the prospect of self-flagellation because it builds character, "The Boss" is the man for you. If you admire the sartorial tastes of ascetics and penitents who don hair shirts, George is the employer of your fantasies. Maybe.

In his first 23 seasons as majority owner of the Yankees, Steinbrenner changed managers 20 times. Like privates under Pickett, Ralph Houk, Bill Virdon, Billy Martin (five times), Bob Lemon (twice), Dick Howser, Gene Michael (twice), Clyde King, Yogi Berra, Lou Piniella (twice), Dallas Green, Bucky Dent, Stump Merrill, and Buck Showalter all fell. Strikingly, the list of dismissed Yankees managers includes a wide panorama of personality types, a generous variety of strategic preferences, and an impressive range of baseball experience. All of these baseball leaders, though, were joined by a common thread: they could not satisfy the bizarre demands of George Steinbrenner, at least not for long.

Even worse than his predilection for hasty managerial changes was Steinbrenner's addiction to publicity. He absolutely *had* to meddle. Steinbrenner interfered with trades, maligned his managers in the media, second-guessed during games, telephoned the dugout in critical situations, and basked in a life of high anxiety and relentless pressure. Unsurprisingly, he was quick to take credit for success and never implicated himself in failure. To call him "The Boss from Hell" is to slander Hades.

Into this caldron of confusion, mistrust, and hypertension knowingly walked the man the newspapers dubbed "Clueless Joe." At this point in his baseball career, Joe Torre held an unenviable record, not likely to be broken: He had played in 2,209 games and managed in 1,901—a total of 4,110 games — without participating in a World Series. With this background of team failure, Torre strolled down the organizational aisle to join the most demanding, imperious owner in professional sports. The over and under on Joe Torre's seemingly certain firing was around 120 games.

Even a casual sports fan knows the rest of the story. From 1996 to 2005, Torre's Yankees went 982–634, winning 4 World Series, 6 American League Pennants, and 9 American League Eastern Division Titles. All fair statistical analyses conclude that his 1998 squad enjoyed one of the five greatest seasons, if not the greatest, in major league history. The team stormed through the regular season at 114–48 (.704), setting an American League record for victories. They held opponents to a league-low 656 runs, while scoring a league-high 967 runs. The Yankees slashed their way through the playoffs, winning 11 of 13 games, including a four-game sweep of the San Diego Padres in the World Series. Torre was the obvious choice as American League Manager of the Year, an award he had also earned in 1996.

As I type this work in August 2006, Joe Torre remains the manager of the New York Yankees, who are in first place in the American League East, leading the Boston Red Sox by two games. George Steinbrenner, perhaps mellowed a smidgen by age and a shred by four world championships, has been less intrusive. Steinbrenner has also moderated his knee-jerk bellicosity and obnoxiousness when defeated.

What happened? Torre was fortunate to arrive on the scene when a handful of talented Yankees prospects — Mariano Rivera, Derek Jeter, Bernie Williams, Andy Pettitte, Jorge Posada, Ramiro Mendoza — were just coming into their own. Trades and free-agent signings of solid performers such as Chuck Knoblauch, Tino Martinez, Scott Brosius, Orlando Hernandez, David Wells, Tim Raines, and Joe Girardi helped. But Torre, himself, must be credited for being a superior manager of talent. He provided the calm assurance and steadfastly positive attitude that facilitated team success. Under Torre, the Yankees have consistently exceeded their Pythagorean projections.

> Torre's hands-off managerial style was a perfect fit for the experienced professionals assembled.... He taught his players to be aggressive on the base paths and patient at the plate. He modeled his never-panic philosophy with an imperturbable presence in the dugout, slouching stone-faced on the bench, never becoming visibly upset or excited, regardless of the score. Never abandoning his by-the-book approach to managing, Torre took occasional risks and learned to ride the hot hand rather than always playing the percentages. While few baseball professionals regard Torre as a managing genius, he has been perfect for his team.[5]

The Intimacy of Friendship

Friendships are intimate relationships of varying degrees, typically less so than romantic loves and more so than polite acquaintanceships. One of the functions of friendship is to control access to ourselves and to regulate our privacy. Intimacy is mutually nurtured in several ways: through privileged self-disclosure, participation in shared projects, discerning and advancing each other's best interests, and having a roughly similar system of values. Bonds of trust, far beyond the level we enjoy with strangers, flow from the heightened mutual vulnerability distinguishing deep friendships.

I disclose information about myself to my friends that I keep shrouded from the general public. In so doing, I regulate my privacy — permitting more access to those whom I choose — and both acknowledge and reinforce the bonds of trust between my friends and me. By participating in shared projects, friends reveal and sustain the projects of their most profound concern. Friends share activities at least partly for the sake of sharing them. Friends often strive to advance each other's interests. I can advance my friend's interests only after appraising what my friend's best interests are. Throughout all these processes, the values of the parties are paramount. Sometimes friends come to their relationship with roughly similar values. Sometimes they develop roughly similar values as a consequence of their relationship and shared activities. In any case, friends mutually influence each other's values in proportion to the closeness of the relationship.

I may be drawn to or try out a new value or project simply because my friend already embodies the value or pursues the project. But my initial attraction need not translate into final acceptance of the value or project into my life scheme. We should recognize a distinction between what motivates my desire to try out a new project or examine a new value — I pursue them just because they rivet my friend's concern — and the grounds upon which I will decide whether to adopt the value or project as my own. My friend's values and projects never fully define mine. I must make a relatively independent assessment of the new value or project at some point.

Friendship is also an exercise in self-making in proportion to the closeness of the relationship. Aristotle insisted that human beings are social animals. A person alone on a desert island might be a beast or a god, but not a human being. We need others to help understand and define ourselves. Those closest to us play a disproportionately strong role. The annoying parental warning — "Be careful who your friends are, don't associate with the wrong crowd" — hits the mark squarely. Friends influence the people we are becoming.

Friendship is, accordingly, a process, not a fixed condition. It begins in lack and is grounded in power. But the grandeur of friendship is that it is not a commodity: it cannot be bought or sold, yet it isn't costless. Friendship struggles to overcome its internal paradoxes of consolation and growth, dependency and freedom. The uniqueness and specialness of the friends — not in terms of their facility in guiding the mutual quest for individual perfection — forms the core of the relationship. Friendship is a mysterious mixture of choice and discovery that changes our perception of the world without actually changing the world. Friendship is transformative but not redemptive. But, mostly, it is an acknowledgment of bonds not fully chosen.

Friendship cannot be an arm's-length, mutual aid exercise in individualism. Friends cannot be creators in *lontananza*. No, friendship widens our subjectivity and creates a new identity that immediately embodies its own unrealized ideals. And the unrealized ideal possibilities of friends-bound are never merely the sum of the unrealized ideal possibilities embodied by the two individuals. The friendship is not two minds thinking or valuing as one. Even the closest of friends, like the most committed lovers, must keep a salutary amount of independence.

The Risks and Benefits of Friendship

Friendship is also dangerous. Other than our spouse or a blood relative, no one can betray us more hurtfully or thoroughly than a close friend. Any time we heighten our vulnerability through revealing special information about ourselves, sharing intimate activities, forging bonds of trust, and relying upon the good will of others, we not only enjoy the fruits of positive self-making but also risk treachery. My friends know more about me, have shared and helped to shape my values, and benefit from my trust. They are in a better position than the general public to advance my best interests but also to extinguish my deepest aspirations.

Are the risks worth the value of friendship? Friendships increase our flow experiences by energizing our efforts in the projects at hand. Shared activities and commitments are also necessary for moral and intellectual growth. Friends, following Aristotle, help us accurately evaluate the quality and meaningfulness of our lives. The sense of belonging and intimate validation friendships produce soften our fears that we are alone and powerless. Because we are social animals friendships are valuable for their own sake, not just for benefits directly derived from the relationships.

The Torre Method

Behind the demeanor and presence lies Joe Torre's theory of personal relationships, sharpened by his experiences in a troubled home, tested during his playing days, and refined during his managerial career. Here is the Torre method distilled:[6]

General Qualities: Strive for patience, tranquility, resilience, steadiness, commitment, optimism, and conviction. Leaders must retain their poise even if everything around them is chaotic. The Stoic virtues are crucial over the long haul. The cliché is accurate: you are never as good as first seems after a victory, you are never as decrepit as first seems after a loss. Focus on the task at hand. We cannot change the past, the future should be approached in small increments. Approach your projects with a positive attitude, throw yourself into them with conviction, refuse to allow inevitable setbacks to mar your confidence. *Pazienza* (patience) and *elasticità* (resilience).

At first blush, the preceding paragraph reeks of platitudes. Its only purpose appears to be sketching the obvious. But first impressions, like first loves and souped-up European cars, are not always what they seem. Most human beings too easily fall prey to the four horsemen of failure: anger, frustration, disappointment, and self-pity. Of these, the worst is self-pity. Becoming better athletes and better people requires overcoming these natural, but self-defeating, human impulses. The four horsemen of failure do not permit us to actualize our ideal possibilities. Instead, they diminish us.

Making excuses, a progeny of the four horsemen of failure, deflates character. By evading responsibility we posture as victims of cruel fates, incompetent teammates or umpires, or other circumstances beyond our control. We make ourselves small by underplaying our own agency and exaggerating the power of external forces. By standing up and assuming responsibility we acknowledge our power to change the future. The present error need not be repeated. We have the power to change our fate.

Too many of us, like George Steinbrenner, embrace an asymmetry of results. When we achieve our immediate goal by getting a hit, making a fine play, pitching effectively, or cleverly running the bases, we puff out our chests and assume full credit. We deserve the credit because we are responsible for the happy result. Through our efforts honorable goals have been reached. But when less welcome results dog our efforts, we look to place the blame on bad luck, the shortcomings of others, the position of celestial bodies, or a conspiracy of evil-doers.

The adage, "Victory has many fathers, defeat is an orphan" is instructive. We gleefully accept full credit for success, while fervently making excuses for failure. The close calls that went our way in victory are soon forgotten. The close calls that went against us provide the introduction for our book of excuses in defeat. In the end, we attain full membership in the congregation of the miserable, gypped by external fates or incompetent other people from attaining the full glories we deserved.

We cannot alter the past, although we can change our perceptions of it. Once a teammate's error, an umpire's misjudgment, or an unlucky bounce occurs, the play is set. Obsessing over our misfortune only compounds the problem. If obsessing on the immediate past makes things worse that is our responsibility. We are then unwitting collaborators in our own uncomfortable situation. Who promised a ballplayer or a manager a universe without errors, mistaken judgments, or bad bounces? All such obstacles to success are predictable, although we cannot foresee the exact moments they will occur.

But no one can be defeated against his will in baseball. We can lose against our will on the scoreboard, for that is never entirely within our control. Losing on the scoreboard, though, is not automatically a defeat unless those on the short end of the score permit it to be. A defeat happens when we succumb to the four horsemen of failure, when our spirits sag, when our souls surrender, when our heads hang. No opponent on the planet can force us into such postures. That is one of the beauties of baseball. Opponents can murder us on the scoreboard, they can demonstrate greater skills, experience, and talent, they can deny us championships. But no opponent on the planet can force us to welcome the four horsemen of failure into our bosoms. We are the only ones who can accept this most devastating defeat. When it happens we do it to ourselves. We are, usually unwitting, collaborators in our own agony. If we go belly up, if we perceive ourselves only as helpless victims before overwhelming power, that is our choice for which we are responsible.

Much the same can be said of life. Whose life is an endless series of triumphs and glories? Whose life is bereft of tragedies and sufferings? Yet it is in our responses to triumphs and tragedies that we reveal and sustain our characters.

This is the deeper message underlying Joe Torre's list of desirable human qualities. What at first seems platitudinous blossoms into a strategy for approaching baseball and for living a robustly meaningful life.

Relations with Players. The first set of considerations is epistemological, and requires knowledge of your players' and your own skills, character, and ability to deal with competitive pressures. Personal relations are not conjured from a vacuum. They require accurate self-assessment and evaluation of others. Managers must find the proper role for each player, define that role for the player, and afford players enough opportunities to show they can fulfill their roles. Managers should give players a clear understanding of their expectations, provide support, show confidence in players' ability to fulfill expectations, and underscore players' value to team success.

Again, if this first seems platitudinous, we should dig for the deeper message. We all have experienced verbally abusive coaches, the sort of ready-to-blow-a-gasket, gosh-I-love-Bobby Knight, I-am-a-tough-guy-and-you-better-be-too, why-aren't-you-perfect-you-little-SOB pepperpot who must comment in stentorian bravado after every pitch. He is especially prevalent at the youth and high school levels. When he is coaching third base, he is a master of the obvious. Swing and miss at a high pitch and he will scream, "That is not a strike, bear down, you are killing us." When off the field watching one of his pitchers throw balls out of the strike zone, he will holler, "Get the ball down, throw strikes." Worse, he actually thinks he is being helpful. As if the batter has not already realized he swung at a bad pitch or the pitcher has not figured out that he is supposed to throw strikes. At his worst, the verbally abusive coach berates his players when things are not going well: "You lack heart, you are a bunch of chokers. You are gutless, I am tired of coaching losers." Sometimes expletives spice these negative messages. The verbally abusive coach, of course, is convinced that his tactics toughen his players, making them better players and men.

The inability of coaches to control what is taking place on the field — they are not players, only coaches — intensifies their frustration. Their best hatched schemes are foiled by the shoddy execution of their ungrateful, hapless charges. Because such coaches have not mastered the four horsemen of failure, verbal abuse is their outlet.

Buster Olney, in *The Last Night of the Yankee Dynasty*, describes New York Yankees owner George Steinbrenner's verbal abuse of employees during times of stress.

> The better the team did, it seemed, the more he had to lose and the more panicked he became, his hyperventilating beginning in the first innings of each postseason series and evolving into anger and hopelessness. When Steinbrenner had publicly praised his players for their resilience, his comments had amused many of his front-office employees; they thought *Steinbrenner, at heart, was a quitter*.[7] (Emphasis added.)

Too often, those who verbally abuse others are merely struggling with their own demons. Unless we are diligent and disciplined, the four horsemen of failure will ride roughshod over players, coaches, owners, officials, and fans.

Why is verbal abuse rarely helpful? Let's count the ways. First, verbal abuse contaminates the process of playing, making athletics less enjoyable and more demeaning. Second, verbal abuse sends a dishonorable message: Play well and I stand behind you, even love you. Play poorly and I will berate you, even hate you. Third, verbal abuse lacks educative value. If verbal abuse were sound then we should expect classroom teachers to use it liberally: "Billy, you *&%$#&*, 4+3 is not 6. What is the matter with you? Are you gutless? Do you lack heart? Are you less than a man?" Imagine what would happen to such an instructor. He would lose his job quicker than Tony Kornheiser lost his hair. Fourth, verbal abuse usually impairs performance. Players, imbued with worthless, negative messages become angry or fearful or anxious. They lose whatever self-confidence they had. Baseball rewards the loose, confident player. Baseball further punishes the insecure, doubting, abused athlete. Verbal abuse rarely nurtures relaxation and confidence. Fifth, verbal abuse coarsens the person who spews it. Such coaches desensitize themselves and make themselves less worthy human beings.

All verbally abusive messages are negative, but not all negative messages are abusive. Coaches convey, through their body language and verbal messages, confidence or frustration. They send positive or negative messages. Instead, of telling players, say, not to swing at high pitches or to stop walking batters or to stop throwing wildly, coaches are better advised to instruct them to get a good pitch to hit, throw strikes, and take their time and make good throws. Accentuate the positive and soften the negative is solid advice.

Consider the difference between two former Yankees farmhands, Ricky Ledee and Derek Jeter, who both were considered can't miss prospects.

> Ledee and Jeter played in Tampa together in 1992, and Denbo [a Yankees batting coach] recalled that when they performed badly, both of them would come out for early batting practice the next day. Jeter would work at his swing till he regained the feel he wanted and then walk away from the batting cage confident he would get hits in the game that night. Ledee would remain, frustrated, still searching, still unsure. It was an early insight into one player absolutely certain he was destined for greatness, Denbo thought, and another no less dedicated but lacking a similar self-confidence.... No matter what Jeter did in his first at-bat in a game, he would come back to the dugout with his confidence still running over.[8]

Such confidence is rarely, if ever, the product of verbal abuse or a steady diet of negative messages from authority figures.

The second set of considerations regarding player relations pertains to general virtues: fairness to all under your command, nurturing trust and loyalty, valuing mutual respect. Again, the deeper message is that the best managers and coaches are the best teachers. This is a commonplace within sports, but its implications are too often ignored. Consider high school sports and teaching. In the classroom, would you want teachers to verbally abuse or publicly ridicule their students for a disappointing score on a test? Would you want teachers who had whipping boys who were blamed for every perceived shortcoming in the class regardless of their amount of responsibility? Would you want teachers who belittled the students of a neighboring school? Who constantly and publicly disparaged administrators? Who figured out ways to cheat that would enhance students' performances? Who glad-handed in times of triumph and deserted in adverse times? Who showered affection on successful students while laughing at mediocre and poor students?

The third set of considerations regarding player relations focuses on communication: rely on positive messages to the greatest extent possible; recognize the range of players' emotions, including fear, anxiety, doubt; strive for civility; deal with grievances openly and immediately; express anger occasionally, if appropriate, but without tirades and tantrums. Torre is, clearly, deeply influenced by his dysfunctional communication with his father. He came to understand that negative emotions such as fear and self-doubt are natural, and should not be denied. Instead, acknowledging them can be used for practical advantage: strengthening personal relations.

The fourth set of considerations relate to perspective: focus on the task at hand, learn from mistakes, retain a sense of humor, maintain an even keel, remember that consistency yields calm, control what you can, do not agonize over what you cannot control. Torre reaches back to the Stoics when defining what he can control:

> [I can control] all strategic decisions during ball games; how I relate to and teach my players; how I utilize my coaches and support staff; how prepared I am for every ball game; how I speak to the media and react to their stories; how I relate to George Steinbrenner and others in our front office; how I react to what George says or does regarding the Yankees; my input regarding player personnel decisions, though I have no final say over those decisions.[9]

All else is either entirely or largely out of a manager's control, including how his players actually perform when on the field; how much they are paid; when and how severely they are injured; and what the media and general manager say or do regarding the team.[10]

Distinguishing what is and what is not under our control is crucial to our accountability. We cannot control the ability or conduct of the other team. We cannot control the weather, the favorable and unfavorable bounces of the ball, the judgment of officials, and a host of factors that affect the outcome of sporting events.

Conscientious players and managers judge their performances by how well they executed the things, mostly or entirely, under their control. Whether we have played well or not is not invariably connected to the final score. We can play admirably in defeat, dishonorably in victory. At times, players can fool spectators and coaches. Players should not fool themselves. To defeat an over-matched and less experienced team by a wide margin does not automatically confer glory. To lose to a highly skilled opponent is not always humiliating.

Sportswriter Grantland Rice famously intoned, "It is not whether you won or lost, but how you played the game." If invoked without qualification and too often, this slogan invites parody. Whether you won or lost the game is relevant. We do keep score for a reason. But often whether we won or lost depends on variables outside our control, while how we played the game — in terms of effort, intelligence, enthusiasm, and relentlessness — is under our control. While scoreboard results do count, they should not be the primary way we judge our performance. This is the power of Rice's message.

More important, how we react to defeat measures our character. Sports, like life, are never an ever-ascending series of victories and glories. And that is good news. If all we experienced in sports were triumphs, victory itself would begin to lose its luster. Life eventually brings suffering and death, sometimes sooner not later. Sports bring heartbreak, usually sooner not later. Think about it. How do almost all sports seasons end? With an "L." Even if your team wins a championship this season, the odds are it will not repeat. The *Wide World of Sports* promo, "The thrill of victory, the agony of defeat," underscores the uneasy marriage of elation and frustration in sports.

But amid the changing fortunes of sports, some constants are available. In victory or defeat, our conduct in those matters under our control provides the ballast for our character in sports and, possibly, for our general character. Properly understood and nurtured, sports can help develop and strongly rein-force praiseworthy general character. The connection is not automatic. In fact, supporting the connection requires uncommon understanding, superior teaching, and learning. But the opportunity should not be wasted.

Examples of those who take care of the things under their control and avoid the distractions of those things that are not are easy to find. Derek Jeter began the 2004 baseball season in a slump, then he really went south. His batting average drooped to about .180, twenty full points below the dreaded Mendoza line.[11] Articles, predictably, were written about his batting problems. He endured countless interviews that included questions and commentary that often highlighted his puny average. His own parents — who are annoyingly well-known to the Yankee Stadium camera crew — seemed unable to conceal their disappointment at their son's ineptitude. Despite eight previous years of inspiring play, remarkable contributions to six pennant-winning and four championship teams, the unthinkable happened: Jeter was sometimes booed by Yankees fans. By mid-season, though, Derek Jeter slowly but surely raised his average to .280. His final average was .292. Throughout his travail, teammates were amazed that his personality never changed. He did not become depressed, he did not take out his frustrations against others, he did make excuses or point fingers, his body language never revealed defeat, he did not surrender. Baseball rewards the loose, confident player, the relentless competitor, the performer who can stare adversity in the face and hold his head up high. Baseball rewards the Derek Jeters of the world.

Yogi Berra may have said, but probably did not say, "Baseball is 50 percent physical and 90 percent mental." The kernel of truth in this mathematical distortion is that the mental dispositions and psychological profiles required to succeed in baseball at the highest levels are rarer than the athletic skills demanded.

The fourth set of considerations regarding player relations centers on sustaining optimism: our responses to setbacks are more important than the losses themselves; recall high achievements in the past and draw strength from those memories; focus on your strengths, not weaknesses, and pursue goals relentlessly. All such factors, though, repeat lessons sketched in the first three sets of considerations.

Game Strategies and Winning. "The Book" is the name given to a list of principles that supposedly defines percentage baseball: the strategies to employ in different situations to maximize the probability of victory. Sabermetricians provide compelling evidence that much of The Book is unwise, particularly in the use of one-run strategies, in the way relief pitchers, especially closers, are called upon, and in managerial preoccupation with the traditional batting order. One of the early criticisms of Torre was that he managed closely by The Book, he played safely in order to avoid censure from second-guessers. He now understands that sound in-game strategies are conclusions arrived at by consulting The Book, the statistical record, and intuition. Intuition is grounded in observation and understanding of the general and immediate psychology of your own team and the competition. Sometimes what appears unorthodox is the proper choice. For example, instead of bunting automatically with runners on first and second and no outs — a classic small-ball strategy extolled by The Book — Torre will, at times, use the hit-and-run play. Another nuanced ploy is to turn an opponent's strength into a weakness. In a 1998 playoff game against the Texas Rangers, the Yankees led 1–0. With runners on first and third, one out, and two strikes on the batter, Torre called for a double steal. The Rangers' catcher, Ivan Rodriguez, had one of the strongest arms at that position in major league history. Predictably, he threw to second base, the runner got himself caught in a rundown, and the runner on third was able to scamper home. The Yankees won the game 2–0. Torre turned one of the strengths of the Rangers — the superior ability of their catcher to throw out base runners trying to steal — against them.

> Ivan Rodriguez has a gun for an arm. I figured that if Brosius [the runner on first base] broke for second, Rodriguez would take the challenge and fire the ball to second base. Curtis [the runner on third base] would break for home on the pitch, with a good shot of scoring. But if Rodriguez held onto the ball, Curtis would be a dead duck at the plate.[12]

A lesser catcher would have played it safe and either held onto the ball or thrown directly to third base. The clever manager always looks for ways to transform the opposition's points of pride into his own advantage.

Joe Torre, in short, has parlayed his understanding of successful human relationships into a certainty that will be enshrined in the Major League Baseball Hall of Fame for his accomplishments as a manager. Aristotle would approve.

Does Friendship Violate Morality?

Sometimes — well, this only occurs when academic philosophers are present — critics argue that the partiality of friendships impairs the principle of moral equality. That principle insists that the interests of all human beings are, other things being equal, morally equivalent and should be afforded like consideration. From the impartial vantage point of the principle of moral equality the fact that, say, Rocco is my friend should not mean that Rocco gains special consideration in any moral calculus.

Moralists who subscribe to the ideal of impartiality based on the principle of moral equality can point to a distinguished history for support. In the West, we are familiar with the biblical injunction to *Love Thy Neighbor as Thyself*.[13] This moral ideal was clearly meant to extend self-love to all other human beings, or at least all those with whom one comes into contact.[14] Taken at its most uncompromising, this injunction commands us to manifest the same degree of concern to others that we lavish upon ourselves. Although it is inartfully crafted — as it holds out the possibility that if one is filled with self-hate or ersatz self-love such dispositions are legitimately transferred to others — it offers a powerful moral aspiration. In the eyes of the Supreme Being, the ultimate ground of morality, we are all equal and none of us merits privilege on the basis of identity alone. Instead, human beings all share claims to equal mutual concern based on their humanity. To transfer this principle into the language of affection: love for all humanity must be unconditional and unwavering.

But one need not be a fervent subscriber to Judeo-Christianity to find historical support for impartiality. Four hundred years prior to the birth of Christ, the Chinese sage Mo Tzu counseled a universal human love that did not distinguish between families, friends, and strangers.[15] Mo Tzu explicitly advised that we have as much regard for strangers as for our immediate families, and suggested that until we renounce partiality to immediate families and friends we will be saddled with an incoherent and inferior moral code: recognized duties among family members could only be understood coherently as particular cases of our duties to humanity.[16] Thus, to differentiate strongly between the degree of concern we show to intimates and to strangers undercuts the ground of all morality and fragments social life.

Taken at its most uncompromising, the impartiality thesis demands that we assume the perspective of an ideal, detached observer when arriving at moral judgments: I must attach no special weight to my own interests when determining moral action. Moreover, the fact that another person is my spouse, my child, or my intimate friend is morally irrelevant; it provides no moral reason to favor such a person over a complete stranger. An eighteenth century English philosopher, William Godwin, sums the view up well when he considers whom he should save in a fire, an archbishop or a chambermaid, when he can save only one: "[If the chambermaid is my wife or mother] that would not alter the truth of the proposition [about whom to save] for of what great consequence is it that they are mine? What magic is there in the pronoun 'my' to overturn the decisions of everlasting truth?"[17] We may from a moral viewpoint discriminate between people — Godwin would save the archbishop, not the chambermaid — but this may be done only on the basis of nonrelational characteristics, those that would attract the assent of an ideal, detached observer.

The Case for Impartiality

As we have seen, impartialists can point to much in our moral traditions that supports their position. Yet, at first glance, the position of impartialists seems completely ridiculous when applied at the level of concrete moral action. There are few aspects of human experience celebrated as intensely as family love and intimate friendships. What could be more preposterous than morally requiring impartial treatment as between one's child and an utter stranger? Is there even a plausible case that can be made for such a posture?

James Rachels argues that the partialist position, even if deeply embedded in conventional moral wisdom, is fatally flawed because it wrongly privileges irrelevant considerations, such as luck, with moral significance: "Suppose a parent believes that, when faced with a choice between feeding his own children and feeding starving orphans, he should give preference to his own. This is natural enough. But the orphans need the food just as much, and they are no less deserving. It is only their bad luck that they were not born to affluent parents; and why should luck count, from a moral point of view?"[18] Moreover, Rachels endorses the view that "universal love is a higher ideal than family loyalty, and that obligations within families can be properly understood only as particular instances of obligations to all mankind."[19] Finally, the conception of morality captures "something deeply important that we should be reluctant to give up. It is useful, for example, in explaining why egoism, racism, and sexism are morally odious, and if we abandon this conception we lose our most natural and persuasive means of combating those doctrines."[20]

Impartialism, though, has an impoverished concept of the value of personal relations. Imagine a nation of universal benevolence and sympathy. All others are equal objects of concern. Intimacy, in the sense of exclusionary and partial relations such as friendship, vanishes. In such a nation, aspects of life that are deeply embedded with moral significance are relinquished. To suppose that almost everyone would choose our present situation over the hypothetical nation is reasonable. A country lacking deep friendship and family affection is unappealing even if it produces slight gains in overall happiness.[21] Impartialism is inconsistent with the sort of personal relations that almost everyone desires, at least almost everyone who has a reasonably satisfying network of friends and loved ones.

Is it possible, much less desirable, to act, on emotional and spiritual levels, like someone is your intimate friend and thus special, and to remain impartial when allocating paramount material and service goods? Is it plausible to act as if someone is your friend, to tell that person that you are friends, yet at the moment of need toggle to a default moral position of impartiality? ("Mary, we have been close for years, we have shared a common history and exchanged numerous intimacies, but, hey, you are only a chambermaid while the other guy is an archbishop! I must either be a Godwinian and save the chief or remain fully neutral and flip a coin to see whom I should rescue. Either way, our friendship over many years cuts no moral ice!")

The most reasonable rendering of impartialism recognizes that personal relationships embody a degree of independent moral relevance. Thus, Rachels writes: "Bonds of affection are more than just instrumental goods. To be loved is to have one's own value affirmed; thus it is a source of self-esteem. This is important for all of us, but especially for children, who are helpless and more vulnerable than adults.... Loving relationships provide individuals with things to value, and so give their lives ... meaning."[22]

It may seem that this interpretation coincides with the basic tenets of partialism and thus its distinctive status evaporates. But this appearance is deceiving. Rachels continues: "When considering similar needs, you may permissibly prefer to provide for the needs of your own children. For example, if you were faced with a choice between feeding your own children or contributing money to provide food for other children, you could rightly choose to feed your own. But if the choice were between some relatively trivial thing for your own and necessities for other children, preference should be given to helping the others."[23]

Obviously, where we draw the line between the trivial and the important is highly contestable, but the main thrust of this proposal is that partiality, at least in the allocation of material benefits, must be limited to situations where the needs of conflicting potential recipients are similar, when one potential recipient has greater need than another the fact that the latter is my child or intimate friend is morally irrelevant. Accordingly, Rachels, unlike Godwin, would rescue his mother the chambermaid and not the archbishop, but the presence of personal relationships triggers moral currency only when the needs of the potential recipients are similar: "You may provide the necessities for your own children first, but you are not justified in providing them luxuries while other children lack necessities. Even in a fairly weak form [one in which necessities are broadly defined], this view would still require much greater concern for others than the [partialist] view that is most common in our society."[24]

The Case for Partialism

But the moral enterprise, understood properly, presupposes the partiality in personal relations. That is, the sorts of dispositions and virtues that comprise the moral enterprise can be acquired only through the experiences and habits learned in personal relations characterized by partiality. Personal relations are nonfungible: if X has a personal relationship to Y, then Y is one of X's ends and that end is precisely Y and not any other person. The particularity of the other person grounds the value and bond of friendship, at least in part. Also, the intimacy of friendship promotes general virtues such as honesty, loyalty, empathy, and self-making. Intimacy requires partiality — by definition, we cannot be intimate with everyone — and treating family and friends preferentially is sound.

We must recognize that the unique and valuable ends of family and personal relations cannot be achieved without the socially recognized institutions of family and friendship. While the precise nature and strictures of these institutions are reimaginable, some form of family and friendship are necessary lest important values evaporate. By viewing morality merely as a set of abstract rules and principles, impartialists open themselves to the charge that they ignore paramount functions of morality such as developing and nurturing personal relationships as well as trusting local communities.

Partialists also illustrate the alleged poverty of viewing the value of personal relations in purely instrumentalist terms. If some impartialists are willing to admit a certain level of partiality only because doing so has an instrumental value for the general moral enterprise, they miss the mark. Personal relations bear value for their own sakes. Imagine being in a personal relationship and discovering that the other party has done certain actions for you only out of a sense of duty or from an ideal of universal beneficence or for reasons of general moral development. You would likely conclude that the other has misunderstood the nature of personal relations. Personal relations are not merely different in degree from impersonal relations, they are metaphysically different in kind: the metaphors of mutual bonds, connectedness, attachments, although faintly capturing the truth, are too effete.

Rachels, though, accepts (a limited) partiality in personal relations on explicitly noninstrumentalist grounds. Is the limited bias permitted by his version of impartialism — I may prefer my family and intimates to strangers only when the conflicting interests at stake are equally important, or when family interests are nontrivial and stronger than the competing interests — sufficient to rescue the impartiality thesis from the charge that it wrongly devalues and misunderstands intimacy?

Personhood presupposes partiality in the sense that one's identity and personal integrity must consist in part of projects, aspirations, and life's plans that have unique status in one's priority of values simply because they are hers. To require people to calculate impartiality would be to alienate them from their attitudes, convictions, projects, and actions. Also, a world in which I considered everyone's interests equally would be a world in which profound affection for others no longer existed, a world that eliminated the values of specialness and belonging. Intimate friendships involve the parties' recognition of each other as special, non-interchangeable people. They and only they have certain unique qualities, or combinations of them, or ways of embodying and expressing them. We do not live in a sea of undifferentiated humanness.

Torre and Aristotle

The most fundamental message of the baseball manager and the Ancient Greek philosopher is that worthy human relationships elevate us. One test of our relationships is whether we are better in the presence of our friends or teammates than we are in their absence. Contra Aristotle, "better" does not have to mean "superior in moral goodness." That our greatest value is measured by our moral dispositions and actions may be true, but human worth is gauged by several other dimensions as well: our connection to cognitive, aesthetic, scientific, social, even athletic value. Our fruitful relationships with friends and teammates should increase our value in one or more of these dimensions.

Another test of our relationships is whether we are sometimes willing to advance the interests of our friends or teammates when doing so does not advance — and may even hinder — our own interests. This is, admittedly, a tough standard. I once unveiled this idea to a colleague. She was too polite to tell me that she thought I was crazy, but her involuntary facial reaction spoke volumes. She was convinced that friendship surely involved caring about others, wishing them well for their own sakes, providing comfort in troubled times, sharing joys in triumphant moments, and the like. But to ask that we sometimes put the interests of friends above those of our own struck her as tyrannical.

I held my ground. To me, the most penetrating relationships, the ones most implicated in transforming the self, must accept this stringent test. The baseball manager and the Ancient Greek philosopher, I suspect, would agree.

SIXTH INNING

Jackie Robinson and Antonio Gramsci

"Robinson did not merely play at center stage. He was center stage; and wherever he walked, center stage moved with him."

— Roger Kahn, author

"Robinson didn't just come to play. He come to beat you. He come to stuff the damn bat right up your ass."

— Leo Durocher, manager

"He was the most difficult ballplayer I had to deal with ... he could never accept a decision."

— Jocko Conlan, umpire

"Jackie was the kind of man who had to make his presence felt."

— Don Newcombe, teammate

"I felt he was fiercely racist. I thought he saw racism and prejudice under the bed and I'd get out of patience with things he'd say and do."

— Red Smith, sportswriter

Antonio Gramsci (1891–1937) was a Marxist of a special stripe, one who advocated social change in a generally nonviolent but relentless fashion. Jackie Robinson (1919–1972) was a great social reformer who broke the color barrier in major league baseball in 1947. By showing how Robinson was unwittingly engaged in a Gramsci-style revolution, we can better understand Jackie's significance in 20th century America.

Jackie Robinson and the Color Barrier

Born in Cairo, Georgia, Jackie Robinson moved with his mother and four siblings to Pasadena, California, in 1920, after his father deserted the family. Mallie Robinson, a deeply religious woman who believed that she and her children could advance socially, washed and ironed clothes for more privileged people. Welfare relief supplemented her meager savings.

After graduating from high school, Jackie Robinson attended Pasadena Junior College and later, UCLA. There he played baseball, basketball, football, and track with exceptional skill. He led the Pacific Coast Basketball Conference in scoring for two years, was a national champion long jumper, an All-American football halfback, varsity baseball shortstop, and UCLA's first athlete to letter in four sports. Because of financial pressures, he withdrew from college in his senior year, only a few credits short of earning an undergraduate degree.

After leaving UCLA, Robinson worked for a short time as an athletic director in the National Youth Administration. In the fall of 1941, he journeyed to Hawaii to work construction and play semipro football with the Honolulu Bears. After returning to the mainland USA after the attack on Pearl Harbor, Robinson entered the Army and was assigned to a segregated unit in Fort Riley, Kansas. He tried to enter Officers Candidate School (OCS), but was rejected because of his race. Prominent black men, such as heavyweight champion Joe Louis, who was then stationed at Fort Riley, and Truman Gibson, advisor to the secretary of war, protested the policy excluding African Americans. The policy was rescinded and Robinson entered OCS. He graduated as a first lieutenant in 1943.

Assigned to Fort Hood, Texas, Robinson defied a bus driver's instruction to sit at the rear of the bus. Robinson was charged with public drunkenness, conduct unbecoming an officer, and willful disobedience. The allegations sparked curiosity in light of the fact that Robinson did not drink alcohol and the army had earlier decreed the desegregation of military buses. Robinson, supported by numerous fellow servicemen, the NAACP, and the African American press, earned an acquittal at his court-martial. He was honorably discharged from the military in 1944.

After a short stint coaching a college basketball team, Robinson joined the Kansas City Monarchs of the Negro American League in 1945. Events soon conspired on behalf of Jackie Robinson to confer upon him the honor of breaking the color barrier in Major League Baseball.

In the 1880s, around two dozen black players had graced the rosters of professional baseball. Moses and Weldy Walker, George Stovey, and Frank Grant were among the more prominent. In 1887, Cap Anson, manager and star of the Chicago White Stockings, threatened not to play an exhibition against Toledo if its star hurler, George Stovey, took the field. Anson may not have been the most vicious racist extant at the time, but, if not, he certainly was a powerful challenger to whoever was. Stovey withdrew. Anson rallied support for what became the baseball version of Jim Crow policies: informal gentlemen's agreements that no black players would henceforth be included in professional baseball. By 1892, the color line had solidified. With a few, scattered exceptions in the 1890s, only white players could apply for professional baseball jobs.

In response, the best black ballplayers soon formed a handful of teams such as the Cuban Giants, the Cuban X Giants, and Columbia Giants. By 1906, nine professional black teams were centered within a 100-mile radius of Philadelphia. These squads, all named Giants, each with a different modifier, journeyed in search of games. Barnstorming was the foundation of black professional baseball.

Then along came Arthur "Rube" Foster, pitcher, manager, owner, baseball commissioner, visionary *par excellence*. Rube founded the Negro National League in 1920. For six years, Foster's benevolent dictatorship held the eight-team league together: "This universe of black baseball was run by African Americans and was largely dependent on an African American fan base, though it appealed to a cross-section of fans."[1]

Barnstorming, though, remained a staple: "Only a third of a season's 200 games counted in the league standings. To survive, a team had to travel. Most major franchises were located in the North, but 90 percent of the nation's black population lived in the South."[2] Black ballplayers traveled throughout the United States, Cuba, Venezuela, and Mexico.

Foster understood what most baseball people refused to admit: integration with the major leagues would eventually happen. He schemed for the day when the strongest teams in the Negro League would be ushered into the major leagues.

> [Foster's] innovation wasn't being the first black in a white-defined institution.... He wanted a professional league of black baseball that was owned, organized, managed, and played by African Americans.... His theory was that the league's strongest teams would be absorbed intact, not picked apart like a carcass by so many buzzards.[3]

In December 1926, Foster, worn down by stress, pressure, and relentless labor, suffered a nervous breakdown. He died four years later at the age of 51: "Without Foster to push every button, plug every hole, whip and intimate, the Negro National League floundered and finally died in 1932."[4]

The following year, Gus Greenlee, czar of the numbers racket (which when legalized under the auspices of state government morphs into the lottery) of the North Side of Pittsburgh and owner of the Pittsburgh Crawfords, initiated the second Negro National League. The new league endured numerous membership changes, but persisted for over twelve years. In 1937, the Negro American League was formed and lasted over ten years.

The Negro Leagues, however, were leagues in name only. Black teams still derived the bulk of their income from barnstorming games not counted in the standings.... Athletes repeatedly jumped from team to team or to Latin American clubs and back. Many players worked without contracts.... Underfinanced and overextended, few, if any, Negro League franchises registered profits before World War II.[5]

World War II, however, animated attendance at professional baseball games. For example, the East-West All-Star game, created by Greenlee and an aide in 1932, drew over 51,000 fans in 1943: "At the war's end, the Negro Leagues reached their peak — a two million dollar empire, one of the largest black-dominated businesses in the United States."[6]

Meanwhile, the major leagues coasted along, smugly oblivious to the possibilities of integration. Over 75 percent of the black population lived in the South, while major league franchises were in the North. Admitting black players to the majors offered no obvious economic gains to owners. Also, most clubs held their spring training in the Jim Crow states of the South. Admitting black players invited problems with Jim Crow laws and customs. Despite objections raised by the black press, members of the Communist Party, and a few white sportswriters, the prospect of integrated professional baseball was greeted with resounding indifference.

The aftermath of World War II, though, augured change. How could the United States sanctimoniously condemn Hitler while promoting racial prejudices at home? And what about the heroic military service of African Americans during the war? Why should a person, solely because of skin color, be able to die on foreign soil for a country's cause but be banned at home from an opportunity to play professional baseball?

Such questions were not new. But coupled with a dramatic shift in population trends — in the 1940s, African American population in northern states increased by 50 percent — and increased attendance at Negro League contests, they took on added significance. The engagement of economic opportunity for major league owners to high-minded moralism seemed possible. The perfect marriage broker, though, had to step forth to seal the deal.

Antonio Gramsci and Social Change

Gramsci aspired to loosen Marxism's scientific and material inclinations and reinstate the importance of cultural and ideological change. He was inspired by Marxism's democratic impulses and by the need to translate ideas into political action.[7]

Earlier Marxist thinkers insisted that the working class was an inherently revolutionary force, that capitalism's collapse was inevitable, and that the manner of collapse was predictable. Gramsci rejected these convictions. Instead, he believed that liberal-capitalist regimes were able to transform and reproduce themselves despite their persistent economic contradictions. They did this, according to Gramsci, by establishing ideological hegemony.

An ideological hegemony consists of values, cultural attitudes, beliefs, social norms, and legal structures which thoroughly saturate civil society. Whereas earlier Marxist theorists stressed the role of the state and the way economic forces molded dominant ideas, Gramsci emphasized the active role ideas play in class struggle and denied that a single cause, such as economics, could explain all social development.

Major social institutions — the state, legal systems, schools, workplaces, churches, families, media — transmit the dominant ideas and the practices they support. A nation's popular consciousness is thus transformed. The most solid ideological hegemonies receive general acceptance and come to be viewed as natural, appropriate, perhaps even inevitable. In this manner, the ruling ideas become so deeply embedded in social relations that they are internalized by citizens as common sense. An ideological hegemony conceals the sources of its ideas and practices — particularly its power relations and specific historical circumstances — and presents itself as a historical truth.

For Gramsci, the state mobilizes both force and consent. As a forum of ideological and political dispute and a major medium through which the dominant classes lure popular consent, the state plays a major role in solidifying ideological hegemony.

But instead of relying mainly on the dominant Marxist analyses of economic base ideological superstructure and state power, Gramsci introduces the notions of historical bloc and ensemble of relations. A historical bloc is formed by popular groups built around a common ideology which challenges the dominant set of ideas. Economic, social, and ideological forces combine to change social conditions. Social forces intrude on existing class domination and coalitions are formed to shift the ensemble of relations, the totality of social relations in historical context, to a new social order. While not ignoring the important role of economics in social change, Gramsci refused to view all cultural and ideological reality as caused only by economic factors.

Gramsci contrasted passive revolution with popular political struggle. Conducted mainly through state agency, passive revolutions respond to a perceived crisis by changing the economic structure from above. In contrast, popular political struggle requires the active participation of the masses.

Popular political struggle requires a crisis of authority. Revolution must undermine the spiritual power of the ruling classes by penetrating the false appearances tied to the dominant order and by creating a new set of beliefs, cultural attitudes, and social relations. A counter-hegemony must challenge and augur the collapse of the old authority patterns. At early stages of revolt, we can expect mass apathy, cynicism and confusion as the gap between the promises and the performances of the dominant order widens. Next, we can expect overt, political forms of class struggle: the spread of anti-authoritarian norms, the development of new social relations, anti-establishment subcultures, new language codes, and emerging ways of life. State repression and force may follow. Such a response may serve to quell rebellion if the underlying counter-hegemony is weak, or ennoble the rebels by drawing new supporters if the counter-hegemony is strong. Successful revolution requires the unsettling of the old ensemble of relations and the transformation of civil society, which prefigures a new state system built on nonauthoritarian foundations. The revolutionary process will involve lengthy transition periods and much unpredictability.

Such revolutionary strategies constitute a war of position in which the civil society of a developed nation is the object of attack. In contrast, in primitive societies Gramsci advised wars of movement in which the state is the object of frontal attack.

But what will energize a revolution? Marxists were divided between two answers: spontaneity and vanguardism. Advocates of spontaneity theory held that the working class would rise up to overthrow the state once capitalism could no longer mask its economic contradictions. A time would come when capitalism's relations of production could no longer efficiently use developing technology. Economic conditions would be so bleak that workers would no longer be mystified by the ideological superstructure and they would solidify into a revolutionary class. In contrast, advocates of vanguardism were less likely to view workers as an inherently revolutionary class. Instead, they stressed the role of the Communist Party in actively promoting and organizing political struggle.

Although Gramsci at various times was drawn to each of these models, his considered judgment was that each was fatally flawed. His relentless commitment to political inclusion undermined vanguardism by an elite force, while his equally strong conviction about the revolutionary role of ideas unsettled spontaneity theory. Instead, he advanced the notion of organic intellectuals.

Gramsci viewed traditional intellectuals such as writers, artists, philosophers, and the clergy as an independent social class typically divorced from social action. Instead, he emphasized how all human action is inherently political and how all reflective human beings are intellectuals. Although not necessarily the bearer of special technical knowledge, working class intellectualism is woven into the fabric of everyday life. Gramsci was also convinced that there exists a general historical process that tends continually to unify the entire human race. Once he combined his inclusive vision of politics, his conviction that history tended to extend high culture, and his belief that all human action is political, his notion of organic intellectuals followed.

Thus, the underclasses must generate their own intellectual base, revolutionary consciousness, and political theories from self-activity. The solution to lagging revolutionary consciousness among workers is not a vanguard elite who seek to impose a rebellious spirit externally. Nor is the solution blind insistence that communist revolution is inevitable and working-class consciousness will arise on cue at the appropriate historical moment. The solution is for workers to become revolutionaries through activity in the workplace, in the home, and in civil life generally. Decades prior to contemporary feminism, Gramsci insisted that the personal is political. Again, Gramsci highlights the importance of extending democracy through ideas which translate to social activity. The revolutionary party must be a mass party rooted in everyday existence. It must be an agent of social change which coordinates historical forces already in motion. Most important, it cannot be a force of external imposition if it is to prefigure a classless, radically democratic social order.

Gramsci, perhaps more than any other Marxist thinker, understood that political ends are prefigured in the means used to achieve them. If the goal is a classless, sharply democratic society which absorbs the functions of the modern state, then revolutionary activity must itself assume that form. Rather than advancing a universal model of communism, as did Joseph Stalin, Gramsci counseled popular movements which paid careful attention to existing national character and differences in historical circumstances. Because he understood theoretical activity as a changing, dialectical part of mass struggle, he was sensitive to novel ideas, ambiguity, unevenness, and indeterminacy. His own work reflects little dogmatism and a robust sense of the inherent contestability of political strategies and ideas.

Gramsci has had great influence, particularly in Italy, among leftist thinkers who are suspicious of the scientism of early Marxism, the tyrannical excesses of the Soviet model of communism, and the doctrinal posture of Communist parties generally. Perhaps it is not merely a coincidence that for decades Communists in Italy, inspired largely by Gramsci, gained consistent political influence through parliamentary means. A dispute will remain, however, whether this shows that political activity inspired by Gramsci's work is easily co-opted by liberal-capitalist regimes, or whether we are witnessing the building of a counter-hegemonic force capable of eventually unsettling the dominant ensemble of relations in Europe.

Gramsci's political genius, though, goes beyond his commitment to Marxism. His theory contains lessons for social revolutionaries positioned on all points of the ideological spectrum. To understand his war of position as tied only to Marxism is to permit opportunities for social change to breeze past.

Jackie and the Mahatma

Pompous, religious, unscrupulous, vain, parsimonious, moralistic, hypocritical, brilliant, overbearing, hard-working, messianic, opportunistic, intuitive, manipulative, highly principled, conspiratorial, a windbag, prescient.... Branch Rickey, general manager of the Brooklyn Dodgers, embodied all these attributes and much more.

Rickey was famous for inventing the farm system in the 1920s while he was general manager of the St. Louis Cardinals. He, as usual, was two steps and twenty years ahead of his peers. Under his farm system, St. Louis signed young talent cheaply then assigned the players to minor league teams owned by or under contract to the Cardinals. The previously dead-end Cards promptly won National League pennants in 1926, 1928, 1930, 1931, and 1934. Rickey's farm system was quickly mimicked by other teams. Leaving the Cardinals after a series of disputes with owner Sam Breadon, Rickey joined the Dodgers and lifted them out of Palookaville into contention. Brooklyn won a pennant in 1941 and tied for one in 1946 but lost the playoffs to the Cardinals. During the 1940s, Branch Rickey was dreaming and scheming for one more big score, yet another maneuver to get the edge over the competition.

Rickey decided that the best economic interests of the Dodgers lay in securing players from the Negro Leagues. He saw with clear eyes that the talent was there and available cheaply, the time was right to unsettle segregation in the major leagues, and he sensed that the country would inevitably integrate. Whether motivated primarily by moral outrage at the historical treatment of African Americans or fueled by his obsession with advancing the interests of the Brooklyn Dodgers (and therefore his own), Branch Rickey was ready to make the move.

Still, major transition must be planned carefully. Too many things can go wrong. Major disaster can too easily be wrenched from lofty social crusading. So Rickey sketched a list of necessary personality and athletic traits the African American who crashed the major league color barrier had to possess. He had to be a superior athlete with exceptional mental toughness. He would have to perform uncommonly well, while suffering verbal and physical abuse from opponents, fans, and, perhaps, teammates. He had to bear up under the pressure of serving as the standard bearer for his race. He had to have the discipline and self-control to step away from confrontation without yielding his dignity and integrity. He had to conduct himself as a gentleman off the field. He had to be under 30 years old because he might have to toil for a few years in the minor leagues prior to ascending to a major league roster. Yet he had to be mature, articulate, and intelligent, with varied life experiences in integrated settings.

Rickey soon realized his list was so daunting that few, if any, human beings would qualify. Finally, he settled on Jack Roosevelt Robinson, college man, Army officer, athlete *extraordinaire.* Jackie, though, exhibited one potential flaw: a ferocious temper leavened by an indelible rage against racial discrimination.

> Proud, courageous, and defiant, Robinson was never reluctant to assert his rights as an American and as a black man, even in the face of personal risk.... [He] was the most aggressive of men, white or black. This characteristic nurtured his greatness and encouraged him to rise to challenges and advance where others might retreat. But this same coiled tension, increased by Robinson's constant and justifiable suspicions of racism, led to eruptions of rage and defiance, which at times exceeded accepted — and even necessary — bounds.... Robinson's hair-trigger disposition led many Negro League players to doubt that he would be able to withstand the pressures of racial pioneering.[8]

The remaining issue would be decided through personal interview. Branch Rickey — mincing no words and spewing, as usual, thousands more than were strictly needed — would put Jackie Robinson to the test.

On August 28, 1945, a skeptical Jackie Robinson strolled into the office of the man called "Mahatma," "El Cheapo," and, especially during contract negotiations, tons of unprintable phrases. Robinson had received a sham try-out with the Boston Red Sox earlier that year and was in no mood to be jerked around any further by Branch Rickey–double talk. Rickey, the ever cautious, calculating predator, focused keenly on Robinson's character and demeanor.

The precise report of this meeting has undoubtedly been embellished, distorted, and mythologized with each telling. We can be confident, though, in the following. The two men began by silently sizing one another up. They eye-balled each other, each trying to detect even a hint of insincerity, weakness, or disingenuity in the other. Rickey played his first card and straight-forwardly let Robinson know why he was called in: the color barrier must be broken in major league baseball and Robinson might well be the man to crash through. He convinced the wary Robinson that Branch Rickey was not spending time just to slid Jackie through the rhetorical grease.

Act two consisted of Rickey lecturing Robinson for at least three hours — barely a warm up for the voluble mountebank — on the social and athletic responsibilities facing the first black ballplayer. Much more was at stake than just baseball. The entire nation would be watching, judging, testing, and measuring the man, not just the athlete.

Act three was a Branch Rickey masterpiece. Alternating between portraying a hostile teammate, abusive fan, racist opponent, and Jim Crow–tempered hotel worker, Rickey laid into Robinson with theatrical flair. Cajoling, challenging, insulting, taunting ... Branch Rickey was play-acting with purpose. Robinson controlled his first, second, and third impulses to respond in kind. Finally, he sputtered, "What do you want, a ballplayer who is afraid to fight back." Rickey tossed his trump, "No, I want a player with guts enough not to fight back."[9]

The evangelical Rickey underscored his position by having Robinson read sections on nonresistance in Papini's *Life of Christ*. He concluded with a non-negotiable demand: the first black ballplayer would have to shrink back from all confrontations for at least the first three years of his major league career.

Jackie Robinson, "the most aggressive of men," thoughtfully cogitated on this condition for at least five minutes prior to responding. He intuited what breaking the color barrier in baseball might mean generally for African Americans. He reimagined the abuse he would have to endure. He wondered if he could walk away, turn the other cheek, niftily skirt the mean-spirited challenges hurled his way. He weighed the costs and benefits.

Finally, he spoke. Robinson assured Rickey that he would neither initiate any incidents nor be drawn into confrontation. He would accept Rickey's nonresistance condition. Before leaving the office, Robinson signed a contract to play for the Montreal Royals, the top Dodgers farm club, in 1946.

Jackie the Pro

The Montreal Royals traveled no farther south than Baltimore during the regular season, but Robinson was still subjected to the full monty of Jim Crow segregation in Florida during spring training. Often denied use of facilities and services enjoyed by the rest of the team, Robinson presented a troubling dilemma for entrepreneurs in Florida: They aspired to ingratiate themselves with the Brooklyn Dodgers for commercial and entertainment purposes, but most were deeply wed to segregationist traditions.

The Dodgers eventually signed an African American pitcher, John Wright, and assigned him to Montreal to ease Robinson's social burdens. Throughout his minor league season, Robinson endured the predicted reactions: more than the usual number of brushback pitches, verbal taunts from bench jockeys and fans, suspicion and hostility from some teammates, great expectations from black fans, and microscopic attention from the media.

He responded spectacularly — leading the International League with a .349 batting average and in runs scored with 113, while finishing second in stolen bases and earning the highest fielding percentage among second basemen, and leading his team to the pennant. Not fully quantifiable by statistics was the scintillating Robinson style of play: base running that exuded daring, hard-nosed hustle at all times, clever use of the bunt, and a winning presence teammates could access for their own benefit. To call Jackie Robinson determined is understatement. Robinson was not just focused, he seethed.

The effort, as it would throughout his professional baseball career, exacted an extravagant price. While outsiders marveled at his "effortless dignity,"[10] Robinson churned and burned: "There were the stresses of just knowing that you were pulling a big weight of a whole lot of people on your back."[11] Robinson's personal baseball success or failure was small potatoes compared to the social implications for African Americans. Baseball was the context to test Robinson's resolve, but the findings would spread expansively beyond the diamond. By late August, a medical doctor concluded Jackie Robinson — unable to eat or sleep properly, beset with recurrent nausea — was on the verge of a nervous breakdown. Two playing days after the diagnosis, Robinson was back on the field.

In 1947, Robinson would debut with the Brooklyn Dodgers. A shortstop in the Negro League, a second baseman at Montreal, he was asked to play first base for the Dodgers. He lacked the arm to unseat future Hall of Famer Pee Wee Reese at shortstop, and second base, Robinson's best position, was safely in the hands of Eddie "The Brat" Stanky. Robinson complied, but not happily.

His rookie year, like D-Day, was eventful. Certain Dodgers players circulated a petition declaring their refusal to play with Robinson. The petition soon died from failure of key players, such as Reese, to sign and Branch Rickey's "play with Robinson or be traded" manifesto.

Philadelphia Philly manager Ben Chapman, along with his jive time chorus of bench jockeys, rained racial taunts down on Robinson: "Chapman mentioned everything from thick lips to the supposedly extra-thick Negro skull ... [and] the repulsive sores and diseases he said Robinson's teammates would become infected with if they touched the towels or combs he used."[12] The venomous, unbridled attack backfired. Chapman unwittingly solidified Dodger support for Robinson, and invited a torrent of general condemnation against Chapman and his loudmouthed minions. So powerful was the backlash, that team owners asked Chapman and Robinson to shake hands and stand for a conciliatory photo. The resulting picture is comical as both parties look as comfortable in the other's presence as pre-teens at their first dance.

In May, another alleged scheme, a player strike targeted against Robinson, was conjured by stalwarts on the St. Louis Cardinals. Facts about this supposed venture were difficult to separate from fictions even in 1947. Today, myth and reality are firmly intertwined. Some argue that the entire tale is fabrication. Others insist the strike was hatching, but the heroic efforts of National League president Ford Frick and Cardinals owner Sam Breadon crushed the miscreants prior to fruition. Still others maintain that strike talk did occur, but player solidarity was insufficient to generate anything other than sound and fury signifying little.

As expected, Robinson also suffered from a passel of death threats, written typically by fans who were barely literate, flying spikes from runners crossing first base, and weekly indignities at the hands of service providers: "May 9, 1947, marked perhaps the worst day of Jackie Robinson's baseball career. Threats on his life, torment from opposing players, discrimination at the team hotel, and rumors of a player strike simultaneously engulfed the black athlete."[13]

He, nevertheless, persevered. Attendance rose at Dodgers games, home and away. One sportswriter observed, "Robinson dressed himself in a cloak of humility and made it a perfect fit through one of the greatest acting jobs in baseball history."[14] Brooklyn won the National League pennant. Robinson was named Major League Rookie of the Year, smacking a solid .297, spiced with a league-leading 29 stolen bases and 74 walks. His base running and impact, as usual, cannot be captured fully by numbers.

> Breaking, Robinson reached full speed in three strides. The pigeon-toed walk yielded to a run of graceful power. He could steal home, or advance two bases on someone else's bunt, and at the time of decision, when he slid, the big dark body became a bird in flight. Then, safe, he rose slowly, often limping, and made his pigeon-toed way to the dugout.... The rundown was his greatest play. Robinson could start so fast and stop so short that he could elude anyone in baseball, and he could feint a start and feint a stop as well.[15]

Backlash, in the form of sympathetic understanding, from the excesses of the likes of Ben Chapman, deranged fans, and the daily debasements of Jim Crow, was forthcoming. At the end of Robinson's rookie year, an annual nationwide public opinion poll named him the second most popular person in the United States. Perhaps, though, the competition was not stiff: crooner Bing Crosby finished first.

More black ballplayers entered the major leagues. Larry Doby was signed by the Cleveland Indians and played a few months after Robinson's debut. The Dodgers, under the triumphant Rickey's supervision, signed Roy Campanella, Don Newcomb, Joe Black, and Jim Gilliam in short order. The Indians, spurred by iconoclastic owner Bill Veeck, enrolled the great Satchel Paige, Al Smith, Dave Hoskins, Minnie Minoso, and Luke Easter. The New York

Giants added Monte Irvin and Willie Mays. The St. Louis Browns inked Hank Thompson, Willard Brown, and Piper Davis to contracts. And so it went. Major League owners gleefully picked the ripest fruit from the Negro Leagues, but rarely compensated the management of those teams. The Negro Leagues soon withered away.

Meanwhile, Jackie Robinson was flourishing. After his second year as a Dodger, Rickey released Robinson from his promise to avoid confrontation. Jackie cast off the "cloak of humility." He became one of the most cutting bench jockeys in the league, the scourge of umpires and opposing players. Few slights, real or imagined, went unavenged. Robinson freely and passionately held court on the injustices and remedies of American society. Upon being asked, he charged that the New York Yankees were prejudiced against Negro ballplayers (he was undoubtedly correct). He accused some umpires of being biased against him. He criticized Dodgers management freely. His critics accused Jackie of viewing all disagreements along racial lines and suggested he was paranoid. Robinson became a lightning rod for controversy.

For example, in one game in spring 1955, Sal "The Barber" Maglie, ace hurler of the New York Giants and renowned for his success against the Dodgers, was again working his curveball magic. The Barber, celebrated for his brushback pitches and fearless confrontations, had buzzed a few tosses high and tight to Dodgers batters, including Robinson. Spurred on by teammates, Robinson sought revenge. He bunted towards first base, hoping Maglie would be forced to cover the bag. Instead, second baseman Davey Williams took the throw from first baseman Whitey Lockman, who had corralled the bunt. Robinson smashed into Williams: "[Jackie's] knee crashed into Williams' lower spine and Williams spun in the air, twisting grotesquely, and when he fell he lay in an awkward sprawl, as people do when they are seriously injured."[16] Davey Williams, an excellent defensive second baseman, injured his back so severely on the play that he was forced to retire at the end of the season at age 27. Was this justified retaliation within the informal rules of major league baseball? Or was it a cheap shot, disproportionate response on an innocent, well-respected ballplayer?

The Dodgers won pennants in 1947, 1949, 1952, 1953, 1955, and 1956, with near misses in 1950 and 1951. "Next year" finally arrived in 1955 as they defeated their nemesis, the New York Yankees, in the World Series. Jackie Robinson carved out a Hall of Fame career, winning the National League Most Valuable Player award in 1949, when he swaggered his way to a league-leading .342 batting average, 124 runs batted in, 16 homers, 12 triples, league-leading 37 stolen bases, 86 walks, a .432 on base percentage, and .528 slugging percentage. After the 1956 season, he was traded to the New York Giants, but retired from the game instead of reporting. Jackie Robinson had a 10-year career batting average of .311, playing on 6 pennant-winners and 1 World Series championship squad.

Robinson and Retirement

Upon retirement, Robinson became an executive in the Chock Full O'Nuts restaurant chain. He later participated in a handful of black-owned local businesses such as the Freedom Bank in Harlem and the Robinson Construction Corporation. He struck the old guard Negro establishment as too militant and eventually resigned from the NAACP. Younger black militants — who celebrated Malcolm X, the Black Panthers, and separation flowing from strength — decried Robinson as an Uncle Tom because of his call for black capitalism, his flirtations with Republican politicians, and his integrationist commitment.

Robinson aged poorly. The inferno of pressure and stress that dogged him during his playing days took vicious retribution on his health. He suffered from the effects of heart disease, high blood pressure, and diabetes. When he was 40 years old, he appeared 20 years older. When he was 50, he looked like a 75 or 80 year old man. In 1971, one of his sons, who had become a drug addict and undergone two well-publicized arrests, died in a car accident at age 24, shortly after successful drug rehabilitation.

In 1972, Jackie Robinson appeared at Dodger Stadium in Los Angeles to participate in events commemorating the 25th anniversary of his major league debut. He was only 53 years old but was virtually blind and barely able to walk. Later in the year, he threw out the first ball at the World Series at Riverfront Stadium in Cincinnati. He expressed his desire to see the first black manager in the major leagues. Nine days later, Jackie Robinson died of a heart attack. On his tombstone is inscribed his signature belief, "A life is not important except in the impact it has on other lives."

Robinson and Gramsci

Gramsci, to the best of my knowledge, was unfamiliar with baseball. Moreover, his commitment to refashioning Marxism is irrelevant to our concerns. What is crucial, though, are Gramsci's insights regarding effective social transformation.

Phase One. If popular political struggle requires a crisis of authority, so, too, does social transformation. The authority of Jim Crow segregation was unsettled by the aftermath of World War II, changing African American population patterns, and the growing perception that the abuses of Jim Crow were indefensible. Television, which burst on the scene shortly after the signing of Jackie Robinson, would soon bring into John and Jane Doe's living room graphic scenes of racial injustice that had previously been, at best, abstractions to most white Americans.

Baseball was the national pastime. Sure, black athletes such as Joe Louis and Jessie Owens had already risen to become national heroes. But their sports were episodic and dramatic — Louis's first round knockout of Max Schmeling, Owens's remarkable Olympic games performance in Berlin with Hitler watching. Black prizefighters and track stars had been present for some time. Baseball, though, was the great national sport, capturing the rhythms of everyday life and standing as a metaphor for America itself. Baseball was played almost every day in spring, summer, and early fall.

The crisis of authority was major league baseball's right to operate under informal rules excluding black ballplayers. Led by Robinson, Rickey, and Commissioner Happy Chandler, the slogan, "If he was good enough to fight and possibly die for his country in war, he is good enough for the opportunity to play professional ball" gained currency. Yes, a clear economic motive underwrote the efforts of white management, but even coarsened cynics must admit Rickey and Chandler were putting themselves on the line, risking the disapprobation, even ostracism, of their peers, especially if Robinson failed.

In 1949, the Grand Dragon of the Ku Klux Klan was appalled at the prospect of the integrated Brooklyn Dodgers playing exhibition games in Georgia during spring training. He muttered, then sputtered, later threatened a boycott, and spiced his rhetoric with allusions to possible violence. Branch Rickey, though, had made up his mind to enter Georgia and Florida, to skip into the mouth of Jim Crow and loosen a few teeth. Once Rickey made up his mind only God had a chance to change it and God had better have an exceptional argument.

The Dodgers came, played, and reaped a windfall of attendance money. Robinson played uncommonly well, fans packed the stadiums, and the Mahatma's Cheshire grin could not have been wider: "Robinson's 1949 conquest of Atlanta reflected a subtle shift in race relations in the postwar South. Despite the sporadic violence and Klan growth, the rule of Jim Crow was softening."[17]

In 1949 in addition to the Dodger breakthroughs, racial barriers fell in Norfolk, Virginia, Shreveport, Louisiana, and several Texas cities. In 1950 St. Petersburg, Florida, Columbia, South Carolina, and Mobile, Alabama, succumbed. In 1952 Chattanooga, Tennessee, New Orleans, and Montgomery, Alabama, accepted black players. Many smaller cities followed suit.[18]

Phase Two. Revolution must undermine the spiritual power of the ruling classes by penetrating the false appearances tied to the dominant order and by creating a new set of beliefs, cultural attitudes, and social relations. The phony, self-serving appearances, carefully nurtured by repeated social messages had crystallized into false consciousness: "Negroes will fold under pressure," "They aren't smart enough to play the game," "They can't act properly, on or off the field," "Outside of, maybe, Paige and Josh Gibson, both of whom are well past their prime, they just aren't good enough," and the like.

Jackie Robinson took hold of these dominant ideas and squeezed the life out of them. Although he was not considered the best player in the Negro Leagues, the crafty Rickey was correct in anointing him the best player to smash the color barrier.

New social beliefs were nurtured by laws and reactions against mindless racial cruelty and hate.

> In July 1948, President Truman had initiated the desegregation of the armed forces, affecting military installations throughout the nation. A series of Supreme Court decisions in 1950 limited segregation on railway cars and in higher education. At the same time many southern communities rejected the most visible trappings of racial intimidation, passing anti-mask laws aimed at the Klan. In several states blacks returned to the polls and took their places on juries, school boards, and in colleges and universities.[19]

Phase Three. A counter-hegemony must challenge and augur the collapse of the old authority patterns. At early stages of revolt, we can expect mass apathy, cynicism and confusion as the gap between the promises and the performances of the dominant order widens. Next, we can expect overt, political forms of class struggle: the spread of anti-authoritarian norms, the development of new social relations, anti-establishment subcultures, new language codes, and emerging ways of life.

Robinson played with a style that challenged the dominant strategies of the game and animated new possibilities:

> He revolutionized major league baseball by injecting an element of "tricky baseball," so common in the Negro Leagues. In an age in which managers bemoaned the lost art of bunting, Robinson [in 1947], in forty-six bunt attempts, registered fourteen hits and twenty-eight sacrifices, a phenomenal .913 success rate. His tactics often went against the time-worn conventional wisdom.[20]

Socially, the participation of blacks in integrated competitions kept edging aside the authority of Jim Crow and unsettled southern racial traditions. Once Rickey released Robinson from his promise of non-confrontation, Jackie was able to press hotels and restaurants servicing the Dodgers for more racial inclusion. Change was marginal and incremental, but progress was made. The counter-hegemony was on the move. The dominant ensemble of relations were being challenged.

Phase Four. State repression and force may follow. Such a response may

serve to quell rebellion if the underlying counter-hegemony is weak, or ennoble the rebels by drawing new supporters if the counter-hegemony is strong.

Robinson met stiff resistance from certain opponents, umpires, fans, and
teammates. The most vicious and indefensible of these attacks were greeted
by a sympathetic backlash from reasonable people of all races. Robinson, typically, gained supporters as right-thinking people were repelled by the mean-
spiritedness and bigotry of his tormentors.

In 1954, after the Supreme Court declared school segregation illegal in
Brown v. Board of Education, a new wave of racial violence engulfed the south.
Lynchings, racially-motivated murders, and an emboldened KKK appeared
on the scene. From 1955 to 1958, over forty people were beaten and almost
thirty shot or wounded in racially-charged incidents. As Gramsci would have
predicted, repression and force reared their ugly faces.

But the counter-hegemony, led by the symbolism of Rosa Parks and the
rhetoric of Martin Luther King, showed its power and the civil rights movement attracted new disciples. Television now played a crucial part in dissem-
inating the most vicious abuses of segregation, bias, and racial hate. Many
people who had been indifferent or uninformed could no longer stand passively by.

> King and his people were conducting the most perilous undertaking imaginable,
> for they knew that the more skillfully they provoked their enemies, the more dra-
> matic the footage they would reap, and also the more likely they were to capture
> the high moral ground.... [King] needed some measure of white backlash, and he
> needed, among other things, proper villains. He wanted ordinary white people to
> sit in their homes, and watch blacks acting with great dignity while Southern offi-
> cials ... assaulted them.... Racial prejudice had been like a giant beast that never
> came out in the daytime.[21]

The movement was not a linear, ever-progressing advance to better days.
Twists, turns, backward steps were evident. But America would never return
to the old hegemonic mindset. Opportunities for racial minorities increased
to the benefit of the nation. We can imagine Gramsci cheering.

Phase Five. Successful revolution requires the unsettling of the old
ensemble of relations and the transformation of civil society, which prefigures
a new state system built on nonauthoritarian foundations. The revolutionary
process will involve lengthy transition periods and much unpredictability.

We have a long way to go to achieve a new state and social system built
on nonauthoritarian foundations. Hierarchy and division remain, smugly
enjoying the bounty of their misdeeds. Official policies such as affirmative
action coalesce uneasily with subtler, cleaner-appearing forms of racial bias.
The social revolution remains in process. Carl Erskine, Robinson's teammate
on those great Dodgers teams, sums up the convictions of many: "Jackie gave

momentum to the civil rights movement in modern times by reenergizing it and setting it upon a new, strong course. I believe Jackie single-handedly kicked off the civil rights movement."[22]

Gramsci would probably conclude that "single-handedly" is too extravagant a description — a historical bloc that sires a counter-hegemonic ideology capable of unsettling the established ensemble of relations is rarely, if ever, initiated by one person or group. Erskine's hyperbole, though, is easily forgiven when we fairly assess the glorious contributions to civil rights bestowed by Jackie Robinson.

Regrettably, but predictably, Robinson remains a controversial figure. Contemporary criticism spews from the political left. Branch Rickey — a complicated, robustly complex man — is portrayed as a greedy, grasping opportunist who shrewdly shrouded his raging capitalism in the cloak of humanitarianism. Robinson is painted as an unwitting accomplice in Rickey's master plan to destroy a successful black institution. Thus, sociologist Harry Edwards concludes: "The baseball model implied that overall Black integration into the mainstream of American life [would] necessarily demand the denigration, abandonment and ultimate collapse of parallel Black institutions."[23]

William T. Rhoden carries the attack further:

> Rickey exploited a psychological soft spot within the African American community — the desire to "measure up" — that made the invasion [of the Negro Leagues by the major leagues] go infinitely smoother.... A black institution was dead, while a white institution grew richer and stronger. This was the end result of integration.... [Integration] pulled black athletes back into the mainstream, but in a way that kept them on the periphery of real power, safely within sight.... Robinson did not realize the complex effects of segregation on black and white communities, and failed to balance the goals of integration and empowerment. In the end, he achieved one without the other.... [Integration] had worked its magic on what was once a thriving black-owned industry, stealing its talent base and laying waste to its power.[24]

The attack bears a germ of truth: Robinson's efforts did not bring with them an African American presence in league offices, team ownership, management, or coaching. At the time he died, Jackie had not witnessed even one black manager in the major leagues, much less an African American owner. Today, the situation remains uninspiring. Black managers have arrived, a general manager, a few prominent league executives, but no owners. In that vein, Edwards and Rhoden score an important point.

Defenders of the integrationist model counter with a slogan, "The Negro Leagues should never have existed." If blacks had not been denied access to the major leagues, if they had not been wrongly banned from playing, the Negro Leagues would not have been necessary.

The Negro Leagues, from the comforts of retrospective falsification, are now too often seen as an always viable, economic boon for African Americans. This was not the case. The determined, benevolent despotism of Rube Foster kept things running for a few years in the 1920s, the league — depending on barnstorming more than established institutions — was hit and miss through the 1930s. Only at and after World War II were the Negro Leagues truly flourishing.

Jules Tygiel marks an important distinction between the Negro Leagues and other black institutions: "Unlike other African American entities such as black churches, music, and colleges that survived and flourished after the civil rights years, The Negro Leagues lacked any legitimacy outside of a segregationist context. Robinson's critique of the Negro Leagues stemmed ... from his perception of these teams as Jim Crow institutions."[25] As African American sportswriter Wendell Smith wrote in the 1950s, "Nothing was killing Negro baseball but democracy."[26]

Most important, the connection between Jackie Robinson's integration of major league baseball and wider social change sometimes eludes writers such as Edwards and Rhoden. Robinson always knew it was not only or even primarily about baseball. The more important venue was what came to be known as the civil rights movement. As sportswriter Leonard Koppett observed in his eulogy to Robinson, "By challenging the caste system in baseball, the pre-eminent pastime of the age, Jackie compelled millions of decent white people to confront the fact of race prejudice — a fact they had been able to ignore for generations before. Robinson accomplished more than any other individual to focus attention on the inequities of American society."[27]

I cannot resist closing with an *ad hominem* attack: Harry Edwards teaches at the University of California at Berkeley, not Morgan State. William T. Rhoden is a sportswriter for the *New York Times*, not the *Amsterdam News*. They should both thank the legacy of Jackie Robinson for their opportunities. If they had met Robinson in his prime ... well, Leo Durocher probably could have guessed at what would have happened.

Mickey Mantle and St. Thomas Aquinas

"Watching [Mantle] take his freshman swings [in 1951] against major-league pitching, [his fellow rookies] must have felt the same blend of awe and envy Salieri experienced when he first heard the adolescent Mozart tinkering at the piano."

— Richard Lally, author

"[Mantle] runs so fast in the outfield, he doesn't bend a blade of grass."

— Casey Stengel, manager

"Sometimes I think if I had the same body and the same natural ability and someone's else's brain, who knows how good a player I might have been."

— Mickey Mantle

"Mickey Mantle is the only baseball player I know who is a bigger hero to his teammates than he is to the fans."

— Clete Boyer, teammate

"I'd have to say DiMaggio [was the greater center fielder] because he played right handed and the park [Yankee Stadium] wasn't built for him, and he didn't need a manager."

— Casey Stengel, manager

"If I'd known I was gonna live this long, I'd have taken better take of myself."

— Mickey Mantle

Mickey Mantle (1931–1995) had an ambiguous relationship with his fans. Although often curt and insulting, Mickey had legions of admirers based on his performances and other aspects of his personality. Although leading a life that was predominately self-absorbed and self-indulgent, he gained stature by the way he dealt with his terminal illness. What is it about the faith of a fan that vivifies such reactions? St. Thomas Aquinas's (1225–1274) analysis

114

of the relationship between faith and reason is helpful in understanding the Mantle phenomenon.

Mantle the Phenom

Elvin Clark "Mutt" Mantle was an admirable man. Born to poverty, he labored at the Blue Goose lead-zinc mine in Commerce, Oklahoma. Mutt had been an able semi-professional ballplayer in his youth, or the few years that passed for his youth. In the first quarter of the 20th century, uneducated, unsophisticated, impoverished men such as Mutt married young, bred frequently, and were tethered to the yoke early and endlessly. Mutt was a serious man, not given to foolishness. When you are responsible for six children and a wife, and laboring under unspeakable conditions designed to shorten your life, you grow up early or you run like a cheetah to escape reality. Men such as Mutt Mantle could have been Karl Marx's poster boys for alienated labor under laissez-faire capitalism.

He was no saint. He drank and smoked more than advisable. But Mutt had a dream. Not for himself, of course. Mutt was ignorant of most things, but he wasn't a fool. He was and would remain a serf to the Blue Goose mine until he was beaten down by time or died. Mutt, though, had a son named Mickey, after Hall of Fame catcher Gordon "Mickey" Cochrane. Mickey Mantle exuded stunning athletic talent even as a little boy. Mickey just might have a way to get his ticket punched out of the mines, into the bright lights and clean air far beyond Commerce.

Mutt, though, understood dreams are foolish pastimes unless underwritten by hard work. Mutt Mantle held a Ph.D. with honors from the University of Hard Knocks & Harder Labor. After returning from a day at the mines, Mutt threw right-handed batting practice to Mickey who would bat left-handed, while Mutt's dad threw left-handed to Mickey who would bat right-handed. Mutt had heard about platooning in baseball-batting left-handers against right-handed throwers and batting right-hand hitters against lefties — and he imagined that this strategy would become more common. Mickey would learn to hit both ways.

Mickey Mantle adored his father and loved baseball. He practiced long and hard. If Mutt could put in the time and expend the effort after a grueling day at the mines, Mickey had no reason to complain. The years passed. Mickey was small but powerful. His foot speed was breathtaking, his power unprecedented, his general athletic ability was a gift only nature could bestow. Mutt had Mickey work a couple of stretches in the mine to impress upon him that the alternative to baseball stardom was stone cold misery.

When Mickey graduated from Commerce High in the spring of 1949, he was signed by Yankees scout Tom Greenwade for a $1,000 bonus. Mantle spent the next two seasons at Independence and Joplin, lower level Yankees farm clubs. Tall tales, mostly true but some hyperbolic, of his prodigious minor league feats and spectacular talent filtered to New York City. During spring training with the Yankees in 1951, Mantle was a marvel. He smashed balls farther than anyone had ever seen. He ran from home to first in 3 seconds batting left-handed and 3.1 seconds batting right-handed. No baseball player had ever shown greater speed. As a shortstop, though, he was scattered-armed and unreliable. Phil Rizzuto, veteran Hall of Fame Yankees shortstop, had worried about his job when he first heard the embellished yarns and later watched Mantle crack tape measure shots over the fence. But after watching Mantle play shortstop, the Scooter knew he was still employed.

Casey Stengel, Yankees manager, envisioned Mantle as the successor to Joe DiMaggio in center field. Joe was on his last legs as a ballplayer and Mantle had the raw talent to become even greater than the Yankee Clipper. When the Yankees left spring training, Mickey Mantle was on the roster.

> He was a child, timid, self-conscious, and completely overwhelmed. Among his teammates he was well-liked from the start because he had a ready smile and was pleasant company. All the young kid wanted of life was to be liked.... The image of a country rube gaping like a moron in his first face-to-face encounter with an urban society he never could have imagined seems trite, but in Mantle's case it's completely true.[1]

Starting in right field, next to the aging DiMaggio, and making the huge jump from Class-C ball to the major leagues, Mantle, not yet 20 years old, oscillated between flashing greatness and flailing ineptly at seasoned big league hurlers. By mid–July, the Yankees, world champions the previous two years, had stumbled to third place, behind the Red Sox and White Sox and only a game ahead of the fourth-place Cleveland Indians. Mantle was slumping, but his batting average was around .260 and he had driven in 45 runs. True, Mickey had struck out 52 times in less than 250 at bats, but that proportion, it turned out, would reflect his lifetime rate. All in all, he was performing quite well for a teenager adjusting to radically new social and athletic contexts. Nevertheless, Mantle was sent down to the Kansas City Blues, the top Yankee farm club.

His first time at bat with the Blues, Mickey bunted for a base hit. Instead of the expected pat on the back, he received a tongue lashing from manager George Selkirk. Mantle had been sent back to the minors to regain his knack of crushing the ball, not to reinvent himself as a punch-and-judy stroker. Mantle stumbled into a valley of depression. He did not get a hit in his next 19 at bats. Mantle telephoned his father. Desperate, anxious, panic-ridden, the most gifted natural ballplayer of his era spoke to Mutt Mantle about quitting the game. Mutt drove immediately to Kansas City, about a five hour trip. In a scene reminiscent of *The Godfather*— where Marlon Brando (Vito Corleone) slaps a whimpering Al Martino (Johnny Fontaine)— Mutt started packing Mickey's clothes and assaulted his ego, "I thought I raised a man, not a coward. You can come back to Commerce and work in the mines with me." Mutt got the result he desired. Mickey quickly begged for another chance to play baseball. That night he slammed two monster home runs. He hit over .360 in the following forty games and was recalled by the Yankees.

> The fear that ruled and motivated [Mickey Mantle] as both a boy and a man, as both a player and a husband, had begun as a mixture of fear and respect for his father.... Mutt's influence over Mickey — Mutt's ability to motivate his son through Mickey's fear of disappointing him — would extend far beyond Mickey's childhood, as well as beyond baseball ... anything short of perfection would have failed his father.[2]

Prior to joining the Yankees, Army doctors declared Mantle ineligible for military conscription because of the osteomyelitis he had contracted after being kicked in the shin during a high school football game. Osteomyelitis was the first of numerous serious injuries, diseases, and afflictions that Mantle endured through his baseball career. The second occurred in the second game of the 1951 World Series against the New York Giants.

Willie Mays sliced a fly ball to shallow right-center. Stengel had earlier instructed Mantle, who was playing right field, to use his great speed to run down any ball to the left of DiMaggio, who was playing center field. DiMaggio was playing his last series and was hobbled by bone spurs. Mantle took off at the crack of the bat, drew a bead on the pop fly, and closed in to snag it. Suddenly, he heard DiMaggio, who despite his physical ailments had retained his uncanny judgment and timing for fielding, call for the ball. Mantle put on the brakes, and caught his right foot in a rubber drain cover. His right knee collapsed as he went down as if shot. Everyone viewing knew Mantle was seriously injured.

The next day, Mutt accompanied Mickey to Lenox Hill Hospital. Mickey was on crutches and grabbed his father's shoulder to steady himself as he got out of the taxi cab. Mutt collapsed. Father and son were rushed into the hospital. Mickey underwent surgery to repair the two torn ligaments in his right knee. Mutt would soon be diagnosed with Hodgkin's disease, the same type of cancer that had killed Mutt's father and two brothers at early ages. Mutt eventually went back to the mines and worked until about a month prior to dying at 39 years of age in the spring of 1952.

> When his father died, Mantle's burdens were compounded by a fear of early death. His two uncles and now his father, all were dead before they were forty. Mickey

was convinced that he, too, would suffer an early demise. And from that year on, quite logically, he lived his life as though each day would be his last, and he did party a great deal, and he enjoyed his liquor, and he enjoyed his fun.[3]

Prior to dying, Mutt Mantle insinuated himself one final time into his son's life. He urged Mickey to dump his showgirl dalliance in New York, Holly Brooke, and marry his hometown fiancée, Merlyn Johnson. Merlyn was an unsophisticated country girl who was Mickey's "own kind," according to Mutt. Mickey, as ever, complied with Mutt's judgment. Mutt, though, did Merlyn no favor. Although she loved Mickey passionately and bore him four sons, Merlyn's marriage was scarred by Mickey's relentless womanizing, physical abuse, and occasional public humiliations. The details of these ugly incidents are better suited to supermarket tabloids than to this text.

Thomas Aquinas and the Nature of Faith

Born at Roccasecca, Italy, Tommaso D'Aquino, began his schooling under Benedictine monks in Montecassino. He became the greatest Christian theologian in history and one of the finest interpreters of Aristotelian philosophy in the medieval world. The influence of this Dominican monk is difficult to overstate. Of the countless contributions Aquinas made to the history of Western thought, I will focus only on his discussion of the relationship between faith and reason.

Some of the early church fathers, such as Tertullian (160–220), argued that faith is supreme. Divine revelation, as codified in the Bible and official church doctrine, reigns supreme over all other knowledge. Philosophical speculation is either superfluous or heretical. If philosophical theorizing confirms what is known by faith — which rarely, if ever, happens — then it is unnecessary. If the findings of philosophical theorizing contradict what is known by faith, then it is heresy. "The simplest believer knows more than the greatest philosopher," insisted Tertullian. The opposition of faith and reason, then, was established. Reason will not confirm the most profound truths of revelation and those infatuated with logical machinations jeopardize their own souls.

Thinkers more profound than Tertullian emerged. Augustine (354–430) and Anselm (1033–1109) initiated and refined the view that faith is a presupposition of understanding: "I believe in order that I might understand" (*credo ut intelligam*). Faith is the starting point, but reason can deepen our understanding. Reason, though, does not create new religious truths. But to eliminate natural reason from faith is to impoverish our consciousness and remain a simple believer. For example, we begin with belief in the existence of God.

By constructing rational arguments and by adducing reasons why God exists, we sharpen our awareness of God's existence. Natural reason cannot establish the existence of God *ex nihilo*. We started with faith, but by adding natural reason we rise to the level of enlightened believers. If reason leads to conclusions contrary to revelation, we have reasoned poorly. The crucial point is that both faith and reason are needed for religious understanding, the hallmark of the enlightened believer. The simple believer still knows religious truth — through revelation — but does not understand it thoroughly. To eliminate natural reason is to choose to grasp religious truths weakly. Non-believers, of course, can neither know nor understand religious truths.

Aquinas aspired to harmonize faith and reason. Faith and reason have different domains. Faith is agreement, by act of will, to a proposition because it was revealed by divine authority. Reason is agreement, by act of intellect, to a proposition because it was established by rational demonstration. One proposition or event cannot both be an object of reason and an object of faith simultaneously. Aquinas challenged the distinction between the simple faith of the masses ("simple believers") and the enlightened faith of those with understanding ("enlightened believers"). As believers, all human beings are equal.[4]

Some religious truths, sometimes called the preambles of faith, *are* attainable by reason alone. The existence of God, the divine attributes, the existence and immortality of the human soul, are examples. Even if God had not revealed such truths, at least a *few* human beings would have been capable of deriving them. God revealed these truths so *everyone* could know them. Such elements of revelation are the presuppositions to the mysteries of faith. Aquinas advances the stunning claim, then, that the religious truths that are knowable by reason alone (at least by a few) are the necessary starting points to the mysteries of faith.

Some articles of faith, the mysteries, surpass the range of human reason. The notions of the trinity, incarnation, and redemption, for example, cannot be proven true or false by natural reason. Faith remains a safe guide to truth and a warning against error: if faith and reason differ, then reason has gone astray. Faith is the unshakeable certitude that God has spoken. Faith is not assent to rational probability, not mere opinion, not understanding. Reason is defined by necessary, rational demonstrations. The objective cause of faith — divine revelation — is more certain than the products of human reasoning. But faith's grasp of its object is less certain than rational knowledge because faith's connection to truth lacks independent demonstration.

The articles or mysteries of faith function as first principles. They do not cascade down to us *ex nihilo*, though. The preambles of faith, knowable to all through revelation and a few through rational demonstration, are starting points that lead to the mysteries of faith, which are only revealed. We can then use them, as axioms, to prove other things are true. Just as the first principles of one discipline are not provable from within that discipline, they may be established by appeal to the methodology of a higher discipline. Aquinas reminds us that the first principles of music, for example, can be demonstrated by mathematics. The mysteries of faith are, accordingly, established by the knowledge and authority of God.

The harmony, then, of faith and reason rests on the truth of four propositions:

- Faith and reason have different domains of knowledge.
- The preambles of faith are knowable to all human beings, at least in principle, through divine revelation, and are knowable to a few through rational demonstration.
- The mysteries or articles of faith are knowable to all human beings, at least in principle, through divine revelation only. The mysteries can be neither proved nor disproved through rational demonstration.
- Any rational argument that results in a conclusion that is inconsistent with the mysteries of faith is invalid or unsound.

The Mantle Legend

Mickey Mantle's major league baseball career was inspiring. Despite osteomyelitis, the horrible knee injury suffered in the 1951 World Series, and countless other impairments, Mantle became a legend. He smashed 536 career home runs, hit .298, slugged .557, with an on-base percentage of .421. Mantle was a 16-time all star, won the MVP three times, and the triple crown in 1956 (.353 batting average, 52 home runs, 130 runs batted in). He played on 12 pennant winning and 7 world champion Yankees teams.

Along the way, he was idolized for a bunch of tape-measure home runs he rifled into the ozone. In 1953, Mickey launched a ball tossed by Chuck Stobbs over the 55-foot-high wall in Washington's Griffith Stadium. The rocket soared over the 391-foot mark, deflected off a 60-foot-high sign on the stadium's football scoreboard, and skipped to a home owner's lawn. The Yankees publicity director paced off the distance at 565 feet.

In 1960, Mantle powdered Detroit Tigers pitcher Paul Foytack's offering over the right-field roof at Briggs Stadium to a distance estimated at 643 feet. In 1964, he hammered a shot against Chicago White Sox hurler Ray Herbert to straightaway center field at Yankee Stadium judged to travel 502 feet. Twice, he almost did the impossible: slam a home run out of Yankee Stadium. The 1956 clout, off Pedro Ramos of the Washington Senators, was still rising as it slammed 18 inches below the stadium top. The 1963 blast, off Bill Fischer of the Kansas City Athletics, was still soaring when it crashed into the top of the façade. Estimates of the distance the ball might have traveled but for the presence of the façade ran as high as 620 feet. While the measurements blend truth and hyperbole recklessly, the reality of Mantle's long-distance prowess compelled awe. The specter of super-human power housed inside of an ever-fragile body added to the legend of Mickey Mantle.

He did not merely play hurt, he played injured. And everyone knew it. He never complained about his injuries. If Mutt could work the mines until a month before his death, what right did Mickey have to beg out of a baseball game? Sure, some injuries might have healed more quickly or done less damage if Mickey had pursued his rehabilitation exercises more seriously and sat on a barstool less frequently. But Mickey Mantle was ravaged by fear — of not meeting his father's perfectionist standards, of dying young, of not measuring up — and he was not going to be cheated by a short life. Sadly, his idea of not being cheated never rose above the crudest of hedonisms — more liquor, more women, more mindless laughter: desperate, unconscious rebellion against a dead father leavened by self-destruction. At times, Mantle understood this, at least dimly. Years before he died, he cajoled country star Roy Clark to promise to sing "Yesterday, When I Was Young," a lament about a life squandered in puerile adventures while hopelessly devoid of reflection, at his funeral. Mantle lacked the discipline, resources, and will to break his shoddy behavior patterns.

Mantle's deepest aspiration, eventually reflected on the epitaph of his monument in Yankee Stadium, was to be recognized as a great teammate. If anything, achieving that goal was his crowning glory. More outgoing and willing to extend himself to others than DiMaggio, less self-absorbed and obsessed with his statistics than Williams, Mickey Mantle may well have been the perfect teammate. He welcomed and encouraged rookies, played pranks on veterans, always picked up the tab, generously praised others in victory, and took the blame upon himself in defeat. He was genuinely humble, never thought he achieved his potential (translated: he was convinced he failed to meet his father's perfectionist standards), and refused to take himself or his athletic feats too seriously. Mantle did not have to feign modesty or manufacture self-deprecation for disarming effect. That all came naturally to this fearful, highly social, enormously talented, fun-loving, unsophisticated manchild. Mickey Mantle was an abject failure as a husband, father, and role model for youth. But no better teammate ever strode a major league diamond.

His relations with media and fans were more ambiguous. Throughout the 1950s, Mantle was often booed mercilessly by disappointed spectators. He struck out a lot during an era when strikeouts were less common than they are today. He often acted like a two-year-old brat after doing so: hurling equipment, kicking water coolers, stomping helmets.

At times, his statistics puzzled his admirers. In 1959, a year in which the Yankees finished in third place, he knocked in only 75 runs even though he batted 541 times. While runs batted in are context-driven data — much depends on teammates being on base frequently — the Yankees on-base percentage was quite close to the league average and Mantle batted in the power positions of the lineup, either third or fourth: "The booing of Mickey by Yankees fans became so strong that at one point he simply gave up. After striking out twice in one game, on his third time up he intentionally took three straight strikes. The displeasure of fans in the stadium was matched only by Stengel's own outrage. Mantle on several occasions had shown his own disgust by saluting his tormentors with a defiant middle finger of an upraised fist."[5] How could the great Mickey Mantle manage only a paltry 75 RBI?

Fans and autograph-seekers were sometimes put off by Mantle's churlish behavior, as were media representatives. Mantle could be rude, crude, and insulting.

> There were all those times when he'd push little kids aside when they wanted his autograph, and the times when he was snotty to reporters, just about making them crawl and beg for a minute of his time. I've seen him close a bus window on kids trying to get his autograph. And I hated that *look* of his, when he'd get angry at somebody and cut him down with a glare ... "like the nictitating membrane in the eye of a bird." And I don't like the Mantle that refused to sign baseballs in the clubhouse before the games. Everybody else had to sign, but [the clubhouse man] forged Mantle's signature.[6]

As author David Halberstam would note about Mantle and the press:

> His anger, his ability to look right through men he dealt with every day, men whose reporting had in general helped build the myth of Mantle as the greatest ballplayer of his era, could be shattering. Once when Maury Allen, the beat writer on the *Post*, was standing near the batting cage and Mantle was taking batting practice, Mantle turned to him and said, "You piss me off just standing there."[7]

Faith and Doubt

Religious faith can always be called into question. First, no religion can be proved. Proofs for the existence of God are often energized by fear of an infinite regress, for example, a chain of causation and movement that never ends unless an unmoved mover or uncaused cause stops the chain. Infinite regresses terrify some philosophers because they provide no ultimate explanation of events on earth. But all such proofs, at best, can conclude only that there is an uncaused cause of some sort, not that the God of Judeo-Christianity or Allah of Islam is that first cause. Aquinas was wrong in thinking that the existence of God, as a preamble of faith, could be demonstrated independently by rational argument. Augustine and Anselm were closer to the mark in thinking that proofs for the existence of God will convince only those folks already committed to a deity with certain attributes.

Moreover, even the conclusion that there is an uncaused cause depends on eliminating, usually by logical fiat, the possibility of an infinite regress. Perhaps an infinite regress is the (non)explanation. Finally, the supreme being of Western religion can itself be viewed as an anthropomorphic infinite regress. Eternal and complete with no origin, the Supreme Being is every bit as mysterious an explanation of the cosmos as an infinite regress. Has religion substituted a living, eternal, infinite being for the infinite regress of causation and motion it feared? Insofar as a supreme being or nature itself is a first cause it invites further questions: What is God's purpose in creating a meaningful world? Does a more ultimate purpose even than God's purpose exist? Theists might respond that as the ground of all being God would not be *in a relationship* with Truth, Goodness, Meaning, and the like. God would be *identical* to and His being the ground of these values. But that identity and ground remain mysterious and beg the question against the nontheist.

In sum, proofs for the existence of God typically beg the question against the possibility of an infinite regress and after concluding that an uncaused cause exists affirm faith in a supreme being. Therefore, these exercises do not demonstrate independently the existence of a first being.

Second, scriptural accounts and religious experiences are likewise unreliable. The methodology of appealing to scriptures in sacred texts as divine revelation is questionable. Often, advocates take single scriptural passages as decisive for all moral cases that might relate to the passage. But there are grave difficulties in doing so. Questions about the original context in which the passage was used, about how the passage's context may have been shifted by later authors, and about how a scriptural passage relates to other passages on the same topic abound. Much like the proclamations of the Delphic Oracle, the writings in sacred texts admit different interpretations. Such writings have a deep historical dimension, they arose at a time in a place under social circumstances. The existence of scriptures shows at best that certain people deeply believed certain things, including the existence of a supreme being, and interpreted certain events in certain ways in their time.

Religious experiences fare no better as demonstration of theism's truth. Having unusual experiences can be interpreted and can be accounted for in different ways. They provide little or no evidence for the existence of divinities.

Even a visit from a seemingly powerful being, one who can perform extraordinary deeds beyond human efficacy, does not establish the qualities of the Western God. Is this powerful being a demon, a semi-god, or truly all-powerful, all-knowing, all-good?

Third, explanations other than the reality of gods can be offered for the prevalence of religious commitment. In the nineteenth century, the masters of suspicion undermined theism with relish. Karl Marx (1818–1883) called religion "opium for the masses," a way to divert the pain of proletariat life by focusing on a better world after death.[8] Part of the ideological superstructure that serves the interests of the dominant classes, religion distracts the disenfranchised from the misery of their social condition, forestalls revolutionary fervor, and reinforces prevailing economic systems. Marx, himself pursuing a quasi-religious grand redemption of the human race, argued that the functions religion serves will wither away once the communist paradise on earth is realized.

Sigmund Freud (1856–1939), although far from original on this issue, argued that we create gods, they do not create us.[9] We project our own deepest yearnings and fears on an indifferent universe, conjuring up various theisms to soften the human condition. Religion is thus an illusion that makes life palatable for many people.

Nietzsche viewed the creation of the major Western religions as the revenge of the herd.[10] The masses of human beings, resentful and fearful of those more noble and excellent, devise religion as a way of humbling their betters. Slogans such as "the meek will inherit the earth" and "the wealthy are as likely to pass through the gates of heaven as a camel is of passing through the eye of a needle" warm the cockles of the resentful masses and calm the haughtiness of the powerful. Religion, under this view, is a method born of ill motives to install and reinforce a particular system of values that glorifies equality, mediocrity, and social domesticity. Fueled by a lowest-common-denominator mentality, religion honors herd values to the detriment of potentially noble types. To ensure general compliance with these values, religion invents an all-powerful supreme being with strong retributive leanings: to fall out of line is to risk eternal suffering. Such an enforcer, who knows everything and can do anything, gives pause to even the most powerful on earth. Nietzsche concluded that the rise of science and the disaggregation of fervent religious conviction, the kind that truly animates everyday social life, showed that belief in God is no longer worthy. Human beings have created social conditions, including technological achievements, that undermine intense religious commitment. Priests, ministers, and rabbis now preside over the "death of God" as they orchestrate rituals that lack the power to energize daily life.

Fourth, the major religions invariably have tensions, ambiguities, and conflicts within their fundamental doctrines. The good news is that these frictions permit flexibility and adaptability to changing social circumstances. The bad news is that they diminish the clarity of the theistic message. Take the Christian notion of heaven. The state of eternal bliss is paramount in the theology because it is the final culmination of a meritorious life, the clear connection to Meaning, Truth, and Value, and the ultimate demonstration that the cosmos is rational and just. Heaven must conjure satisfactions that are understandable now. So the theology maintains that the bodies of those earning redemption shall be restored in a new, glorified form. Also, we retain our past histories, cleansed of imperfection and sinfulness. Thus we retain our affections for our backgrounds and contacts, we have continuing knowledge and love of the created beings with whom we had relationships in our earthly lives. But heaven is nonmaterial and unchanging so its crux is the intuitive apprehension of God as He is in Himself, and love. As a complete state, heaven permits our desirous spirits to attain eternal serenity.

From an earthly standpoint the notion of full actualization, having all one's potentials realized, is, happily, impossible. The process of life would end if human beings were somehow complete. If boredom is the shriek of unused capabilities can it also be the murmur of no more capabilities to use? Would heaven be boring after, say, the equivalent of five or six million years of apprehending the same?

None of this demonstrates logical error in the Christian notion of heaven. Surely it is reasonable to hold that there will be considerable mystery in describing and understanding a transcendent phenomenon in earthly terms. But the questions highlight the difficulty of even conceiving of what many take to be the highest human aspirations: the link with eternal Value, Meaning, and Rationality. Is the quest by its very nature outside the human condition?

Fifth, religious conviction may be taken as a matter of faith. But faith is not the absence of reason. Instead, faith is conviction and action not fully supportable by reason. Faith is not mysterious. Faith is required for life. Reason cannot establish itself. Even robust reliance on reason requires a certain faith. Faith, then, is not the opposite of reasons, evidence, and probable belief. Religious faith is a type of but does not define faith. Religious faith is not created out of nothing. People who claim such faith can trace it back to a religious experience, acceptance of sacred texts, a particular socialization process, events in their lives from which it emerged, and the like. The basis of religious faith, then, is one or more of the sources already discussed. Religious faith, by definition, can neither be rationally proved nor disproved. But it does not follow that religious faith is immune from examination. The sources of faith are always subject to scrutiny. One cannot invoke religious faith as if it were a safe, unassailable oasis that ends discussion.

Nevertheless, Marx was incorrect in thinking that religious conviction would wither away once an ideal social scheme was realized. While religious conviction may well serve the functions Marx alleges, it also reflects a more enduring human concern: the search for meaning, understanding, and an antidote to finitude. Even in an ideal social scheme, human beings must struggle with their mortality, and their need to connect with enduring value, an ultimate culmination, and a rational, just cosmos.

Neither theists nor nonbelievers can rationally prove their claims or conclusively disprove the counterclaims of their opposites. Nonbelievers, though, will observe that technological and ideological developments in the twentieth and twenty-first centuries have radically intensified persistent human conflicts. Many find themselves alienated from the comforting, if often illusory, theistic certitudes of the past. Marx, Freud, and Nietzsche had earlier disaggregated the redeeming unassailability of religious meaning by pressing their suspicions that latent economic, psychological, and cultural motives underwrite, indeed create, religious conviction. Later, the rise of Fascism, Nazism, and Socialism amplified the risks inherent in state control of the individual and family. The explosive hegemony of instrumental reason and abstract systems of control facilitated a crisis of the spirit as anxiety transformed itself to addiction. Refined technology mocked itself by producing weapons which threaten a humanly inspired apocalypse. Lived experiences, especially of the body, are too often eclipsed by ersatz media-inspired substitutes: virtual realities, blatant commodifications, and images understood vicariously. The enormous increase in information finds no parallel in expanded wisdom. Too many of us seem unable to reconnect ourselves with or to re-create wholesome realities. The human search for meaning is caricatured by capitalist hucksterism, pop psychology, the sham transcendence of a drug culture, and craven flight from individual responsibility. Cynicism and thorough skepticism are falsely enshrined as insight. The citadel of the self is under siege.

Many people will forsake the religious solution for reasons good or bad. Some people will argue that if God exists then God would not insist on human beings following only one creed and set of rituals. Other people will not separate the historical record of Western religions from the belief in God. The institutions of organized religions will repel them. Utterly convinced of cosmic meaninglessness, the absence of any preordained or inherent purpose in the world, these critics of theism will still feel the urgency of the human yearning for a connection to enduring value, an ultimate culmination, and a rational, just cosmos.

Not all faith, though, is religious. Believing in ourselves, accepting ourselves unconditionally, and being deeply committed to projects transcending our own concerns all nurture happiness. Nietzsche's highest value, *amor fati*, a maximally affirmative attitude toward life, required faith. Neither he nor anyone else can prove, deductively, that such an attitude is the greatest objective value. On Nietzsche's own standards, this is impossible. His highest value requires, instead, an act of faith defined as conviction, choice, and action in the face of epistemological uncertainty.

Living a robust life requires faith of some sort. Even the most pious worshipers at the shrine of reason must admit that reason cannot prove its own standards noncircularly; reason cannot prove itself. So even the idolaters of reason require faith. Part of the human condition is the lack of certain answers to our most pressing questions about life. Religious believers accept a series of answers, but faith is at the core of their acceptance. Nonbelievers in the religious answers must develop other values, principles, and narratives that can sustain their connection to the life force. A maximally affirmative attitude toward life also has faith at its core.

That faith — whether religious or secular — is required for the good life, then, is not earth shattering news. Through faith we not only connect to values greater than ourselves, but we bond with others who are likewise committed. For without faith in a project or being larger than ourselves we lose the ballast for living. Where there is no faith there is no hope. Where there is no hope there can be no happiness.

Mantle's Fall and Redemption

Much changed for Mickey Mantle in 1961. Mantle and teammate Roger Maris, who was playing only his second year as a Yankee, were both slamming home runs at a pace that threatened Babe Ruth's record of 60 in one season. Maris soon developed larger public relations problems than Mantle had ever known. Shy, distrustful, suspicious, and inarticulate, Maris was overwhelmed by the media attention. His reluctance to jolly up the press was interpreted as pettiness, self-worship, and arrogance. Maris was ripped in the press daily — about his attitude, relatively low batting average, impatience, bluntness, and almost everything else. The press openly sided with and cheered for Mantle in his race with Maris. Fans picked up the drift and followed suit.

Mantle was, characteristically, an excellent teammate and played down any sense of rivalry. The two men were roommates and genuinely liked each other. Mickey seemed to soften his approach to the media and this added to the transformation of Mantle from mixed bag of attributes to folk hero. Late in the season, Mantle contracted a virulent flu. He was urged, probably by Yankees broadcaster Mel Allen, to visit a doctor, Max Jacobson, in New York who often treated celebrities. Although not clearly understood at the time,

Jacobson specialized in feel-good medicine. He was more of a drug pusher with a medical license than a physician in the Hippocratic tradition. Jacobson administered a shot in Mantle's hip that immediately pained the superstar. Soon thereafter, Mantle developed a rapidly-spreading infection and had to be hospitalized. A physician lanced and drained Mantle's hip. The resulting hole was over three inches in diameter. Mantle's regular season was over. He finished with 54 home runs. Maris smacked 61 homers, but in a 162 game season. Ruth had hit 60 in 154 games. What should have brought extravagant glory to Maris was tainted by controversy. The unwitting benefactor was Mickey Mantle, who was now idolized by fans and media in lockstep. The booing stopped. The cheering resounded.

The last seven or eight years of Mantle's baseball career chronicled the eroding of his skills, the increasing severity of his injuries, steadfast endurance in the face of unbearable pain, punctuated by exhilarating deeds of baseball. Mickey Mantle retired after the 1968 season, adored by fans, celebrated by media.

Mickey Mantle's off-the-field baseball life was almost solely the pursuit of crude hedonism. At retirement, his entire life was defined by the consumption of alcohol, habitual sexual conquests, and horseplay more appropriate to 20-year-old males at a toga party. His romance with bottled spirits matured into alcoholism. By 1980, he and Merlyn had separated. Along the way, she and their sons had become alcoholics, either trying to keep up with Mickey or out of desperation that he was not there for them in any meaningful way. A few years later, Mantle was living with Greer Johnson, a school teacher turned celebrity agent.

Mickey Mantle, boy wonder, was a stumble-bum, the village idiot with a glittering resume. For example, he was renowned for strolling into the restaurant of an exclusive Dallas country club and ordering a drink. That he was nude was noteworthy. Mantle sometimes moseyed into the club's pool in his birthday suit. These incidents were frequent enough that the club's membership committee had to inaugurate a rule that prohibited anyone from entering or hanging around the restaurant in the nude. We should hope that most folks had already figured out that common courtesy prior to applying for membership, and that drinking in the buff in public was not exactly a fad.

Mantle's public displays of vulgarity, inappropriate sexual overtures, and general obliviousness to the interests of others increased. His self-destructive, unconscious performance of the script he had concocted at his father's death — I am going to die young, I won't be cheated — ensured his prophesy would prove correct. Most embarrassing incidents went unreported. Fans and the press continued to find ways to honor him. The memorabilia business courted him for signings. Mantle continued to drink himself toward death.

By December 1993, he was examined thoroughly and told by a physician that his liver was in such wretched condition that "your next drink might be your last."[11] Mantle checked into the Betty Ford Center, the Mecca of substance-abuse rehabilitation-seekers. This final act to Mantle's life would soon bring him his greatest, most deserved cheers.

Mantle discussed his career and life with Bob Costas on national television. A story in *Sports Illustrated* sympathetically, but accurately, testified to his demise. Mickey's summary refrain never varied: "I have let everyone down. I was a terrible role model. Live your life differently from me." Americans love to forgive repentant, fragile, flawed heroes who reach out to us. Mickey Mantle the hero on Olympus was now one of us, born to suffer and die, and not sure why. We responded with love and admiration.

He made appearances to the extent possible. The crude hedonism, his only past connection to the meaning of life, had evaporated. Now, he was a poster boy for substance abuse, a living reminder that the piper would be paid. Our job was to make sure he knew how much we loved him, warts and all.

In the spring of 1995, tests revealed he had cirrhosis, hepatitis C, and cancer of the liver. Mantle would need a liver transplant. Within a few months he was already close to death — his kidneys had shut down due to liver failure. Mantle received a new liver only two days after being placed on the transplant waiting list. Whether he received wrongful preferential treatment in receiving a transplant so quickly became controversial.

He was released from the hospital a month later. Even after his release, Mantle suffered as cancer grew. The anti-rejection medication required for the transplant made him vulnerable to cancer cell growth. Chemotherapy and blood transfusions followed. Mantle lost 40 pounds and was anemic. Looking frail, thin, and old, he addressed the public:

> It seems to me like all I've done is take. Have fun and take. I'm going to start giving something back. I'd like to say to kids out there, if you're looking for a role model ... don't be like me. God gave me a body and an ability to play baseball. God gave me everything, and I just ... pffttt."[12]

Just over two months after his liver transplant, Mickey Mantle died at the age of 63. Merlyn, his estranged wife, held one of his hands, while son David, held the other. The last eighteen months of his life were courageous. Roy Clark sang at his funeral.

Mantle and Aquinas

Michael Novak has argued that sports in our nation amount to a natural religion:

Sports flow outward into action from a deep natural impulse that is radically religious: an impulse of freedom, respect for ritual limits, a zest for symbolic meaning, and a longing for perfection.... There are many ways to express this radical impulse: by the asceticism and dedication of preparation; by a sense of respect for the mysteries of one's own body and for powers not in one's own control; by a sense of awe for the place and time of competition; by a sense of fate; by a felt sense of comradeship and destiny; by a sense of participation in the rhythms and tides of nature itself.[13]

Following that vein, the faith of baseball fans in Mickey Mantle and Thomas Aquinas's faith in Christianity bear similarities.

Historical amnesia or historical secrecy. The foundations of divine revelation — scriptures, religious experiences, inspired prophets — were invariably cast in distant centuries. We lack accurate historical records of exactly what happened, when, and in what context. Religious doctrines and policies that were hammered out hundreds of years after the supposed divine presence graced the earth take on the aura of direct revelations. We either forget the historical genesis of what now passes as the sacred word or that process is obscured in secrecy. We treat, for example, a complicated, often conflicting, historically-bound text such as the Bible as if it embodies one clear interpretation of divine imperatives. In fact, the dominant interpretations themselves were the consequences of councils, conferences, and scholarly disputes that bore most of the trappings of political conventions: negotiation, compromise, strategic maneuvering. We also forget that many of the accounts of the divine presence on earth were written generations after the historical events they purport to chronicle. Aquinas's confidence in divine revelation as a source of truth and the basis of faith leaves such issues unexplored.

In Mantle's case, historical secrecy was crucial. Mickey's mindless, desperate chase after self-defeating crude hedonism went underreported or unreported. We knew about the excruciating pain, the numerous injuries, and his steadfast commitment to playing. We knew little or nothing about his lack of discipline during rehabilitation and his relentless dedication to the bar stool. We heard about his occasional small acts of kindness toward fans and media. We were shrouded from his more frequent mean-spirited and ungracious moments. We saw the boyish grin and the country simplicity. We were screened from the cutting glare and uninventive profanity. After he retired, only a few witnessed his unspeakable boorish escapades, unworthy of a 20-year-old college boy pledging Sigma Chi. The faith of his fans took on a life of its own based on the mostly positive athletic feats we directly observed and media accounts that were mainly favorable. "Divine revelation" was partial and provisional. The holy book of scripture was crafted in a historical context self-consciously distorted by an obliging press. What we wanted and needed from our heroes became the first principles — our articles of faith —

that allowed us to derive deeper "truths." The mythology of Mickey Mantle was largely a function of our projections. Freud conjectured that God did not create us, we created God. Perhaps, we also created Mickey Mantle.

Belief in impossibles. Aquinas accepted, among other things, miracles as historical events, the virgin birth, the resurrection of Jesus, Jesus as both divine and human, and God as both a unity and a trinity. The last two of these convictions appear to be logical contradictions. The first three seem to be empirically and scientifically impossible. For Aquinas, all five are divine revelations — articles of faith. Admittedly, none of the five can be independently proven by rational argument. Yet they are knowable to everyone, in principle, because they have been divinely revealed. For Aquinas, rational arguments that lead to conclusions incompatible with these articles of faith are unsound or invalid.

Tape measure home runs and blinding speed were the hallmarks of Mickey Mantle. Who can hit a ball 643 feet? Only Mickey Mantle, baby. Maybe this year he will swat one out of Yankee Stadium. Who can turn a drag bunt into a double? Mickey Mantle can (at least until the leg injuries sapped his gettyup). My Uncle Frank saw him do it last spring. Faith in the attainment of hitherto impossible athletic feats was the core of the Mantle legend. Evidence that disputed these tall tales — Was it 643 where it landed, after two dozen bounces on concrete? Didn't the catcher throw the ball past the first baseman on that bunt? — was denied or suppressed. Without articles of faith, mythology is impossible.

Baseball fans enlarge their own lives and extend their identity by affiliating with a favorite team and special player. They belong to something larger and more potent than themselves and spice up their own lives. Their membership in a group of fans aids their self-understanding and permits comparative judgments. The scoreboard is the ultimate adjudicator. Faith has numerous practical dimensions.

Faith and doubt. Yet faith is fragile. Articles of faith, generously sprinkled with logical contradictions and empirical impossibilities, test our resolve. Soren Kierkegaard (1813–1855) celebrated the knight of faith, the person who renounced universal norms in service of a higher calling. He understood the danger in doing so, and the lack of guarantees the leap of faith required to renounce the general demands of reason and the moral law. These risks, he insisted, promised greater rewards for those willing to take them in service to the religious life. Aquinas would argue that faith is secure because it is based on divine revelation. But the phenomena of divine revelations are themselves gravely problematic. From the litany of objections to religious belief I sketched earlier, we might well conclude that the commitment to divine revelation is itself a matter of a second-order faith.

Aquinas tried to harmonize the tensions between faith and reason. Theologians such as Tertullian and Kierkegaard luxuriated in the conflict. The dedicated religious adventurer sneers in the eye of reason when science denies religion. The leap of faith, for Kierkegaard, is the grandest form of individual authenticity: no guarantees, plenty of critics — this is where I stake my being. Nevertheless, doubts are part of the bargain. If we could embrace faith once and forever, and extinguish all reservations, faith would be purchased too cheaply. Instead, faith must be won continually. Faith is never safely in our satchels. We must swallow recurrent doubt. We must renew our allegiances, while the sirens of natural reason continue to whisper competing messages in our ears.

Baseball fans doubted Mickey Mantle, at least through the 1950s. Despite his miraculous feats, growing legend, and undeniable charisma, competing messages abounded. He struck out too much. His RBI rate was below snuff for someone batting in the middle of the order for championship teams. He often sulked when in a slump. His fielding might be acceptable, but he was no Willie Mays or Joe DiMaggio. Would he be able to overcome the latest injury?

The test of faith may well be its survival in the face of serious misgivings. A faith that is too comfortable, too smug in its truth, is insufficiently robust. The knight of faith becomes the lockstep conformist.

Selection of the better alternative. Part of the renewal of faith is (an often subconscious) assessment of the alternative. The human yearning for a connection to enduring value, an ultimate culmination, and a just cosmos is natural. Such links are not obviously available on earth. But religious faith resonates with our yearnings. Faith offers a link to enduring value in the form of an eternal deity or absolute, an ultimate culmination on the day of judgment, and a rational cosmos as the judgments of an infallible ruler or karmic justice prevail. The alternative? Perhaps a sea of cosmic meaninglessness where our tiny, finite lives act out their few moments in "sound and fury, signifying nothing." Perhaps the routine futility of Sisyphus pushing metaphorical boulders up contrived mountains only to have them roll back down, again and again. Perhaps the knight of faith is less the romantic risk-taker and more the cautious supplicant before safer, more consoling convictions.

Fans choosing Mickey Mantle as their athletic object of concern selected the better alternative on two levels. First, in the early 1960s the choices for Yankees fans seemed to be Mantle or Maris. Maris, though, was the interloper, the johnny-come-lately who had not yet earned his stripes. Mantle was the veteran, a stalwart on numerous championship teams, the golden boy. Maris was portrayed as sullen, sometimes surly, rarely communicative. Mantle was the perfect teammate. Second, sports without heroes, without those in which we invest our faith, become diluted recreations. Pastimes in an effete sense, unworthy of intense commitment, unable to sustain our bond to the meaning of life. Sports fans must have faith in their heroes, whose mythology speaks more to the projections of the worshipers than to the reality of the idols. Why? Because the alternative is unbearable and underscores the feebleness of our "lives of quiet desperation."

Novak reminds us:

> [Sports] recreate symbols of cosmic struggle, in which human survival and moral courage are not assured. To this extent, they are not mere games, diversions, pastimes.... Sports are mysteries of youth and aging, perfect action and decay, fortune and misfortune, strategy and contingency. Sports are rituals concerning human survival on this planet: liturgical enactments of animal perfection and the struggles of the human spirit to prevail.[14]

Fans make commitments of faith in part because they are convinced that the object of their concern is worthy. With Mantle, that judgment was based on his undeniable skill and inspiring effort despite harsh injuries. We didn't know much about his off-the-field exploits, but probably would have brushed them off as the tolerable excesses of a young man blowing off steam. We suffered through the strikeouts, we were often riddled with doubt, but the nature of faith admits that the road to redemption cannot be easy or guaranteed.

Grand redemption. We labor steadfastly. The world too often seems irrational and unjust. Bad things happen to good people. Good things happen to bad people. The relationship between moral goodness and earthly reward is sporadic and unreliable. Faith promises redemption. Moses led his people out of enslavement into the promised land and pointed the way to eternal salvation. Jesus died to redeem human beings from our sins and guaranteed eternal life to all true believers who acted on their convictions. The Buddha gently prods us to aspire to universal states and to edge away from the desirous individual ego. Nirvana, union with the Absolute, will be our reward.

Novak elaborates:

> You need to have heroic forms to try to live up to: patterns of excellence so high that human beings live up to them only rarely, even when they strive to do so.... The root of human dissatisfaction and restlessness goes as deep into the spirit as any human drive — deeper than any other drive. It is the human spirit. Nothing stills it. Nothing fulfills it.... The hunger for perfection in sports cleaves closely to the driving core of the human spirit.[15]

Mickey Mantle was redeemed by his response to terminal illness. The perpetual adolescent, the simpleminded pursuer of crude hedonism, the wayward son abandoned by the authoritarian father who died too soon, grew up. Mantle reflected and repented. He understood, finally, the poverty of his approach to lifelong fear and insecurity. Bereft of self-pity, brimming with fortitude in the face of the inevitable, resolute in confrontation with his finitude, Mickey Mantle regained his dignity. He even confided to his former teammate Bobby Richardson that he had accepted Jesus as his lord and savior. For the first time since Mutt Mantle died, Mickey had reclaimed his faith — secular and religious.

EIGHTH INNING

John Franco and William James

"Superstition is the religion of feeble minds."
— Edmund Burke, philosopher

"Superstition is the poetry of life."
— Johann Wolfgang Von Goethe, poet and dramatist

"Men become superstitious not because they have too much imagination, but because they are not aware that they have any."
— George Santayana, philosopher

"Only in superstition is there hope. If you want to become a friend of civilization, then become an enemy of the truth and a fanatic for harmless balderdash."
— Kurt Vonnegut, Jr., novelist

"If it comes true, it's not a superstition."
— Yogi Berra, wordsmith

John Franco (1960–) has several superstitions that he claims energize his athletic performance. By studying William James's (1842–1910) arguments about human will and belief, we can understand how many superstitions, although seemingly based on false beliefs, can actually enhance athletic performance. In so doing, the relationship between truth, belief, and human action is sharpened.

Fireman Franco

John Franco was born and raised in Bensonhurst, a predominantly Italian section of Brooklyn. Although modestly sized at 5'10" and 185 pounds,

135

he was blessed with a powerful left arm. After a brilliant high school career, he starred at St. John's University. After brief minor league seasoning, he joined the Cincinnati Reds in 1984, and began a career as one of the most durable, consistent relief pitchers in major league history. Relying on a hard fastball and sharp-breaking slider, he spent two years as a left-handed setup man before inheriting the closer role. He saved 132 games in his four years as the closer for the Reds, with sparking earned run averages (ERAs) of 2.18 in 1985 and 1.57 in 1988. He was traded to the New York Mets after the 1989 season. John Franco had returned home. His fierce competitiveness, unbridled enthusiasm, and unmistakable street-smarts made him a team leader and fan favorite.

Franco eventually set Mets franchise records for games pitched and games saved. Over a 21-year career, the last year with the Houston Astros, Franco saved 424 games (third on the all-time major league saves list, although in 2007 Mariano Rivera will pass Franco), pitched in 1119 games, and compiled a standout 2.89 ERA. Along the way, he led the league in saves three times. As age sapped the velocity of his fastball and sharpness of his slider, he developed a sinker and change-up. Franco made the transition from under-sized power pitcher to crafty southpaw. Through career highs and lows, Franco was widely admired for his courage, refusal to make excuses, and tight identification with the greater New York metropolitan area and its fans.

In many ways, John Franco's career was uncommon — in respect to its duration, the relative consistency of his performance, and his success. But in one respect his career was prototypical: John Franco was superstitious. Superstition to a baseball player is like water to a halibut, a requirement of survival.

William James, Will, and Belief

Conventional wisdom, grounded on scientific method, insists that, in order to be rational, our belief in the truth of an event or proposition must flow from adequate evidence. Our assent must be compelled by the evidence. To believe anything upon insufficient evidence is to flirt with irrationalism. We should first regard a hypothesis with grave suspicion, subject it to rigorous tests, and adopt only those that survive.

William James assaulted conventional wisdom. At times, we must believe and act as if something is true — prior to adequate evidence — in order to help make that something true. The belief that a stranger will treat us honestly may occasion that quality from her. Some possible truths will be denied us if we are unwilling to anticipate their reality. Trust, love, friendship, for examples, cannot be realized if we begin with maximum skepticism, hostility, and distance. Humans have the right to choose for ourselves between the risks of falling into error, if our antecedent belief goes unrequited, or missing out on a great good, if our skepticism prevents the good from materializing.[1]

A sports cliché reminds us that "the person who thinks he will succeed and the person who thinks he will fail are both right." Often, positive thinking, even if based on inadequate evidence, can enhance our chances of succeeding. A batter, for example, must be convinced prior to every at bat that he will get a hit. But look at the evidence: no major leaguer has batted as high as .400 since 1941; even a .400 hitter is more likely to make an out than get a hit; an average batter, about .270, fails to get a hit 73 percent of his official at bats! How could the scientific method support the batter's belief in the case at hand that he will get a hit? Maybe, if conditions are typical, the average batter is warranted in believing he has a 27 percent probability of getting a hit. But, paradoxically, a batter who has the *correct* probability constantly in mind will end up batting *below* .270. In order to hit .270 the average batter must be convinced, contrary to all evidence, that he will get a hit prior to every plate appearance. If a pedantic statistician insists that the hitter's belief is irrational, not warranted by the evidence, and not adequately supported by reason, so much the worse for math. Our mathematician does not have to stare down Roger Clemens or Mariano Rivera. At those times, buckaroos, the batter requires all the positive thinking, however irrational from the standpoint of probability, he can muster. Score a point for William James.

James did not advance the simpleminded thesis that believing something strongly enough will ensure its reality. If life were so facile, most of us would be smarter, younger, stronger, and more beautiful. Children would enjoy Christmas every day and potato chips would be nutritious. Instead, James suggests that our antecedent belief allows us to *test* hypotheses that involve uncommon experiences.

> If these hypotheses, when they unearth the data of new experience, prove to be inept, incomplete, or simply wrong, then they should be abandoned. We cannot know the worth of a belief until it is pressed forward into the crucible of new experience. James holds that the willingness to risk belief in possibilities that are often scoffed or mocked by common sense generates an energy that frequently leads to paths of insight otherwise closed off from us.[2]

For James, rationality implicates not only cognition but feelings. If two hypotheses are equally consistent with the facts, the one that fulfills our drives and aesthetic impulses is the more rational. Human needs are crucial to our conception of the world and to our notion of rationality itself.

He is arguing for a *right* to believe, on broadly rational grounds, in something that narrow rational evidence has not yet sustained. James does not conclude that we *must* believe, that we are duty-bound to trust all strangers, befriend all acquaintances, and declare love prematurely in order to maximize the possibility that we can facilitate healthy relationships. Instead, he claims that we often face choices in which belief in either alternative is permissible, but both bring risks. We should be aware of the dangers and possible benefits, but we should not automatically be intimidated by those who insist that one alternate is not yet supported by adequate evidence.

James discusses *genuine* choices, those that are live, forced, and momentous. A *live* choice has emotive appeal to the agent. Emotive appeal is internal to the agent and not compelled by universal, rational standards. A *forced* choice is an either-or context: either X or not-X, we cannot avoid choosing one way or the other, we cannot avoid the choice by selection Y or Z. A *momentous* choice has significant consequences: matters of life and death, crucial once-in-a-lifetime circumstances, and life-altering situations.

When we face a genuine choice that cannot be decided solely on cognitive grounds, our passions must rule. We have the right to believe, at our risk, any hypothesis that is sufficiently live to lure our will. The right to believe refers to living choices which are unresolvable by cognition.

> We can either take the stance that avoiding error is most important and then we will hesitate to decide on such grounds, or we will take the position that losing the truth is the worst consequence and that the chance of gaining the truth outweighs the risk of being duped.[3]

James's agenda mainly concerns religious faith. He aspires to demonstrate that belief in God is not blind irrationalism, but a voluntary, rationally permissible, genuine choice. For those who exercise their right to believe in God, the choice is live, forced, and momentous. The existence of God can neither be rationally proved nor disproved, so the passions must decide. Whereas the person of science would argue that belief in the hypothesis of God's existence is unworthy because that hypothesis is unsupported by enough rational evidence, James would rejoin that belief in God is a genuine choice for those with the requisite subjective impulse.

A critic might respond that whatever currency beliefs based on genuine choices in the areas of trust, friendship, and love bear, their worth is discounted in the domain of religious faith. Although it is true that antecedent beliefs in trust and the like, not coerced by reason, often help bring their objects into being, faith in God will not help create that which is believed. If God exists, God exists independently of human beliefs.

Also, we might press James on how much evidence is required to nullify a genuine choice. To say that the evidence is not sufficient to disprove X is vague. Enough evidence may be available to, say, conclude that the possibility of X is only 20 percent or less. In that case, does the right to believe in X still hold sway? Do we have a right to believe *anything* that cannot be proven

100 percent false, as long as believing it is a genuine option for us? Is it rational to make ourselves vulnerable — to trust, to curry friendship — with a stranger or acquaintance where the antecedent probability of success is, say, less than 20 percent? Is belief in God really a 50–50 proposition? Or does the evidence, antecedent to belief, suggest that the existence of God is quite improbable?

James could undoubtedly refine his analysis in terms of probabilities, potential benefits, and risks: generally, the lower the probability of helping to bring about the object of our belief, the greater risk we take in believing. But we should also take into account the magnitude of the potential good we would realize if we are able to help bring about the object of our belief. A further complication: to be a live choice for us, the belief must stir our passions. James might well agree with Camus that life often requires a 100 percent conviction in matters that are deeply uncertain.

Baseball Superstitions

John Franco always wore a bright orange New York City Sanitation Department T-shirt underneath his jersey when he pitched. Franco's father, who died on the job six months prior to retirement, was a longtime member of that department. He also had a particular support cup he wore for luck. Examples of baseball superstitions are easy to find:

- Curse of the Bambino: Babe Ruth was traded from the Boston Red Sox to the New York Yankees prior to the 1920 season. The Red Sox had been an American League powerhouse. They appeared in the World's Series in 1918, but not again until 2004. The Yankees appeared in their first World's Series in 1921 and promptly became baseball's greatest dynasty. Apparently, Babe's curse expired after about 85 years (1919–2004). Similar curses allegedly explained the Chicago Cubs' failure to appear in a World's Series after 1945 (The Curse of the Billy Goat, which still holds strong), and the Chicago White Sox failure to make it after 1919 (The Curse of the Black Sox, whose warranty was recalled in 2005).
- The *Sports Illustrated* Curse: appearing on the cover of this weekly sports magazine dooms a team or player to failure for an unspecified time period.
- Players should not step on the foul lines when running on or off the field to start and end innings. (Perhaps inaugurated by a grounds crew? Or might it be a variant of "step on a crack and break somebody's back"?)

- Following a certain routine before each pitch or at bat (for example, Frank Viola would kick dirt away from the mound four times prior to each inning, but if he was pitching poorly he would change to three or five times. Turk Wendell would brush his teeth, chew licorice, draw three crosses in the dirt, and wave at his center fielder prior to every inning he pitched.).
- Eating the same meal prior to a game (for example, Wade Boggs ate chicken prior to every game).
- Insisting on a particular uniform number for luck. Refusing to wear other numbers (such as "unlucky" 13).
- Teammates not talking about a no-hitter or perfect game in progress lest their pitcher be jinxed.
- Broadcasters not talking about a no-hitter or perfect game in progress lest the pitcher be jinxed.
- Not washing a particular piece of equipment during a winning streak.
- Insisting on using a lucky bat or glove.
- Performing a ritual to extricate a player from a slump (Dave Concepcion, for example, would shower in his uniform to wash away the bad energy of a slump).
- Outfielders stepping on second base when they run in from their defensive position at the end of an inning or making a point not to step on second base when they run in.
- In general, following precisely the same routines during a winning streak or winning season, but changing routines during a losing streak or losing season.

Whether ballplayers harbor superstitions because they want to assume more control over the outcomes of their performances or less control is not clear. One argument would claim that reasons beyond the control of players — jinxes, curses, the mysterious forces of the unknown — govern results and players cannot fully be held responsible. A counter-argument would claim that by following successful rituals of the past and avoiding unsuccessful routines, players are controlling their effect on outcomes to the maximum extent possible.

Superstition and Rationality

Strictly speaking, a superstition is an irrational belief about causality: believing that doing (or not doing) X will cause Y, under circumstances in which X has no objective effect on bringing Y about and *human beings should know this.* The final clause is crucial because otherwise many mistaken beliefs about causality, held in good faith, would be improperly classified as superstitions. Stepping on a crack in the sidewalk has no effect on anyone's sacroiliac. Thinking otherwise is normally a superstition because human beings of full rational capabilities and the requisite age should know this.

Numerous baseball superstitions are misclassified. We can distinguish at least five different categories:

Benign Habits: Some behaviors by ballplayers are habits and preferences, not irrational beliefs. If a player, for example, wears a particular uniform number to honor his favorite player or because he has a favorite number, that is not a superstition. As long as the player does not believe the number has magical powers that energize his play, as long as he recognizes that a uniform number is not the *reason* he plays well or poorly, no superstition operates. Wearing #3 to honor Babe Ruth, #4 to honor Lou Gehrig or Duke Snider, #5 to praise Joe DiMaggio, Hank Greenberg, or George Brett, #7 to celebrate Mickey Mantle, #8 to respect Joe Morgan, Yogi Berra, or Cal Ripken, #9 to remember Ted Williams, or #42 to identify with Jackie Robinson were common preferences of young ballplayers in years past. These preferences were not usually grounded in a conviction that the numbers bore mysterious qualities of greatness, that the uniform number somehow made Babe, Lou, Cal, Joe, Hank, Mickey, Ted, and Jackie great and could do the same for the young player.

John Franco's orange undershirt was probably only a tribute to his father, a reminder of their close relationship and life-long bond. That he believed superstitiously that New York Sanitation Department shirts conferred special powers on wearers is improbable. Now, the "lucky" support cup is another matter.

I always put on and tie the laces of my left shoe, then my right shoe. I hold no superstition about this practice, it is just a habit. Today, in the interests of spontaneity, I reversed my routine. Putting my right shoe on first, I felt peculiar and awkward. So far, though, no unexpected ills have befallen me. Baltimore Orioles manager Earl Weaver always pulled his baseball pants on left-leg first. If he inadvertently began with his right leg, he started over.

A manager's routine of carefully avoiding the foul lines when crossing into fair play may be a superstition — "step on a line and harm will befall my team" — or it could merely be a benign habit, or it might be designed to convey subtle messages to his team — "pay attention to detail, understand the boundaries between fair and foul." The motivation for and purposes behind the routine are crucial to its classification.

Stone Cold Irrationality: Some behaviors are grounded in radically false attributions of causality that we should know are loony. These are superstitions in the clearest sense. Thinking that a sportscaster who mentions that a pitcher is working on a no-hitter or perfect game is going to jinx the hurler is a superstition. If I buy a bobblehead doll of, say, Barry Bonds and drive spikes into it, Barry is not going to be harmed even though the doll bearing his likeness will splinter. Barry Bonds has no idea that I am wasting my time on this empty-headed exercise, just as the pitcher working on a no-hitter is unaware that a broadcaster has mentioned that fact over the air. If Barry or the pitcher knew what was happening, matters might be different. I'll discuss that forthwith. Players cannot be jinxed by fans, broadcasters, or opponents mentioning their hitting streaks or casting their spells out of earshot. The causal relationship between X (the behavior of the fan, broadcaster, or opponent) and Y (the pitcher losing the no-hitter, Barry Bonds contracting strep throat, or the end of the hitting steak) is zero. And human beings of full rational capability and requisite age, who think the matter over for more than three seconds, should know this. The curses of Babe Ruth, some smelly Billy Goat, and the Black Sox are cutesy, after-the-fact explanations for a series of failures that are otherwise explained easily. Again, if ballplayers are deeply convinced of the power of such curses, matters may be different.

Pedro Bourbon, a mediocre relief pitcher, was released by the Cincinnati Reds in 1979. Bourbon, who practiced voodoo, announced that the Reds would never win another World Series because he had placed on a curse on the franchise. Putting aside Bourbon's presumption — he was no Babe Ruth, all of the Black Sox players were superior to him, the Billy Goat was faster — the Reds did not win another National League pennant until 1990. Wags in the media, the only ones who recalled Bourbon's bombast, contacted Pedro and pleaded with him to remove the curse. The surprisingly agreeable Bourbon did so. The Reds defeated the heavily favored Oakland Athletics.[4] The media reaped what they had sown: a good story.

Manager Tony LaRussa sometimes prints the names on his lineup card and sometimes writes them in cursive. If he prints and his team wins, he continues to print until they lose. Only then will he switch to cursive. A silent ode to stone cold irrationality.

Atlanta Braves hurler John Smoltz was munching on a few chicken wings in the clubhouse as the Braves began to rally. He convinced himself that as long as he continued to eat, the hits would flow. The Braves pounded the opposition that inning to the tune of almost four dozen chicken wings. The moral of the story: superstition doesn't cause better luck, but can produce a major league case of *agita*.[5]

I once knew a high school baseball coach who was convinced that any change in his routine would doom his team. He dimmed the lights on the scoreboard to a specified wattage. He insisted that his team have the same number of helmets — usually too few to accommodate players' needs — as his team stocked during the previous season when they played for a state championship. None of these irrational beliefs bore causal power, they were superstitions; none of his players were aware of the coach's unwavering commitment to such irrationality; yet a childish ignoramus who masqueraded as an adult took great pains to ensure such minutiae was in order. During one game, I was working the scoreboard and increased the light wattage for better visibility. The coach almost had a stroke and screeched up at the press box. My reply must go unreported.

William James Rationality: Some behaviors have a *possible* causal connection with bringing about a certain result but only if we first believe that causation will happen. My previous example bears repeating. An average major league hitter, around .270, must believe he will get a hit every time he strides to the plate in order to reach his potential. Thinking, in effect, that he will hit 1.000 will permit him to bat .270. Thinking, prior to each plate appearance, that he has only a 27 percent chance to get a hit will result in his batting much lower than .270. This may not be a precise example of William James–type rationality because the antecedent belief—"I am going to get a hit"—becomes true only 27 percent of the time, but it still illustrates how a belief that is improbable can produce better results than a belief that is more probable.

Placebo, Nocebo and Malocchio *Effects*: In medicine, symptoms are often eased by an objectively ineffective treatment, which patients *believe or expect* will work. Likewise, patients who disbelieve that an objectively effective treatment will work often experience a worsening of symptoms (the nocebo effect). Patients' attitudes and expectations toward their treatments, then, often affect the capabilities of medicines.

The most common placebo is a sugar pill, with no curative power, that patients believe contains medicinal properties that will aid recovery. Studies have shown that the placebo effect typically ranges from 25 to 40 percent. That is, 25 to 40 percent of patients who should not have realized any relief from ingesting the pill gain as much or more benefit than those who were given the proper medicine or treatment. Some scientists argue, for example, that almost 75 percent of the effectiveness of anti-depressant medication is due to the placebo effect instead of the treatment itself.[6] The placebo effect, then is triggered by patients' beliefs in their treatment and their expectation of feeling better, not the treatment itself.

The reason for the placebo effect remains contested. Taking the placebo and expecting it to work may ease the autonomic nervous system and reduce stress chemicals such as adrenaline. Patients' belief in placebos may trigger the release of endorphins, the body's natural painkillers. Placebos may help the brain to remember a time prior to the onset of illness and bring about salutary physiological changes. Perhaps patients re-interpret their symptoms with the expectation of feeling better. Maybe placebos increase patients' motivation to take better care of themselves.

Regardless of explanation, most researchers are convinced of the reality of the placebo effect. What this means outside the medical context is stunning: *Our antecedent belief and expectation that X can cause Y, where X has zero objective causal power to cause Y, can often bring Y about.* This goes beyond William James rationality, which held that X our antecedent belief and expectation in Y, which could possibly but not automatically come about, can *help* bring Y about.

Wade Boggs consumed chicken as his pre-game meal every day of his 18-year major league career. Although we can imagine worse diets, the causal connection between eating chicken and garnering 3,010 career hits is zero. Boggs, though, claimed that "all superstitions are a form of mind relaxation. They distract you from the day-to-day grind and make the day flow that much easier."[7]

Houston Astros second baseman Craig Biggio claims to understand why baseball players are more superstitious than other athletes, "Baseball is the only sport in which players do not control the ball. So in addition to skill, luck is involved ... I'd rather be lucky than good."[8] For Biggio, superstition is the tribute ballplayers pay to *fortuna*.

When I was a child I was astounded to learn that my grandmother and mother believed in the *malocchio* (evil eye), the ability of certain people to place a damning curse on other people through a malevolent stare. My grandmother was convinced of this phenomena, having observed the conjunction of B's stare and C's pain countless times. She could recite the litany of which members of her small town had the power of the *malocchio*, folks to avoid at all costs, especially if you were toting an infant. Infants, presumably, suffered a heightened vulnerable to the dreaded *malocchio* and unwittingly occasioned great jealously from the demonic merchants of the evil eye. Happily, as with most evil, cures were available. All that remained was to master the antidotes for the *malocchio*. These involved olive oil, water, ritualistic gestures, and suitable counter-imprecations. I was proud that my grandmother gained local fame for her unmatched talent of stymieing the *malocchio*.

The entire idea of the *malocchio* is, of course, nonsense on stilts. Ay, but our beliefs and expectations can bring about the seemingly impossible. The placebo effect teaches us that. To those thoroughly convinced of the reality of the *malocchio*, the purported curse of the evil practitioner often *did result* in pain and discomfort to the intended victim. The patsies believed and expected the curse to work and they brought about their own pain with their self-fulfilling prophesies. Later, they arrived at my grandmother's doorstep and hopefully submitted to her antidote. They believed and expected that my grandmother, the village sorcerer, would strike the right note and banish malevolence. Invariably, they were cured. Score a point for the *malocchio* effect. Sing the praises of Grazia Giordano Leonardo, high priestess of street medicine.

The placebo effect involves thinking the sugar pill is something else, say, an antibiotic. The belief is rational given the circumstances under which the sugar pill is administered. The nocebo effect may involve the false belief that a treatment that is objectively curative lacks salutary power. Perhaps the false belief results from radical skepticism in the medical profession or the drug culture. Perhaps the false belief flows from wrongly thinking the curative treatment is other than what it in fact is, from thinking it is inert, like a sugar pill. The *malocchio* effect is the wayward child of superstition — grounded in folklore, ignorance, and cultural hyperbole. Belief in the *malocchio* is always irrational.

Dozens of baseball superstitions fall under the domain of baseball's placebo, nocebo, and *malocchio* effects. If a pitcher deeply believes that his no-hitter will be marred if teammates mention his ongoing effort, that will increase the chances of the pitcher losing focus, feeling pressure, making a mistake. Even though causal connection between the remarks and his failure is lacking, the pitcher deeply committed to the belief will probably cough up the no-hitter. If Barry Bonds thoroughly believes in voodoo, expects it to work, and hears about my actions, do not be surprised if his knees start to ache. If Samson was convinced that his power flowed from his tresses — what physiological connection did he imagine?— then we should not be shocked that Delilah craftily turned him into the before specimen of a Charles Atlas ad with a few snips of her Philistine-manufactured scissors. If a player is convinced his uniform #5 bears special powers and he is assigned #32, his performance may well ebb because of the self-fulfilling prophesy. If players are convinced that crossed bats on the field translate to zero offense, do not be surprised if their resulting loss of confidence and focus manufactures truth out of ignorance. If players who appear on the cover expect the *Sports Illustrated* jinx to work, they will increase their prospects of a slump.

Relief pitcher Rob Murphy wore a pair of women's black silk panties under his athletic supporter. He was given the panties by a friend, wore them as a gag one day, and pitched uncommonly well. Murphy wore them every game thereafter. He claimed that the underwear was part of his "mental preparation."[9] I am not clever enough to have made this up.

Pitching coach Ray Miller observed that superstitious behavior is a coping mechanism, "It's solace. It's about, if I do this, things will be good, so it's a positive thought. You can get carried away with it, though, and go too far."[10]

At least the placebo effect is based on an understandably false belief, held in good faith, that the sugar pill has curative powers because it is not a sugar pill. The placebo effect is not grounded on superstition. Why any of these other nutty propositions should be believed in the first place is puzzling. Perhaps the childhood infatuation with witches, hobgoblins, trolls, demonic forces, mysterious happenings, and the like carries over into adulthood. Perhaps we find it romantic, even inspiring, to conjure a cosmos of unexplained powers. But once believed, such irrational convictions bear expectations that often bring about what should have been impossible.

Conventional Rationality: Many baseball superstitions are grounded firmly in conventional rationality. Consider a batter's elaborate routine of fastening batting gloves, pawing the dirt a certain way, taking a specified number of practice swings, uttering a phrase or word, and the like. This routine is important to trigger the muscle memory, focus, and confidence required to maximize performance. The particular routine the batter uses is a matter of personal preference and habit, but having some sort of routine is crucial. Likewise with pitching routines. Although some of these scripted exercises seem bizarre, they are typically not based on superstitions and irrationalities. The rationality of these practices stems from the objective causal connection between routines that trigger muscle memory, focus, confidence, and optimal performance outcomes.

Brad Ausmus understood that a good catcher must separate his offense from his defense: "When I get to the circle of dirt where home plate is, as I'm crossing over from the grass to the dirt, I put my mask on. That's my mental trigger to forget about the offense and move to defense."[11] No superstition, this. Having a routine that facilitates an appropriate mental attitude toward the task at hand is rational.

Dave Concepcion's bizarre habit of showering in his uniform to end a slump may be more rational than it first seems. Many professional coaches advise players to develop a release for negative thoughts, feelings, and results. The trick is to wipe the slate clean after past failure and renew focus on the present and immediate future.

> Develop a routine or gesture to symbolically release or let go of negative thoughts and feelings.... Pick up some dirt, a rock, some grass, the rosin bag.... Put your anger or frustration into it by squeezing it. Then throw the object away telling yourself that you are throwing away the last pitch, the error you made or whatever is annoying you ... develop a physical action that helps you turn negative thoughts into positive ones.[12]

In this vein, I have seen youth teams make a collective gesture of flushing negative thoughts down the drain. For example, after an error each defensive player on the field will simulate a flush, sometimes simultaneously, to symbolize the release of the negative and renewed focus on the task at hand. I do not recommend this particular method because it looks bizarre and invites misinterpretation or ridicule. Better to have individual or team methods less transparent to the public but that retain great meaning from within.

After throwing a gopher ball, pitchers often use focal points which remind them that we cannot alter the past, that our focus should be on the present and immediate future.

> To get himself under control, [the pitcher] turns his back to home plate and walks to the area behind the mound. He looks out to his focal point, the flag pole in center field, which reminds him that there's nothing he can do about the past or the future, and that he should relax and focus on the next pitch. He takes a good breath, turns around, and walks confidently back up on the mound. Before he steps on the rubber he pauses to make sure he's ready for the next pitch.[13]

Concepcion's routine might well have been in this vein: to symbolically wash away the past and augur a brighter future. After a divorce, the parties often purchase a new wardrobe, get a different haircut, go on a diet. They don't do this superstitiously, but as a way of underscoring their new beginnings.

Sometimes, though, routines are irrational: when they result from superstitious beliefs. If the particular routine a player selects is based on obviously false causal beliefs — brushing my teeth between innings will please the tooth fairy and she will watch over and help me when I hurl — then we return to the realm of the *malocchio*. If players are helped it is only because of their antecedently superstitious belief. If Concepcion held that his uniform was infected with demons sapping his strength, but who were susceptible to soap and water, then his shower was superstitious, but open to the *malocchio* effect. As in the cases of my grandmother's dozens of cured victims of the *malocchio*, such players would probably be much better off not currying the superstition in the first place. The superstitious cure works only because of the superstitious disease.

Suppose players stopped harboring all superstitions, William James rationality, placebo and *malocchio* effects? Would they perform better, worse, or the same? Superstitions that amount to stone cold irrationality have no effect on performance. William James–type rationality is often helpful to performance. Placebo effects, although founded on false beliefs, can facilitate better results.

The biggest dispute centers on *malocchio* effects. Typically, they produce better results only by making their bearer more vulnerable to initial negative influences. But if a player can control access to the object of his false belief he may be able to enhance his performance. For example, if Jones is thoroughly convinced that batting with a rabbit's foot in his pocket betters his performance, Jones's belief is irrational and superstitious. But if he believes it deeply enough, a kind of *malocchio* effect may kick in. Jones's belief may become a self-fulfilling prophecy. As long as Jones can guarantee he has a rabbit's foot — maybe by purchasing two or three gross every spring — his performance may improve due to increased confidence. Unlike the curse of the *malocchio*, which can be placed on victims against their will, belief in the power of rabbit's feet does not make the bearer more vulnerable ("Oops, I lost my rabbit's foot. I am toast today.") as long as he can ensure a ready supply. The belief in the potency of rabbit's feet, though, cannot be simulated. I cannot reason, "Gee, if I start believing in the power of rabbit's feet, even if irrational, then my batting average will go up, so I'll start believing." The irrational belief, on the contrary, must be sincerely held from the start in order to realize the positive effect. The bearer must subconsciously accept the false, irrational belief as true. If so, while the truth may set us free, it will not always raise our batting average.

Jose Canseco and Immanuel Kant

"Steroids produce testosterone levels up to 100 times the normal natural level, which can lead to liver damage, high blood pressure, depression, mood swings and shrunken testicles."

— Linn Goldberg, M.D.

"The problem is steroids 'work.' You do get bigger. You can train harder. There was a lot of bad publicity over Ben Johnson's use of steroids, but he did win races until he was caught."

— Gary Green, M.D.

"Baseball players will take anything. If you had a pill that would guarantee a pitcher 20 wins, but might take five years off his life, he'd take it."

— Jim Bouton, former major league pitcher and author

"Intelligent, informed use of steroids, combined with human growth hormone, will one day be so accepted that everybody will be doing it."

— Jose Canseco, former major league outfielder and unabashed drug consumer

Jose Canseco (1964–) has admitted — and at times seems proud of — his use of performance-enhancing drugs. Immanuel Kant (1724–1804) would undoubtedly conclude that Canseco's actions fail the test of the categorical imperative and were, accordingly, wrongful. Should baseball ban performance-enhancing drugs, such as anabolic steroids? On Kantian grounds? On other grounds?

Jose Canseco: Immigrant makes Good

Jose Canseco's father, Jose Sr., was a manager for Esso Standard Oil in Havana, Cuba, during the Batista regime. After Fidel Castro seized political power in 1959, Jose Sr. understood that the best interests of his family militated that the Cansecos leave their homeland. They were not permitted to emigrate, though, until 1965. Jose Jr. and Osvaldo, his twin brother, were less than twelve months old when their parents, along with an older sister, sought a brave, new world in Miami, Florida.

Jose Sr., was a hard-driving, old-school patriarch who rode his sons mercilessly, especially in athletics. Jose Jr. was far from a prodigy. He was tall and skinny. He lacked the obvious natural talent of contemporaries such as Rafael Palmeiro and Danny Tartabull. Still, Jose had uncommon long ball potential that piqued the interest of former major league pitcher and current scout Camilo Pascual. To Jose's surprise, he was drafted by the Oakland Athletics in the 15th round of the 1982 amateur draft.

Jose understood that he had to develop a stronger body. He had length, but lacked strength. He exercised diligently at a nearby gym and enjoyed modest gains. Two years after Jose was drafted, his mother, who had long suffered from hepatitis and diabetes, died. On her deathbed, Jose pledged, "I'm going to be the best athlete in the world, no matter what it takes. I promise you, Mom, that I will be the best."[1]

Driven by his sacred oath to a dying parent and his recognition that baseball was his only potential ticket to success, Jose Canseco began to learn everything he could about the transforming effects of anabolic steroids and human growth hormone. In a few months, he packed on twenty-five pounds of pure muscle. Maximizing his innate long-ball ability, the new Synthetic Hulk became the terror of the minor leagues. By 1985, he was playing for the Oakland Athletics. He continued to use steroids and growth hormone, and blossomed stronger and larger.

True, cynics will object that Jose's deathbed vow to his mother and subsequent research on and relentless consumption of performance-enhancing drugs (PEDs) is a tad less inspiring than, say, Babe Ruth's alleged promise to smack a home run for a dying child or even Rocky Balboa's mythical determination to go the distance to prove his self-worth. True, Hollywood is unlikely to champion the slogan, "I've got to take a shot of PEDs in my butt for mom" as a marketing device for the Jose Canseco Story: Victory through Chemistry. True, Jose's former high school coach is unlikely to call his current players together, choke out a teary-eyed version of the Canseco saga, and beg them to "Win one for the steroid dipper." But, in the name of charity, let's brush cynicism aside for the moment and continue with the rest of the story.

Canseco played seventeen years of major league baseball. He smashed 462 home runs, slugged .515 and drove home 1407 runs.

> If you are naturally athletic, steroids can enhance whatever you have, both in terms of strength and stamina. And also in terms of hand-eye coordination and perform-

ance.... The psychological effect of steroids is very dramatic. Using steroids properly can do wonders for your confidence ... if you convince yourself that you're a great player, you're going to be a great player.[2]

He won the 1986 American League Rookie of the Year Award. In 1988, he smashed 42 homers, drove in 124 runs, stole 40 bases, slugged .569, and batted .307 with an on-base percentage of .391. He led the league that year in home runs, slugging percentage, runs batted in, and was fourth in stolen bases. He earned the Most Valuable Player Award. Canseco also played in four World Series and was part of two world championship teams, with Oakland in 1989 and with the New York Yankees, in a cameo role at the end of the his career, in 2000.

> If you do steroids properly for long enough and know what you're doing, the powers you gain can feel almost superhuman. Besides the boost to your strength and confidence level, you start running faster. Your hand-eye coordination and muscle-twitch fibers get faster. Your bat speed increases. You feel more powerful, and you can use a heavier bat without sacrificing any bat speed, which is the most important thing.[3]

Along the way, Jose Canseco married and divorced Miss Miami of 1986, married and divorced another beautiful woman, enjoyed countless extramarital affairs, and flirted with Madonna. He owned virtually every desirable Italian sports car — Testarossa, Lamborghini, Ferrari — and numerous other trophy autos. Jose earned millions of dollars, sired a daughter, was charged, at different times, with domestic violence and assault and battery, and spent three months in the slammer for failing a drug test while on probation during two years' house arrest. How much more adventure could one man cram into his first forty years?

Kant's Categorical Imperative

Immanuel Kant was convinced that moral conclusions could be rationally derived. Although a committed Christian, he insisted that belief in a supreme being was not required to understand the moral law. Instead, human beings could discover right and distinguish it from wrong through rudimentary reasoning.

A moral agent must be able to universalize her actions: "I am never to act otherwise than so that I could also will that my maxim should become a universal law." This "categorical imperative" has a rational foundation in logic. Kant gives several examples of the workings of the categorical imperative. One of these illustrations concerns keeping promises. A person may be considering borrowing money, promising to pay the lender back, when in fact she knows that she will not be able to do so. If this person wants to evaluate the morality of her proposed action, says Kant, all she need do is ask the following question: "Can I will that everyone act on a maxim, 'When it is expedient for me to do so, I can make a lying promise to ameliorate my difficult circumstances'?"[4]

Kant insists that we cannot sanction the proposed action because, if universalized, it would destroy the institution of promise-keeping: if the practice were widespread people could no longer rely on promises as signifying much of anything, and even false promises would surrender practical currency. On one hand, a false promise requires the institution of promise-keeping for its intended effect, but, on the other hand, the universalization of false promises eviscerates that very institution. Because we are not allowed to make ourselves exceptions to the moral laws, Kant affirms that the act of falsely promising is shown by the categorical imperative to be inherently contradictory.

Another illustration of the categorical imperative focuses on positive duties. Suppose I am confronted by a person in distress whom I can aid with a minimum of inconvenience to myself. I am not inclined to render aid, but, as a sincere Kantian, I ask whether I can act on the following maxim: "While not harming others I will do nothing to help them when they are in need."[5]

Although I can conceive of a world in which this maxim could be universalized, says Kant, I cannot will the maxim as a universal law because at some future time I may need and desire the help of others. Again, I cannot make myself an exception to the moral law, so logical consistency demands that I render aid now.

Kant contends that one's natural inclinations — love, pursuit of happiness, sentiments of benevolence, self-interest, and so on — are improper motives for moral action. Thus, for Kant, the only unconditional good is a good will: the will to do one's moral duty for its own sake, simply because it is one's duty and because it is required by reason. The goal of moral reasoning, for Kant, is the discovery of truth which silences the voices of irrationality and expediency.

Roger Scruton comments: "Moral reasons close the subject's mind to alternative courses of action ... *because* the moral being is rational, there are certain courses of action which he cannot consider. If Kant is right, it is man's very rationality that leads him to close his mind to actions for which a thousand prudential reasons might be given."[6]

A classic criticism of Kant's view focus on the malleability of his categorical imperative. When one strives to discover rationally "maxims that one can will become universal laws," she will find that logic is more flexible than Kant imagined. The way one poses the question of the categorical imperative to oneself will usually permit several rationally acceptable, but mutually inconsistent, answers. The abstract universality to which Kant aspires is purchased at the cost of specificity and concreteness.

For example, suppose in the first illustration I posed the question as follows: "Can I will that everyone act on the maxim, 'When I am in desperate need of life's necessities, through no fault of my own, may I make a lying promise to extricate myself from the situation if my lie causes minimal harm to others'?" If the situation is described in this way I may find there is no logical contradiction in affirming the proposed conduct. The conduct would not destroy the institution of promise-keeping because it is more carefully circumscribed than the conduct in Kant's formulation of the maxim. Even if readers disagree with that specific conclusion it should still be clear that to arrive at her antecedently desired answer to a moral question, an agent requires only a degree of ingenuity in describing her action and in formulating her proposed maxim. The categorical imperative does less substantive moral work than Kant imagined.

Moreover, there is a paradox deeply embedded in Kant's categorical imperative. Although appeals to consequences are presumably irrelevant to his moral analysis, notice how they play an important role in the application of his categorical imperative. The key questions in his two illustrations focus on the unacceptable *consequences* of everyone's acting on certain maxims and on the moral agent's preferences about her own future treatment. This is not merely logic weaving its impersonal machinations, but, instead, requires attention to desired social consequences and first-person inclinations. Finally, even if Kantian universality were achieved, it is not clear how its rational acceptance is sufficient to provide first-person *motivation* for moral action.

Scruton adds: "If there is [a universal standard of moral validity], then, by its very universality, it must avoid all mention of *me*; in which case, how can it have the motivating force required by a genuine first-person reason? Conversely, if it is such a reason — a reason which motivates *me* — its claim to universal validity must be doubted.... The conflict stems from the contradictory requirements of abstraction and concreteness — the requirements that I be removed from my circumstances, and that I be identified with them.... In abstracting from my values, my everyday aims and preferences, from all that constitutes my contingent condition, I abstract also from the circumstances of my act — and, in particular, from the desires and interests which initially raised for me the question of action."[7]

The moral laws drawn from Kant's categorical imperative, then, suffer from two main defects. First, the methodology of the categorical imperative offers form without content: an abstract formulation that cannot yield substantive moral conclusions without a specific, antecedent moral vision. Users of the categorical imperative must, in effect, put the rabbit in the hat. They must supply the very moral conclusions they claim to be independently deriving. Second, the conclusions of abstract reasons alone may not provide the motivation required for moral action. As Kierkegaard might have said, "what have *universal* standards got to do with *me?*"

Despite such shortcomings, Kant's moral philosophy has been greatly influential. His call to do the morally right action only because it is right, to not make oneself an exception to moral law, to avoid expediency and irrationality, to recognize that the ends do not justify the means, and to place duty above self-interest retains currency in contemporary moral debate.

Performance-Enhancing Drugs and Moral Reasoning

PEDs include a host of medications such as androstenedione, creatine, anabolic steroids, human growth hormone (HGH), erythropoietin (EPO), and a host of others. The dangers and potential performance-enhancing benefits of these drugs are often sport-specific. I'll focus on the two most related to baseball: anabolic steroids and HGH.

The American College of Sports Medicine warns against the serious side effects caused by improper use of anabolic steroids: liver damage, atherosclerosis, hypertension, unwelcome personality changes, lowered sperm count and shrunken testicles in males, masculinization of females, severe acne, higher cholesterol, psychiatric disorders, and the like. Dangers associated with synthetic versions of HGH include sore joints, swollen tissue, thickening of the bones (particularly in the jaw, hands, and feet), and increased risks of diabetes and heart disease.[8]

The performance-enhancing benefits of anabolic steroids include increased muscle mass and strength, quicker recovery from strenuous training, and aggressive feelings that may translate to self-confidence. HGH can increase strength by supporting more bone and lean muscle mass and decreased fat. Both steroids and HGH have legitimate clinical uses and are prescribed by medical doctors for specific conditions.

The following discussion assumes that (1) anabolic steroids and HGH, combined with physical training, facilitate better athletic performances and (2) these PEDs pose potentially serious health risks for committed users. The precise levels of athletic benefits and health risks are a matter of some dispute.

To understand the ying and yang of the PEDs debate, I'll present a catalog of the arguments typically advanced against PEDs and the rejoinders from advocates of PEDs. I'll call those who oppose PEDs "moralists" and those who advocate free choice in using PEDs "cansecos."

We should begin by mentioning one common objection to the use of PEDs: the unprescribed use of PEDs violates the rules of baseball. To use an illegal substance to gain a competitive advantage is unfair because it is a form of cheating. This objection, though, is circular: it uses the current status of PEDs — they violate the rules of baseball — as the basis to conclude that PEDs *should be* against the rules of baseball. A canseco could respond that if PEDs were permitted by the rules of baseball then no competitive unfairness would result.

A cleaner objection could be raised by moralists: unprescribed use of PEDs violates not only the rules of baseball but also the law of the land. Some PEDs are legally dispensed only by prescription from a medical doctor. How can the rules of baseball permit that which the law of the land prohibits? The rules of baseball, for example, could not permit heroin use, or allow the distribution of cocaine, or accept use of any illegal substance. In one way, this objection is decisive: Professional baseball does not even have the option of permitting the use of illegal substances or drug use allowed only through medical prescription. But some milder forms of PEDs are permitted to be placed in dietary supplements because of oversights in the 1994 drug law, while others are readily available on the black market. Moreover, relying upon the illegality argument obscures some of the deeper reasons why use of PEDs may be objectionable.

The Paternalistic Argument: PEDs may be banned from baseball because PEDs harm those who use them

Moralists: Use of PEDs brings enormous potential harm to users. As a sport, baseball should be concerned with the health of participants. The pressure to perform at high levels should not be the prime value of sport. By focusing only on short-time performance and ignoring long-term health risks of using PEDs, sports diminish respect for athletes as people. We should not place a higher value on better athletic performances than we do on the health of our athletes.[9]

Cansecos: The athlete, not the czars of baseball or society, should be the judge of the relevant risks and benefits. Inform athletes of those risks and benefits, but let individuals make their own call. Remember, John Stuart Mill's famous harm principle insists that the only sound reason to legislate is to protect others from harm. The individual is the best judge of his own interests. Society should not be permitted to substitute its judgment or tastes except where doing so protects the well-being of others. Individual autonomy and freedom of choice are paramount. We may rightfully act paternalistically only toward those who lack full rational capabilities because of age or mental incompetence. Besides, taking risks in sports is not automatically foolish. We permit risky sports such as mountain-climbing, sky-diving, professional boxing, and the like.[10] We allow strenuous training that increases risk of injury. Taking risks in sports is as American as a triple-decker burger with blue cheese dressing, topped by a slice of processed cheese, and a side order of fries!

Moralists could rejoin that society does, in fact, often justifiably act paternalistically. The state refuses to permit anyone to agree to his own disablement or killing. The state will not recognize contracts to sell oneself into slavery, or to become a mistress, or a second spouse. Prostitution is illegal almost everywhere. Any citizen may use reasonable force to prevent others from harming themselves or committing suicide. We cannot purchase certain drugs without a physician's prescription. Other drugs, such as heroin, are not permitted at all.[11] The state decrees seat belt laws for automobiles and motorcycle helmet laws. Mill's harm principle is a terrific beginning for understanding the proper scope of regulating conduct, but it is not the final word.

The dangers of paternalism, though, are real. Where do we draw the line? Should we ban whiskey, cigarettes, fried foods, and triple-decker burgers with blue cheese dressing? Once we begin crawling down the slippery slope of paternalistic regulation do we not end up in a conceptual morass?

Not exactly. Numerous arguments end up with someone raising the specter of a slippery slope leading to disaster. Usually, distinctions can be made and tests can be formulated that prevent our stumbling into ruin. We can retain our freedom to pound down deep-fried junk food while accepting the law requiring seat belt use in automobiles.

I would offer the following factors when determining how strong a reason paternalism provides for legislation in a particular case:

- Probability of harm if people do act X
- Severity of that harm
- Immediacy of harm if people do X
- Direct link between harm and doing X
- Benefit people will enjoy if they do X
- Amount of freedom restricted if we prohibit X
- Practicality and feasibility of the legislation (Can it be enforced? Is it practical to prohibit X).

The results of applying this test in good faith would, of course, often be contestable. Some of the factors would sometimes cut in different directions. But that is a function of most regulation. We resolve the matter in the usual way: argument, negotiation, compromise, and the like.

Cansecos are probably correct: the great value we properly place on individual autonomy and freedom of choice suggests that the paternalistic argument cannot conclusively establish a ban against PEDs in baseball. But moralists could point out a difference between risks inherent to sport — those that are an intrinsic part of the competition — and risks that are extraneous to sport — those that are not part of the competition and are brought into play for external purposes. They could argue that the risks of mountain-climbing, sky-diving, and professional boxing are inherent to those sports, they help make the sports what they are, while use of PEDs by baseball players is an extraneous risk. And the argument would continue.

I would urge that readers not fall prey to one rhetoric device common to these debates. Often, once an argument seems unable to establish *conclusively* that PEDs should be banned, the argument is tossed aside. The underlying assumption seems to be the following:

> *If argument N cannot clearly establish that X should be regulated then N is irrelevant to the debate.*

Instead, I would urge that N may provide a *reason* of varying strength, depending on N's power and context of application. So, the paternalistic argument probably cannot conclusively establish that PEDs should be banned by baseball, but the argument is not irrelevant. It provides a (non-conclusive) reason for banning PEDs. Readers should judge what strength they take that reason to bear.

The Argument from Harm Principle: PEDs may be banned from baseball because doing so is consistent with the Harm Principle.

Moralists. PEDs, in fact, could be banned in accord with the harm principle itself. The harm principle is grounded by the primary values of individual autonomy and freedom of choice. But numerous athletes do not consume PEDs after rendering informed consent. Instead, they are subtly coerced into using PEDs because they know opponents are doing so and they cannot afford to yield the competitive edge. These athletes would prefer not to take PEDs, but reluctantly consume PEDs out of fear that they might otherwise lose their livelihood.[12] Accordingly, the choice of some lunatic athletes to risk their health in service of better performances harms others who are coerced into following suit.

Cansecos. Every new training regime, advance in equipment, and athletic technique puts similar pressure on competitors. For example, at one

time, serious weight training in baseball was nonexistent. Once a few players assumed heavy weight programs with clear positive results, competitors
had to follow suit or fall behind. Innovations always carry risks to health, also.[13]
Just because a decision is made more difficult — to pick up the new technique
or to risk falling behind, that is the question?— does not mean the resulting
decision is not free. Athletes of normal human capabilities and above the requisite age can still make informed decisions even though knowing that others are using and benefiting from PEDs must be factored into their decisions.

A typical rhetorical pattern of cansecos is called *tu quoque*: you already
allow X-type activities so you are not in a position to deny privilege to my
favored X-type activity. Moralists have no problem accepting the risks and
subtly coerced choices involved in heavy weight training, and other stressful
physical regimens and techniques, yet they throw up their hands in horror at
the difficult decisions athletes are confronted with involving PEDs. Aren't
moralists being hypocritical and, worse, logically inconsistent?

Maybe. Maybe not. Readers should not succumb to facile application
of *tu quoque*. They should inquire as to whether, for example, heavy weight
training involves the *same likelihood* of harm, *equal severity* of harm, and *similar extra health benefits* beyond enhanced performance as does serious use of
PEDs. If consuming PEDs has a greater likelihood of harm, more severe possibility of harm, and fewer extra health benefits than heavy weight training
and other stressful physical regimens, then *the tu quoque* argument is less
impressive than cansecos imagine. In general, cansecos tend to find a cur-
rently accepted practice that they can claim forces moralists to also accept
PEDs. They claim that accepting the argument against PEDs would also force
moralists to outlaw a host of practices uncontroversially considered permissible. I am cautioning that the claims of parallel risks must be examined more
closely.

The Argument from Naturalness: PEDs may be banned from baseball because they are unnatural additives. They are artificial.

Moralists. PEDs are unnatural additives, they are artificial. Instead of
allowing athletic greatness to be determined by the injection of unnatural,
synthetic substances into bodies we should focus on developing our athletic
talents.[14]

Cansecos. But some PEDs are natural. Testosterone is natural. Those
PEDs that are not natural are manufactured, but so are many accepted foods,

medicines, and vitamins.[15] To call X natural does not automatically prove its merit. To call X unnatural does not automatically discredit it.

Moralists should point out that foods, medicines, and vitamins all have health benefits that PEDs lack. So, PEDs, unlike the other examples, are unnatural and without nutritional value. As always, moralists should not accept counter-examples unless they are truly parallel.

Still, cansecos are correct to be suspicious of the argument from naturalness. There are a variety of possible interpretations of natural: what is statistically usual; statistically frequent; statistically possible; accomplished without human interference; and what is in accord with an entity's essential characteristics. None of these interpretations, however, establishes that use of PEDs is automatically or usually immoral. Notions dependent upon statistical normalcy or statistical possibility, for example, lack necessary moral significance: the mere fact that human beings routinely or often engage in X does not automatically imply that X embodies moral merit, nor does it necessarily imply that — X is immoral. *A fortiori*, the fact that humans *can* engage in X does not establish X's moral credentials: not everything a natural entity can do is automatically moral. Notions of statistical possibility, if they did bear normative significance, could be used to establish the inherent *morality* of PED use. Likewise, an interpretation such as "accomplished without human interference" is insufficient to establish the immorality of PEDs: numerous morally appropriate actions do require human agency, and numerous actions that are not generated by human agency are either without moral significance or are morally inappropriate.

The most promising interpretation of natural for critics of PED use is "what is in accord with an entity's essential characteristics and what facilitates an entity's progress toward its rightful purpose." In this vein, sometimes the term natural is invoked tautologically to mean what is right. But such use of the term disables critics of PEDs in an important respect: conferring the honorific title natural on an action becomes trivial for purposes of *determining* an action's moral merit because natural becomes just another way of *saying* morally sound.

More plausibly, the term natural is invoked functionally: because X is compatible with essential human characteristics and purposes it is natural, and because it is natural, X is morally sound. Nevertheless, this interpretation is fraught with grave difficulties. It can be argued persuasively, for example, that natural laws, at best, merely describe events in the universe, but they bear no necessary moral significance: even if it could be established that X is unnatural is does not necessarily follow that X is immoral. Moreover, attempts to bridge the descriptive and the normative depend invariably on a specialized picture of human nature, on a full account of the proper human *telos,* and on a particular rendering of the genesis of objective morality. These notions, themselves, rest on suspicious metaphysical underpinnings and, often, on question-begging assumptions. Thus, the term natural is most often used in conclusory fashion to express an antecedently held condemnation of a practice, instead of as a conceptual tool for *arriving* at a normative judgment. Furthermore, claims of naturalness often commit the error of reductionism by wrongly postulating that athletics have only one permissible function or appropriate manifestation. Too often, such reductionism does not mirror the imperatives of an alleged objective morality, but the narrow conditioning and historical taboos of one's culture. Accordingly, accusations of unnaturalness expose themselves as feckless analytic instruments for *establishing* the inherent immorality of PEDs. Score a point for the cansecos.

The Argument from Role Models: PEDs may be banned from baseball because young athletes, to their detriment, will emulate the behavior of professional stars.

Moralists. If professional ballplayers use PEDs, young athletes will mimic their behavior. Professional players are role models, whether they choose to be or not. Media and advertising nurture the celebrity of professional ballplayers, and invite young athletes to aspire to that stature. Using PEDs, then, harms others after all — the young athletes of America.[16]

Cansecos. Sports figures should not be role models. Parents, siblings, relatives, and teachers are better candidates. Besides, just because X is a role model does not imply that society should regulate X's behavior. We do not prevent star athletes from divorcing their spouses or using alcohol or smoking cigarettes or gambling in casinos or promoting themselves shamelessly or seeking to maximize their material holdings or a host of other negative actions.[17] Why single out PEDs? Athletes under the age of 18 should not have legal access to many types of PEDs, they are below the age of informed consent. But that should not prohibit use by professional athletes.

Moralists could stress that it is disingenuous to claim sports figures should not be role models when the celebrity and huge earnings of professional athletes depend upon the media and advertising machine. Soften the power of the machine and we decrease the fame and earning potential of ballplayers. The greater celebrity and earnings of players, the more likely they are to be role models. So sports figures are role models whether they like it or not. They receive a package deal: glory, money, and idolization from young folks. While imbibing alcohol, smoking cigarettes, and gambling are adult activities we cannot prohibit, we can prohibit use of PEDs where the will to do so exists.

Cansecos, though, make a strong case that the connection between behavior of professional athletes and the behavior of youngsters is questionable. Just as with claims about the connection between viewing television violence and acting violently, listening to rap music and acting misogynistically, and observing avant garde art and acting promiscuously, the bond between admiring professional athletes and consuming PEDs is speculative.

The Argument from Ideal Competition: PEDs contaminate our best conception of athletic competition.

Moralists. Robert Simon argues that athletic competition is best understood as the mutual quest for excellence through challenge.[18] PEDs taint this ideal because instead of athletic ability determining the outcomes of contests, the efficiency with which a player's body reacts to PEDs becomes crucial. Competition should, ideally, be determined by personal attributes of participants such as dedication, motivation, courage. Insofar as we diminish the power of personal attributes and elevate the influence of efficient use of PEDs, we denigrate athletes as people. PEDs amplify athletic ability without regard for the personal qualities we rightly celebrate in performers such as perseverance, good judgment, poise, and sportsmanship. Athletic competition should honor and be a test of persons, not a contest rewarding those who ingest and can most efficiently use the best pharmaceuticals. Natural ability, how athletes develop that ability, reacting to choices and strategies and abilities of opponents should be paramount. Human traits such as courage, intelligence, and prioritizing should be implicated thoroughly. PEDs make sporting events a duel of competing bodies, not whole persons.

Cansecos. The values of competition are not inherent, but chosen. There is no single conception of sports, much less of ideal sports.[19] We already permit a host of activities that give those with bodies able to more efficiency use them a competitive edge: ingesting vitamins, weight training, stressful diet regimens, equipment itself. Sports ability is not simply, perhaps not even mainly, about personal attributes such as dedication, courage, and motivation. Eye-hand coordination, quickness of reflexes, physical strength, foot speed, agility, mobility, and size are all crucial. Sports, then, are already forums where better bodies excel. Even with use of PEDs, those qualities Simon admires retain their currency. Remember, athletes do not become better merely by injecting or ingesting PEDs. They must train especially rigorously to realize the added performance benefits. If we deny athletes use of PEDs we thereby deny in them precisely the attributes Simon claims to value: self-reliance, personal achievement, and autonomy.

Simon's ideal of competition is contestable from the outset. Even if we accepted its framework, his distinction between persons and bodies is fragile. Cansecos correctly point out that numerous techniques, regimens, and training in sports favor those whose bodies can more efficiently and effectively benefit from them. Also, cansecos score heavily when they insist that athletic contests inherently favor those with better bodies in numerous ways. An athlete can maximize her courage, dedication, motivation, intelligence, ability to strategize, and the like, but if she does not embody ample physical skill — if she doesn't have a good body in that sense — she will not prevail in sports. Moreover, if use of PEDs were allowed, it is unclear to what extent that would infringe on the importance of the personal attributes Simon admires. He sometimes talks as if PEDs of and by themselves produce victories and athletic greatness. That is not the case. The personal attributes cherished by advocates of the argument from ideal competition would remain pivotal even if sports commissioners allowed PED use.

The Argument from Distorted Values: PEDs alter the delicate balance between process values and outcome values in sport.

Moralists. Sports embody inherent goods and values, which are attained by performing in accord with standards of excellence integral to them. The process values of athletics are critical: maximizing one's athletic potentials, striving to do one's best, achieving health and fitness, deserving victory based on superior skill and expenditure of effort, and viewing one's opponent as a necessary partner in mutual self-discovery and self-creation. The use of PEDs pushes process values to the side in a wrong-headed obsession with outcome values: victory at all cost, celebrity, and wealth. Accordingly, PEDs alter the delicate balance between process and outcome values in sport. Sport becomes nothing more than the rush for higher, faster, farther by any means necessary. In so doing, we denigrate the beauty and self-creativity of sport in deference to glory and riches purchased at the cost of our integrity.[20] Such a bargain should be beneath those who view sport as not fundamentally about wins and losses. The old Grantland Rice slogan may seem corny to cynics, but it still reflects a basic truth: it is not whether you won or lost, but how you played the game.

Cansecos. Invoking Granny Rice exposes your desperation. Let me wipe a tear from my eye. Okay. First, we already permit training techniques and regimens (for example, training for marathons at high altitudes, heavy weight training) that help users exercise their skills at higher levels without altering the character of sports.[21] No competitor ignores a new training technique or renounces better equipment or a superior diet because it focuses too much on outcome. Second, PEDs are not magic bullets. Effective use requires extra effort and training, which implicates process values, on the part of athletes. Third, professional and big-time collegiate athletics already stress winning. Coaches and administrators lose their jobs if their teams win too infrequently. Players are cut if their performance wanes. Your ideal of athletics mirrors the rhetoric, but not the actual practice, of sports as we know them. And I would include the Olympics in that category. Medal winners from virtually every country are showered with privileges and acclaim that are withheld from other participants. Use of PEDs does not alter, but merely reflects, the balance between process and outcome values in sport. Of course, I exclude purely recreational sports. But I assume that no one will inject PEDs in order to enhance his performance in flag football played in the backyard.

Moralists are correct in arguing that use of PEDs strains further the balance between process and outcome values in sport. They should insist that strenuous training techniques and regimens, unlike PEDs, do not privilege enhanced performance over the health of athletes. Also, how we achieve victory still matters. Viewing the manner and means of victory as more important than simply attaining victory is reasonable. Still, a canseco might rejoin that this argument is redolent with circularity: it *assumes* PEDs are undesirable and thereby taint the glory of victory, as well as distorting the role of process values in sport. Then it uses the alleged distortion of process values to *demonstrate* the undesirability of PEDs. Cansecos also have a point that in professional and major college venues the relationship between process and outcome values is already other than the ideal extolled by moralists.

The Argument from Kantianism: use of PEDs flunks the moral test of the categorical imperative.

Moralists. The categorical imperative informs us that injecting PEDs is morally wrong. Ask yourself, "Can I will that everyone act on a maxim, 'When it is expedient for me to do so, I can violate the rules of sport to gain a competitive edge'?" Kant would insist that we cannot sanction the proposed action because, if universalized, it would destroy the institution of rule-keeping that is crucial to sports: if the practice were widespread people could no longer rely on others to abide by the rules. Without general compliance with its constitutive rules, participation in sports is impossible. On one hand, a cheater requires general compliance with rules to secure the intended effect: a competitive edge. On the other hand, the universalization of rule-breaking eviscerates that very institution. Because we are not allowed to make ourselves exceptions to the moral laws, Kant would affirm that the act of violating the constitutive rules of sport is shown by the categorical imperative to be inherently contradictory, and thus irrational and immoral.

Cansecos. Your argument is viciously circular in two ways. First, you are using the current ban on PEDs as proof that PEDs should remain banned, a clear case of begging the question. Second, and more fundamentally, I can easily elude the force of the categorical imperative by rephrasing the question. Ask yourself, "Can I will that everyone act on a maxim, 'When I know the dangers of a training aid that will enhance athletic performance, should I be allowed to use that aid if I freely assume the risks where doing so does not endanger others?'" No obvious logical contradiction results from this formulation when subjected to the categorical imperative.

Because we have no independent test to determine which way to phrase the question demanded by the categorical imperative, either description is permissible. So the categorical imperative — true to its reputation as all form, no content — can produce any answer the questioner prefers. Thus, the categorical imperative is just a fancy way of *restating* one's moral preferences, not an independent mechanism to *establish* moral truths.

Granted, moralists could take the way I phrased the question, add some qualifications, and generate a contradiction. So what? Without an independent test to determine which way to phrase the question is best, we wage only a feckless war of description. Nothing conclusive follows.

We must, I would think, award the decision to the cansecos. Kant's categorical imperative works only where a solid moral consensus is in place and where conscientious posers of the question would agree on its proper formulation. Accordingly, the categorical imperative works best where it is needed least.

The Slippery Slope Argument: if we permit PEDs, where do we draw the line?

Moralists. If we permit PEDs we begin a journey down a dangerous road. More and more use of artificial substances and technologic aids would have to be allowed under the same rationale. Bionic implants, artificial bones and organs — the Six Million Dollar Man could come to fruition.[22] Allowing PEDs starts our slide down a slippery slope to the depths of degradation: a synthetic humanoid masquerading as an athlete.

Cansecos. On the contrary, *banning* PEDs begins our journey down the slippery slope of banning other products, equipment, or foodstuffs. Cigarettes, consumption of alcohol, deep fried foods, sports such as sky diving, mountain climbing and professional boxing, and a host of other things are dangerous to consumers or users. Should we ban them all? For every slippery slope fear moralists can raise about permitting PEDs, cansecos can raise a slippery slope fear about banning PEDs. At best, we have a stalemate, an argumentative push.

Slippery slope arguments are almost always a mug's game. We draw the line — we stop our slide down the slope — where we judge appropriate. Because society judges heroin to be too dangerous to be available it hardly follows that cheeseburgers must eventually be outlawed. We arrive at tests to determine which products should and should not be freely available to consumers: What is the probability of harm should people consume X? What is the severity of that harm? What is the immediacy of the harm if people consume X? Is there a direct link between harm and the consumption of X? What benefits will people enjoy from consuming X? What amount of freedom will be restricted if we prohibit the consumption of X? Does the consumption of X bear any health or medical benefits? Is it practicable and feasible to prohibit the consumption of X?

Neither banning nor permitting use of PEDs greases our slide down a terrifying slippery slope. The parade of horrors trotted out by moralists and cansecos, when it suits their respective agendas, marches to a tinny beat.

The Argument from the Prisoners' Dilemma: PEDs should be banned so all competitors arrive at the best situation of choice.

Moralists. The prisoners' dilemma is a well known philosophical puzzle with applications to game theory and the context of free choice. When applied to athletes considering whether to inject PEDs, it illustrates how society and sports officials are justified in banning PEDs.[23]

Suppose two competing athletes, call them Russo and Rossi, must decide whether to use PEDs. Here are the possible results of their choices:

S1: Russo uses PEDs, Rossi does not. *Result*: Russo gets a competitive advantage and bears health risks. Rossi suffers a competitive detriment, but bears no health risk.

S2: Rossi uses PEDs, Russo does not. *Result*: Rossi gets a competitive advantage and bears health risks. Russo suffers a competitive detriment, but bears no health risk.

S3: Both Russo and Rossi use PEDs. *Result:* Neither Russo nor Rossi gain a competitive edge, both bear health risks.

S4: Neither Russo nor Rossi use PEDs: *Result:* Neither Russo nor Rossi gain a competitive edge, nor do they bear health risks.

Although I have restricted the universe of discourse to two competing athletes, the same analysis applies to larger contexts. The best situation for athletes, taken as a whole, is **S4:** players neither gain a competitive edge nor incur health risks. But athletes who are antecedently unwillingly to use PEDs and unaware of how others will choose, will not want to risk competitive disadvantage. As a result, both Russo and Rossi will end up using PEDs and end up in **S3,** the worst possible scenario: Neither player gains a competitive advantage, both incur new health risks. In the larger context, most athletes will choose to inject PEDs and end up, collectively, in **S3.** By enforcing a ban on PEDs, society and sports officials ensure that all competitors end up in the best position, **S4.** To ensure that sports protect athletes from unnecessary risks and maximize competitive equality, they should ban PEDs and enforce the prohibition rigorously.

Cansecos. The prisoners' dilemma looks like a variation of the moralists' earlier claim that consumption of PEDs subtly coerces the choices of athletes who do not want to inject PEDs, but do so to remain competitive with users. The prisoners' dilemma, though, requires independent arguments to sustain its main assumption: that if everyone uses PEDs, everyone is worse off than if no one uses them. The independent arguments available are precisely the previous litany we have examined and deemed problematic.[24] Absent an independent argument to ground its main assumption, the argument from prisoners' dilemma begs the question — it assumes what it purports to be proving.

The argument from the prisoners' dilemma centers on the common good: taking an objective, all-encompassing perspective, what is the best result for competitors, taken as a whole? This approach is especially attractive to sports commissioners and societal reformers who aspire to advance collective benefit. Cansecos are correct in rejoining that an independent argument is required to ground moralists' main assumption — that if everyone uses PEDs, everyone is worse off than if no one uses them. Cansecos are also correct in thinking that the main candidates for that argument are those previously discussed. But cansecos conclude that because the arguments previously analyzed were problematic — they could not conclusively establish that PEDs should be banned — they are irrelevant. I would submit that several of those arguments bear differing weights that should affect our decision making, even if none of them can decisively prove that injecting PEDs must be banned. In life we rarely make decisions from a condition of proof or certainty. Typically, we pursue the action that is supported by the best reasons, even if no single reason constitutes a proof. To stigmatize a reason as problematic is to undermine its capability to establish a proof. But such a reason may well retain enough currency to be useful in discovering what alternative is supported by the best evidence. I'll return to this theme when I advance my own argument against consumption of PEDs.

The Argument from Proper Regulation of the Game: PEDs should be banned because otherwise they upset the structure of athletics.

Moralists. Many prohibitions are permissible in baseball and other sports.[25] For example, a hitter cannot use a bat with a three-inch circumference, a team cannot use an especially tightly-wound baseball while it bats or an especially loosely-wound baseball when it is pitching, an outfielder cannot use a 15-inch mitt, a shortstop cannot play his position while wearing a football helmet, and the like. If players screamed about infringements of their individual autonomy and freedom of choice when, say, their 3-inch circumference bat was removed from play, they would warrant laughter. Games have rules and to participate in the games is to submit to their rules. As in life generally, once players commit to participating they agree to abide by the rules and waive complete freedom to do what they prefer.

Why are such prohibitions put into place? Primarily because sports are structured in precise ways to achieve specific balances — between offense and defense, between challenges and aids to performers, and between innovation and tradition. All sports are susceptible to alterations, but such changes are made carefully. PEDs endanger the health of users and attract widespread disapproval. For example, in 1998, when Mark McGwire and Sammy Sosa locked horns in their historic home run race, the assault on Roger Maris's record, baseball fans were enthralled. A few years later, when fans were virtually certain that both men had injected PEDs during the season of their derring-do, McGwire and Sosa were considered pariahs. In 2006, McGwire was not even asked to throw out the first ball at a World Series game, even though the St. Louis Cardinals, his team in 1998, hosted three games. As I type, over 60 percent of baseball fans hope Barry Bonds, who has almost certainly used PEDs extensively, does not break Hank Aaron's career home run record.

Current prohibitions on equipment and food supplements do not imperialistically presuppose a timeless, static ideal of sport. Instead a core set of understandings, subject to change, regulate the games. Such regulation is necessary for the structure of sport. Changes, of course, occur. Equipment in golf has improved to a degree that golf courses are also being altered to maintain serious challenges to professionals. Still, not all changes are approved. Golf balls cannot be manufactured beyond particular compression standards, club faces cannot exceed certain specifications. And so it goes.

We should adopt the simpleminded view that just because most people prefer X then X is good or right in some unchangeable, objective fashion. But consensus against use of PEDs suggests that, predominantly, people are concerned with not radically transforming certain balances within baseball. Do hitters benefit more from PEDs than pitchers? Do home runs become too easy to smack? Would widespread use undermine the historical continuity of the sport? Would outcome values become too important? Would the health of players be devalued in deference to enhanced offensive performances?

Advocates of PEDs could continue to make their case. With additional empirical work, maybe we'll discover the dangers of anabolic steroids and HGH have been exaggerated. But just as we require an affirmative showing of relative harmlessness from a new drug prior to approving its prescribed use, we must likewise insist upon such a demonstration for use of PEDs. Our default position is not "anything goes," it is "changes are made cautiously and in the best interests of athletes and their sport." For now, at least, PEDs should be banned in baseball.

Cansecos. New advances in equipment, training, and diet regimens occur all the time, even where they make the activity less demanding. PEDs do not artificially aid athletes. Instead, they permit players to overcome performance inhibitions such as muscle exhaustion and passiveness.[26] The existence of a present consensus — which may well be changing, by the way — is based largely on ignorance and fear. Of course, all games have rules. But we do not advocate changing the constitutive rules of baseball, the standards that make the game what it is. Instead, we petition only that players be permitted to use the latest technique to enhance their performance, should they so choose. As for the balances within sport, those are tinkered with continually. From 1911 to 1914, part of the deadball era, Frank "Home Run" Baker led his league with 11, 10, 12, and 9 taters. Today, such a performance would earn him the sobriquet Frank "Ping Pong" Baker. Pitcher's mounds were raised in the 1960s, lowered thereafter. Bats manufactured from maple trees have supplanted white ash. In the 1930s, hitters prevailed. In the 1960s, pitchers reigned supreme. Using a presumed consensus is just another question — begging way to thwart the autonomy and freedom of ballplayers.

The issue here is one of degree and nuance. Neither moralists nor cansecos insist on one fixed ideal of competition or of sport. The question becomes when are changes appropriate and for what purposes. Inevitably, the nature of the change comes into question and many of the earlier arguments and questions seep in. Should we encourage, by sanctioning, use of substances that enhance athletic performance at the possible expense of performers' health? Which changes in competitive balance are advisable? Who bears the burden of proof? Would widespread use of PEDs upset the balances between offense and defense, between challenges and aids to performers, and between innovation and tradition?

I would think that the answers to two of these questions are clear. From the standpoint of the guardians of baseball, the health of athletes should trump enhancement of performance. Also, the burden of proof must rest with the advocates of change, especially in light of the presumed dangers of PEDs. But how heavy a burden should they bear? Preponderance of evidence (just over 50 percent or more)? Clear and convincing evidence (probably around 75 percent certainty)? Beyond a reasonable doubt (close to a practical certainty)? Typically, each side in a debate tries to saddle the other side with the loathsome burden of proof. The rhetorical benefit occurs when the totality of arguments seems inconclusive — neither side can *prove* its case, in the strict sense. At that point, the interlocutor who was successful in hoisting the burden of proof on the opponent, throws up his hands in victory and prances around the debating ring.

In this case, I would think that the burden of proof ladled on cansecos should be clear and convincing evidence. The pull of tradition, the risks PEDs pose that are external to the game itself, and the reluctance to tinker with what is basically healthy suggest the standard of preponderance of evidence is insufficient, while the criterion of beyond a reasonable doubt belongs only to criminal trials and Nostradamus.

In casting the burden of proof upon cansecos, I mosey out of the closet and self-identify as a moralist.

Belliotti's Argument in Favor of Banning Use of PEDs

1. Stipulate that no single argument raised by moralists can conclusively establish (can prove) that PEDs (particularly anabolic steroids and HGH) should be banned by professional baseball officials.

2. That argument N or reason R cannot *prove* conclusion B does not imply that N and R are *irrelevant* to whether B is warranted.

3. When selecting an alternative in a *forced choice* situation — one where we must choose one or the other alternative — we should act on the alternative supported by the best reasons, even if neither alternative can be conclusively established.

4. The following reasons remain relevant to whether PEDs should be banned and bear differing evidentiary value:

   a. Use of PEDs has a *direct* causal link (L) that results in a *definite probability* (P) of producing physical and mental harms of a *specific severity* (S) to consumers. Use of PEDs values enhanced performance over the health of athletes.

   b. Use of PEDs by some athletes subtly coerces other athletes, who would prefer not to use PEDs, to consume PEDs and incur health risks in order to maintain competitive balance (for example, retain a roster spot, continue as a regular, preserve preeminence).

   c. Use of PEDs distorts the proper balance of outcome values and process values in baseball. That is, it fosters an "end justifies the means," "any means necessary," and "victory über alles" mentality that is out of place even in professional baseball.

   d. Prisoner dilemma consideration: Banning PEDs places competitors, taken as a whole, in the best comparative situation — no one gains a competitive edge, no one bears added health risks.

   e. Widespread use of PEDs upsets the balances that constitute the evolving structure of baseball: offense versus defense, challenges versus aids to performance, innovation versus tradition.

   f. In light of (a) through (e), cansecos should bear a burden of clear and convincing evidence to earn a judgment that use of PEDs should be permitted.

5. The reasons, offered by cansecos, militating most strongly that use of PEDs should be permitted center on individual autonomy and freedom of choice; the increased possibilities for some athletes of attaining wealth, athletic success, and celebrity; and greater opportunities for overcoming performance inhibitions such as passiveness and muscle exhaustion.

6. No other training technique, type of equipment, food supplement, or athletic regimen that is counter-indicated by reasons as numerous and strong as those listed in (4) and supported by the reasons listed in (5) is permitted by professional baseball.

Professional baseball should ban use of PEDs

Athletes who use anabolic steroids and HGH do not consume the trace-versions available in tablet form from drugstores and supermarkets. Or if they do, the tablets are used only to supplement more virulent strains contained in serums that are injected. Most such serums cannot be legally obtained without medical prescriptions. A few cannot be legally obtained even with medical prescriptions. Professional baseball, obviously, cannot decree that consumption of these serums is permitted any more than it can allow heroin, cocaine, and morphine. Baseball cannot ratify what the law prohibits.

Although I assign cansecos a burden of proof of clear and convincing evidence, they would be unable to soar over the bar of preponderance of evidence if and only if the rest of my argument is sound. Notice that I have not included in my argument a host of reasons often levied against PEDs (e.g., the arguments from naturalness, role models, categorical imperative, slippery slope, and fixed ideal of competition). The excluded reasons either embody muted evidentiary value or their power is already reflected more vividly in the other reasons upon which I rely.

Pivotal to my argument is the conviction that ongoing use of PEDs such as anabolic steroids and HGH does have a *direct* causal link (L) of a particular strength, that results in an identifiable probability (P) of producing physical and mental harms of a *specific severity* (S) to consumers. But suppose Jose Canseco is correct: that with proper knowledge, ongoing use of anabolic steroids and HGH not only produces better athletic performances, but also results in no significant health risks? If so, only reason 4(e) would be left standing in my argument, and the burden of proof on cansecos would undoubtedly fall to preponderance of the evidence. In this imagined case, the only issue would seem to center on the balances in the current structure of the game. That is, use of PEDs would fall into the same category as considering whether to allow bats with 3-inch circumferences or whether to lower the pitching mound.

But even this observation must be tempered by the practicality of banning PEDs in the imagined case. If PEDs were medically safe, they would be, like vitamin tablets, generally available to consumers. Enforcing a ban in that situation would be impractical. (That is why I would immediately permit in principle the use of the trace-version PEDs available from local pharmacies and food retailers. They have been deemed relatively safe, but consuming them produces undramatic results. Their widespread use would have no discernible effects on the structural balances of baseball. I say *in principle* because if consumption of trace-version PEDs makes it impossible to detect the more virulent serums in users, or makes it impossible to determine whether positive drug tests were caused by trace-versions or by virulent serums, then endorsing the use of trace-version of PEDs would invite widespread abuse of the dangerous, virulent serums.) In contrast, enforcing a ban on 3-inch circumference bats and the height of pitching mounds is relatively simple. Accordingly, we should recognize that the reasons advanced in favor of banning use of PEDs in baseball depend overwhelmingly on the probability of the severe health risks incurred by consumers. Sometimes, as here, seemingly ornate, turgid philosophical arguments rest unsteadily on empirical assumptions.

Chapter Notes

First Inning

1. John Updike, "Hub Fans Bid Kid Adieu," in David L. Vanderwerken and Spencer K. Wertz, *Sport: Inside Out* (Fort Worth, TX: Texas Christian University Press, 1985), 410.

2. Richard Ben Cramer, *What Do You Think of Ted Williams Now?* (New York: Simon & Schuster, 2002), 4.

3. Albert Camus, *The Myth of Sisyphus*, translated by Justin O'Brien (New York: Vintage Books, 1991); *The Rebel* (New York: Vintage Books, 1956).

4. David Halberstam, *The Teammates* (New York: Hyperion, 2003), 109–110.

5. Updike, "Hub Fans Bid," 401.

6. Camus, *Myth of Sisyphus*, 123.

7. Oriana Fallaci, *A Man* (New York: Simon & Schuster, 1980), 129.

8. Robert C. Solomon, *The Joy of Philosophy* (New York: Oxford University Press, 1999), 117.

9. Camus, *Myth of Sisyphus*, 123.

10. Ken Ravizza and Tom Hanson, *Heads-Up Baseball* (Chicago: Masters Press, 1995), 16–17.

11. Mihaly Csikszentmihalyi, *Flow* (New York: Harper & Row, 1990), 4.

12. Ibid., 74, 4.

13. Ibid., 19.

14. Ibid., 16.

15. Ibid., 53, 54.

16. Kenneth Baum, *The Mental Edge* (New York: Perigee Books, 1999), 95.

17. Steve Knight, *Winning State Baseball* (Portland, OR: Let's Win!, 2004), 58–59.

18. Csikszentmihalyi, *Flow*, 46, 47.

19. Cramer, *What Do You Think*, 51.

20. Ibid., 88–89.

Second Inning

1. Peter Golenbock, *Wild, High, and Tight: The Life and Death of Billy Martin* (New York: St. Martin's Press, 1994), 26.

2. Niccolo Machiavelli, *The Chief Works and Others*, Allan H. Gilbert, ed. and trans. (Durham, NC: Duke University Press, 1989).

3. Golenbock, *Wild, High, and Tight*, 45.

4. Legend: G= games played, AB= at bats, R= runs scored, H= hits, 2B= doubles, 3B= triples, HR= home runs, RBI= runs batted in, BB= bases on balls, SO = strikeouts, BA= batting average, OBP = on-base percentage, and SLG = slugging percentage.

5. Machiavelli, *The Discourses*, Book II, Preface, p. 322.

6. Machiavelli, *The Prince*, Chapter 25.

7. Tom Boswell quoted in "Difference Makers: The Top Five Managers in the Major Leagues Today," sportsillustrated.cnn.com., May 23, 2006.

8. Golenbock, *Wild, High, and Tight*, 179.

9. Bill James, *1982 Baseball Abstract* (New York: Ballantine Books, 1982), 60;

Bill James, *1988 Baseball Abstract* (New York: Ballantine Books, 1988), 94.

10. Golenbock, *Wild, High, and Tight*, 336–338.

11. James, *1982 Baseball Abstract*, 168.

12. Tom Holland, *Rubicon* (New York: Doubleday, 2003), 5.

13. Ibid., 33, 109, 113, 143.

14. Machiavelli, *The Prince*, Chapter 26.

15. Casey Stengel, among other things, managed the New York Yankees from 1949–1960, He was noted for double-talk, confusing verbal locutions that went well beyond paradoxes or riddles.

16. Phil Jackson, Foreword, in Jim Thompson, *The Double-Goal Coach* (New York: HarperCollins, 2003), xiv.

Third Inning

1. Leroy "Satchel" Paige, "His Sayings and Baseball Career Highlights, 1906–1982," http://sports-betting-wagering.com., 2.
2. Paige usually claimed he was born in 1908. Sometimes he said his draft card listed 1906. His mother thought he was born in 1903. Some baseball fans insisted they saw him barnstorming in a year that would make him even older.
3. William Price Fox, *Satchel Paige's America* (Tuscaloosa, AL: University of Alabama Press, 2005), 30.
4. Ibid.
5. Ibid., 27.
6. Edward Gibbon, *The Decline and Fall of the Roman Empire,* vol. 1–3 (New York: Everyman's Library, 1993), 89–90.
7. Marcus Aurelius, "The Meditations," in Moses Hadas, ed., *Essential Works of Stoicism* (New York: Bantam Books, 1960), 3.12.
8. Richard Donovan, "Satch Beards the House of David," *Collier's,* June 6, 1953: 21.
9. Epictetus, *Encheiridion,* translated by W.A. Oldfather (Cambridge, MA: Harvard University Press, 1928), 1.
10. Marcus Aurelius, "Meditations," 1.17.
11. Ibid., 7.9.
12. Georg W.F. Hegel, *The Phenomenology of Mind,* J.B. Bailie, trans. (London: George Allen & Unwin, 1949); *The Philosophy of Right,* T.M. Knox, trans. (Oxford: Clarendon Press, 1942). Hegel (1770–1831) argued that finite objects and beings are transitory manifestations of the Absolute, which is called at various stages and in different dimensions Mind, Reality, Reason, Idea. Unlike the Western God, Hegel's Absolute is not a transcendent reality that stands independent from the world and complete from the beginning. Instead, the Absolute develops through time, as the goal and result of a historical process. The Absolute comes to know itself through the movement of finite reality. Every concrete particular is a moment in the development of the Absolute. Thus, human beings make historical contributions to the life of the Absolute and to Its awareness and freedom. We are necessary for the Absolute to become aware of Itself. Unlike the Western God, the Absolute has no meaning apart from the cosmos.
13. Marcus Aurelius, "Meditations," 4.40.
14. Ibid., 4.14, 4.48, 5.13.
15. Richard Donovan, "The Fabulous Satchel Paige," *Collier's,* June 13, 1953: 45.
16. Fox, *Satchel Paige's,* 93.

17. Ibid., 17, 19.
18. Ibid., 34–35, 64–66.

Fourth Inning

1. Joseph Campbell quoted in Dick Johnson and Glenn Stout, *DiMaggio: An Illustrated Life* (New York: Walker, 1995), xi.
2. Michael Seidel, *Streak* (New York: McGraw-Hill, 1988), 2.
3. Gaeton Fonzi, "Why DiMaggio's My Hero," in Daily News, *Joe DiMaggio: An American Icon* (New York: Sports, 1999), 245.
4. Joe Williams, "DiMaggio Becomes Big Town's Top Sports Figure," in Richard Whittingham, ed., *The DiMaggio Albums,* vol. 2 (New York: G. P. Putnam's Sons, 1989), 561.
5. David Halberstam, *Summer of '49* (New York: Morrow, 1989), 48.
6. Friedrich Nietzsche, *Human, All Too Human,* in Walter Kaufmann, trans., *The Portable Nietzsche* (New York: Viking Press, 1954), sec. 2.
7. Friedrich Nietzsche, *Beyond Good and Evil,* Walter Kaufmann, trans. (New York: Random House, 1966), sec. 4.
8. Steven D. Hales and Robert C. Welshon, "Truth, Paradox, and Nietzschean Perspectivism," *History of Philosophy Quarterly* 11 (1994): 101, 106–107.
9. Ibid., 107.
10. Robin Roth, "Nietzsche's Metaperspectivism," *International Studies in Philosophy* 22 (1990): 66, 70.
11. Friedrich Nietzsche, *The Will to Power* (from unpublished notebooks, 1883–1888), Walter Kaufmann, ed., Walter Kaufmann and R.J. Hollinger, trans. (New York: Random House, 1967), sec. 481.
12. Nietzsche, *Beyond Good and Evil,* sec. 34.
13. Peter Golenbock, "Foreword," in Joe DiMaggio, *Baseball for Everyone* (New York: McGraw-Hill, 2002), vii.
14. David Cataneo, *I Remember Joe DiMaggio* (Nashville, TN: Cumberland House, 2001), 63.
15. Richard Ben Cramer, *Joe DiMaggio: The Hero's Life* (New York: Simon & Schuster, 2000), 248.
16. Cataneo, *I Remember,* 108.
17. Ibid., 51.
18. Jimmy Cannon, "The Yankee Clipper," in New York Post, *The Yankees Century,* Part 2 (New York: NYP Holdings, 2003), 3.
19. Stephen Jay Gould, "The Streak of Streaks," in Johnson and Stout, *DiMaggio,* 130.
20. Ibid., 131, 132, 133, 135.
21. John C. Hoffman, "DiMag Worth 100Gs a Year," in Whittingham, *DiMaggio Albums,* vol. 2, 570–571.

22. Cramer, *Joe DiMaggio*, 308.
23. Nietzsche, *Beyond Good and Evil*, sec. 43.
24. Ibid., sec. 4.
25. Friedrich Nietzsche, "On Truth and Lie in an Extra-Moral Sense," in Kaufmann, *Portable Nietzsche*.
26. Mark Kriegel, "DiMaggio Was Perfect Fit for My Song, Simon says," in Daily News, *An American Icon*, 231.
27. John T. Wilcox, *Truth and Value in Nietzsche* (Washington, DC: University Press of America, 1982), 17–21.
28. Ibid., 38.
29. Ibid., 158.
30. Ibid., 158–159.
31. Ibid., 156–157.
32. Arthur C. Danto, *Nietzsche as Philosopher* (New York: Columbia University Press, 1965), 72; Frederick Copleston, *A History of Philosophy*, vol. 7, pt. 2 (Garden City, NY: Doubleday, 1946–1965), 395.
33. Nietzsche, *Beyond Good and Evil*, sec. 39.
34. Nietzsche, *Will to Power*, sec. 172.
35. Friedrich Nietzsche, *The Gay Science*, Walter Kaufmann, trans. (New York: Random House, 1967), sec. 121.
36. Nietzsche, *Beyond Good and Evil*, sec. 22.
37. Ibid., sec. 43.
38. Friedrich Nietzsche, *Thus Spoke Zarathustra* in Kaufmann, *Portable Nietzsche*, "On the Spirit of Gravity," sec. 2.
39. Nietzsche, *Beyond Good and Evil*, sec. 188.
40. Friedrich Nietzsche, *On the Genealogy of Morals*, Walter Kaufmann, trans. (New York: Random House, 1967), sec. 12.
41. Walter Kaufmann, *Nietzsche: Philosopher, Psychologist, Antichrist*, 4th ed. (Princeton, NJ: Princeton University Press, 1974), 204–205.
42. Gay Talese, *Fame and Obscurity* (New York: World, 1967), 91.
43. Cramer, *Joe DiMaggio*, 104, ix.
44. Raymond Angelo Belliotti, *Happiness Is Overrated* (Lanham, MD: Rowman & Littlefield, 2004), 155–160.

Fifth Inning

1. Aristotle, *Nicomachean Ethics*, trans. by W. D. Ross, revised by J. L. Ackrill and J. O. Urmson (Oxford: Oxford University Press, 1980), 1155a3, 1156a16–1156b23.
2. Ibid., 1166a 1–9.
3. James Click, "Is Joe Torre a Hall of Fame Manager?" in Jonah Keri, ed., *Baseball Between the Numbers* (New York: Basic Books, 2006), 142.
4. Bill James, *1983 Baseball Abstract* (New York: Ballantine Books, 1983), 46–47.
5. "Joe Torre," www.baseballlibrary.com, 3.

6. Joe Torre, *Joe Torre's Ground Rules for Winners* (New York: Hyperion, 1999).
7. Buster Olney, *The Last Night of the Yankee Dynasty* (New York: HarperCollins, 2004), 2.
8. Ibid., 217, 216.
9. Torre, *Ground Rules*, 122.
10. Ibid.
11. Mario Mendoza was a notoriously light-hitting shortstop who played in the major leagues from 1974–1982. During five of those years he hit below .200, finishing with a lifetime batting average of .215. He has been informally honored with the Mendoza line, a phrase that designates a batting average of .200.
12. Torre, *Ground Rules*, 175.
13. Galatians 5:14
14. Matthew 19:19, echoing Lev. 19:18. The parable of the good Samaritan, told in answer to the question, "And who is my neighbor?" (Luke 10:29), implies that the commandment applies to any fellow human being: thus "neighbor" must be construed globally.
15. "Teachings of Mo Tzu," in Yu-lan Fung, *A Short History of Chinese Philosophy* (New York: Macmillan, 1960).
16. Ibid., 92.
17. William Godwin, "Enquiry Concerning Political Justice" (1798), quoted in Don Locke, *A Fantasy of Reason* (London: Routledge, 1980), 168.
18. James Rachels, "Morality, Parents, and Children," in George Graham and Hugh LaFollette, eds., *Person to Person* (Philadelphia: Temple University Press, 1989), 49.
19. Ibid., 46.
20. Ibid., 48.
21. Thomas Donaldson, "Morally Privileged Relationships," *Journal of Value Inquiry* 24 (1990): 4.
22. Rachels, "Morality, Parents, and Children," 54–55.
23. Ibid., 59
24. Ibid., 60.

Sixth Inning

1. William C. Rhoden, *Forty Million Dollar Slaves* (New York: Crown, 2006), 100.
2. Jules Tygiel, *Baseball's Great Experiment* (New York: Oxford University Press, 1997), 16.
3. Rhoden, *Forty Million*, 101–102.
4. Ibid., 113.
5. Tygiel, *Experiment*, 22–23.
6. Ibid., 24
7. Antonio Gramsci, *Selections from the Prison Notebooks*. Edited and translated by Quinton Hoare and Geoffrey Nowell-Smith. (London: Lawrence & Wishart, 1971).

8. Tygiel, *Experiment*, 59, 63.
9. Ibid., 66.
10. Ibid., 138.
11. Ibid., 138–139.
12. Ibid., 182.
13. Ibid., 188.
14. Ibid., 214.
15. Roger Kahn, *The Boys of Summer* (New York: Harper & Row, 1971), 394.
16. Ibid., 396.
17. Tygiel, *Experiment*, 267.
18. Ibid., 268.
19. Ibid., 267–268.
20. Ibid., 191.
21. David Halberstam, *The Fifties* (New York: Villard Books, 1993), 691.
22. Carl Erskine, *What I Learned From Jackie Robinson* (New York: McGraw Hill, 2005), 131.
23. Tygiel, *Experiment*, 348.
24. Rhoden, *Forty Million*, 117, 121, 122, 123, 125.
25. Tygiel, *Experiment*, 348.
26. Ibid., 302.
27. Ibid., 344.

Seventh Inning

1. Peter Golenbock, *Dynasty* (Englewood Cliffs, NJ: Prentice-Hall, 1975), 175.
2. Tony Castro, *Mickey Mantle* (Washington, DC: Brassey's, 2002), 100.
3. Golenbock, *Dynasty*, 182.
4. Thomas Aquinas, *Summa Theologica* in *Fathers of the English Dominican Province* (New York: Benziger, 1947), bks. 1–2.
5. Castro, *Mickey Mantle*, 186.
6. Jim Bouton, *Ball Four* (New York: Dell, 1970), 29.
7. David Halberstam, *October 1964* (New York: Villard Books, 1994), 79–80.
8. Karl Marx, *Karl Marx: Selected Writings*, David McLellan, ed. (Oxford: Oxford University Press, 1977).
9. Sigmund Freud, *The Future of an Illusion*, trans. by James Strachey (New York: W.W. Norton, 1961).
10. Friedrich Nietzsche, *Beyond Good and Evil*, trans. by Walter Kaufmann (New York: Vintage Books, 1966); and *On the Genealogy of Morals*, trans. by Walter Kaufmann and R. J. Hollingdale (New York: Vintage Books, 1967).
11. Castro, *Mickey Mantle*, 259.
12. Ibid., 267.
13. Michael Novak, "The Natural Religion" in David L. Vanderwerken and Spencer K. Wertz, *Sport: Inside Out* (Fort Worth, TX: Texas Christian University Press, 1985), 351–352.
14. Ibid., 353, 354.
15. Ibid., 360, 358, 357.

Eighth Inning

1. William James, *The Will to Believe and Other Essays in Popular Philosophy* (New York: Longmans, Green, 1907), 197–236.
2. John J. McDermott, "William James," in John J. Stuhr, *Classical American Philosophy* (New York: Oxford University Press, 1987), 95–96.
3. Barbara MacKinnon, *American Philosophy* (Albany, NY: SUNY Press, 1985), 217.
4. Ken Leiker, ed., *Jinxed* (New York: Ballantine Books), 79.
5. Ibid., 90.
6. A. Khan, H.A. Warner, and W.A. Brown, "Symptom Reduction and Suicide Risk in Patients Treated with Placebo in Antidepressant Clinical Trials," *Archive of General Psychiatry* 57 (2000): 311–317.
7. Leiker, *Jinxed,* 29.
8. Ibid., 125.
9. Ibid., 66.
10. Ibid., 109.
11. Ibid., 68.
12. Ken Ravizza and Tom Hanson, *Heads-Up Baseball* (Chicago: Masters Press, 1995), 52–53.
13. Ibid., 63.

Ninth Inning

1. Jose Canseco, *Juiced* (New York: HarperCollins, 2005), 42.
2. Ibid., 50, 75, 76.
3. Ibid., 180.
4. Immanuel Kant, *Fundamental Principles of the Metaphysics of Morals*, in *Kant's Critique of Practical Reason and Other Works on the Theory of Ethics*, trans. by Thomas Kingsmill Abbott, 2nd ed. (London: Longmans, Green, 1879) sec. 1.
5. Ibid., sec. 2.
6. Roger Scruton, *Sexual Desire* (New York: Free Press, 1986), 322–323.
7. Ibid., 323–324.
8. Robert L. Simon, "Good Competition and Drug-Enhanced Performance," in William J. Morgan, Klaus V. Meier, and Angela J. Schneider, eds., *Ethics in Sport* (Champaign, IL: Human Kinetics, 2001), 119–120.
9. M. Andrew Holowchak, "Aretism and Pharmacological Erogenic Aids in Sport," in M. Andrew Holowchak, *Philosophy of Sport* (Upper Saddle River, NJ: Prentice Hall, 2002), 312.
10. W. M. Brown, "Paternalism, Drugs, and the Nature of Sports," in William J. Morgan, Klaus V. Meier, and Angela J. Schneider, eds., *Ethics in Sport* (Champaign, Il.: Human Kinetics, 2001), 138–139.

11. Joel Feinberg, *Harm to Self* (New York: Oxford University Press, 1986), 24–25.

12. Simon, "Good Competition," 122–123.

13. W. M. Brown, "As American as Gatorade and Apple Pie: Performance Drugs and Sports," in William J. Morgan, Klaus V. Meier, and Angela J. Schneider, eds., *Ethics in Sport* (Champaign, IL: Human Kinetics, 2001), 144.

14. Ibid., 147–148.

15. Ibid., 147.

16. Ibid., 148.

17. Ibid., 149.

18. Simon, "Good Competition," 125–128.

19. Brown, "Paternalism," 139–140.

20. Holowchak, "Aretism," 315–319; Michael Lavin, "Sports and Drugs: Are the Current Bans Justified?" in William J. Morgan, Klaus V. Meier, and Angela J. Schneider, eds., *Ethics in Sport* (Champaign, IL: Human Kinetics, 2001), 176–179.

21. Brown, "American as Gatorade," 149–152.

22. Ibid., 157–159.

23. Ibid., 162.

24. Ibid., 162–163.

25. Lavin, Sports and Drugs," 175–179.

26. Roger Gardner, "On Performing-Enhancing Substances and the Unfair Advantage Argument," in M. Andrew Holowchak, *Philosophy of Sport* (Upper Saddle River, NJ: Prentice Hall, 2002), 304.

Bibliography

Books

Aquinas, Thomas. *Summa Theologica*, books 1–2. Translated by the Fathers of the English Dominican Province. New York: Benziger, 1947.

Aristotle. *Nicomachean Ethics*. Translated by W. D. Ross, revised by J. L. Ackrill and J. O. Urmson. Oxford: Oxford University Press, 1980.

Aurelius, Marcus, "The Meditations," in Moses Hadas, ed., *Essential Works of Stoicism*. New York: Bantam Books, 1960.

Baum, Kenneth. *The Mental Edge*. New York: Berkley, 1999.

Belliotti, Raymond Angelo. *Good Sex*. Lawrence: University Press of Kansas, 1993.

_____. *Happiness Is Overrated*. Lanham, MD: Rowman & Littlefield, 2004.

_____. *Justifying Law*. Philadelphia: Temple University Press, 1992.

_____. *The Philosophy of Baseball: How to Play the Game of Life*. Lewiston, NY: Edwin Mellen Press, 2006.

_____. *Seeking Identity*. Lawrence: University Press of Kansas, 1995.

_____. *Stalking Nietzsche*. Westport, CT: Greenwood Press, 1998.

_____. *What Is the Meaning of Human Life?* Amsterdam, Netherlands: Editions Rodopi, 2001.

Bottomore, Tom, ed. *A Dictionary of Marxist Thought*. Cambridge, MA: Harvard University Press, 1983.

Bouton, Jim. *Ball Four*. New York: Dell, 1970.

Camus, Albert. *The Myth of Sisyphus*. Translated by Justin O'Brien. New York: Vintage Books, 1991.

_____. *The Rebel*. New York: Vintage Books, 1956.

Canseco, Jose. *Juiced*. New York: HarperCollins, 2005.

Castro, Tony. *Mickey Mantle*. Washington, DC: Brassey's, 2002.

Cataneo, David. *I Remember Joe DiMaggio*. Nashville: Cumberland House, 2001.

Copleston, Frederick. *A History of Philosophy*. Vol. 7, pt. 2. Garden City, NY: Doubleday, 1946–1965.

Cramer, Richard Ben. *Joe DiMaggio: The Hero's Life*. New York: Simon & Schuster, 2000.

_____. *What Do You Think of Ted Williams Now?* New York: Simon & Schuster, 2002.

Csikszentmihalyi, Mihaly. *Flow*. New York: Harper & Row, 1990.

Daily News. *Joe DiMaggio: An American Icon*. New York: Sports, 1999.

Danto, Arthur C. *Nietzsche as Philosopher.* New York: Columbia University Press, 1965.

DiMaggio, Joe. *Baseball for Everyone.* New York: McGraw-Hill, 2002.

Diogenes Laertius. *Lives of the Eminent Philosophers.* Translated by R. D. Hicks. Cambridge, MA: Harvard University Press, 1931.

Epictetus. *The Discourses as Reported by Arrian, the Manual, and Fragments.* Translated by W.A. Oldfather. Cambridge, MA: Harvard University Press, 1961.

_____. *Encheiridion.* Translated by W.A. Oldfather. Cambridge, MA: Harvard University Press, 1928.

Erskine, Carl. *What I Learned From Jackie Robinson.* New York: McGraw-Hill, 2005.

Fallaci, Oriana. *A Man.* New York. Simon & Schuster, 1980.

Feinberg, Joel. *Harm to Self.* New York. Oxford University Press, 1986.

Fermia, Joseph. *Gramsci's Political Thought.* Oxford: Clarendon Press, 1981.

Fox, William Price. *Satchel Paige's America.* Tuscaloosa: University of Alabama Press, 2005.

Frankl, Viktor E. *Man's Search For Meaning.* New York: Simon & Schuster, 1959.

Freud, Sigmund. *The Future of an Illusion.* Translated by James Strachey. New York: W.W. Norton, 1961.

Fung, Yu-lan. *A Short History of Chinese Philosophy.* New York: Macmillan, 1960.

Gibbon, Edward. *The Decline and Fall of the Roman Empire.* Vols. 1–3. New York: Everyman's Library, 1993.

Golenbock, Peter. *Dynasty.* Englewood Cliffs, NJ: Prentice-Hall, 1975.

_____. *Wild, High, and Tight: The Life and Death of Billy Martin.* New York: St. Martin's Press, 1994.

Graham, George, and Hugh LaFollette, eds. *Person to Person.* Philadelphia: Temple University Press, 1989.

Gramsci, Antonio. *Selections from the Prison Notebooks.* Edited and translated by Quinton Hoare and Geoffrey Nowell-Smith. London: Lawrence & Wishart, 1971.

Halberstam, David. *The Fifties.* New York: Villard Books, 1993.

_____. *October 1964.* New York: Villard Books, 1994.

_____. *Summer of '49.* New York: William Morrow, 1989.

_____. *The Teammates.* New York: Hyperion, 2003.

Hegel, Georg W. F. *The Phenomenology of Mind.* Translated by J. B. Baillie. New York: Harper & Row, 1967.

Holland, Tom. *Rubicon.* New York: Doubleday, 2003.

Holowchak, M. Andrew, ed. *Philosophy of Sport.* Upper Saddle River, NJ: Prentice Hall, 2002.

James, Bill. *1982 Baseball Abstract.* New York: Ballantine Books, 1982.

_____. *1983 Baseball Abstract* New York: Ballantine Books, 1983.

_____. *1988 Baseball Abstract.* New York: Ballantine Books, 1988.

James, William. *The Will to Believe and Other Essays in Popular Philosophy.* New York: Longmans, Green, 1907.

Jaspers, Karl. *Nietzsche: An Introduction to the Understanding of His Philosophical Activity.* Translated by Charles F. Wallraff and Fredrick J. Schmitz. Tucson: University of Arizona Press, 1965.

Johnson, Dick, and Glenn Stout, eds. *DiMaggio: An Illustrated Life.* New York: Walker, 1995.

Kahn, Roger. *The Boys of Summer.* New York: Harper & Row, 1971.

Kant, Immanuel. *Fundamental Principles of the Metaphysic of Morals in Kant's Critique of Practical Reason and Other Works on the Theory of Ethics.* Translated by Thomas Kingsmill Abbott. London: Longmans, Green, 1879.

Kaufmann, Walter. *Nietzsche: Philosopher, Psychologist, Antichrist.* 4th ed. Princeton, NJ: Princeton University Press, 1974.

Keri, Jonah, ed. *Baseball Between the Numbers.* New York: Basic Books, 2006.

Knight, Steve. *Winning State Baseball.* Portland, OR: Let's Win!, 2004.

Leiker, Ken, ed. *Jinxed.* New York: Ballantine Books.

Lewis, Michael. *Moneyball.* New York: W.W. Norton, 2003.

Locke, Don. *A Fantasy of Reason.* London: Routledge, 1980.

Machiavelli, Niccolò. *The Chief Works and Others.* Edited and translated by Allan H. Gilbert. Durham, NC: Duke University Press, 1989.

_____. *The Prince and Selected Discourses.* Edited and translated by Daniel Donno. New York: Bantam Books, 1966.

MacKinnon, Barbara, ed. *American Philosophy.* Albany, NY: SUNY Press, 1985.

Marx, Karl. *Selected Writings.* Edited by David McLellan. Oxford: Oxford University Press, 1977.

Matson, Wallace I. *A New History of Philosophy,* Volume I. New York: Harcourt Brace Jovanovich, 1987.

Morgan, William, and Klaus V. Meier. *Philosophic Inquiry in Sport.* Champaign, IL: Human Kinetics, 1988.

_____, _____, and Angela Schneider, eds. *Ethics in Sport.* Champaign, IL: Human Kinetics, 2001.

New York Post. *The Yankees Century.* Part 2. New York: NYP Holdings, 2003.

Nietzsche, Friedrich. *Beyond Good and Evil.* Translated by Walter Kaufmann. New York: Vintage Books, 1966.

_____. *Ecce Homo.* Translated by Walter Kaufmann and R.J. Hollingdale. New York: Random House, 1967.

_____. *Thus Spoke Zarathustra.* Translated by Walter Kaufmann in *The Portable Nietzsche.* New York: Viking Press, 1954.

_____. *The Will to Power* (from unpublished notebooks from 1883 to 1888). Translated by Walter Kaufmann and R. J. Hollingdale, edited by Walter Kaufmann. New York: Random House, 1967.

Olney, Buster. *The Last Night of the Yankee Dynasty.* New York: HarperCollins, 2004.

Ravizza, Tom, and Tom Hanson. *Heads-Up Baseball.* Chicago: Masters Press, 1995.

Rhoden, William C. *Forty Million Dollar Slaves.* New York: Crown, 2006.

Schopenhauer, Arthur. *The World as Will and Idea.* Translated by R. B. Haldane and J. Kemp. London: Routledge & Kegan Paul, 1948.

Scruton, Roger. *Sexual Desire.* New York: Free Press, 1986.

Seidel, Michael. *Streak.* New York: McGraw-Hill, 1988.

Shakespeare, William. "Macbeth." In *Complete Works of Shakespeare.* Edited by Stanley Wells and Gary Taylor. Oxford: Oxford University Press, 1988.

Solomon, Robert C. *The Joy of Philosophy.* New York: Oxford University Press, 1999.

_____. *Living with Nietzsche.* New York: Oxford University Press, 2003.

_____, and Kathleen Higgins. *What Nietzsche Really Said.* New York: Schocken, 2001.

Stuhr, John J., ed., *Classical American Philosophy.* New York: Oxford University Press, 1987.

Talese, Gay. *Fame and Obscurity.* New York: World, 1967.

Thompson, Jim. *The Double-Goal Coach.* New York: HarperCollins, 2003.

Torre, Joe. *Joe Torre's Ground Rules for Winners.* New York: Hyperion, 1999.

Tygiel, Jules. *Baseball's Great Experiment.* New York: Oxford University Press, 1997.

Vanderwerken, David L., and Spencer K. Wertz, eds. *Sport: Inside Out.* Fort Worth, TX: Texas Christian University Press, 1985.

Viroli, Maurizio. *Machiavelli.* New York: Oxford University Press, 1998.

Whittingham, Richard, ed. *TheDiMaggio Albums.* Vol. 2. New York: G. P. Putnam's Sons, 1989.

Wilcox, John T. *Truth and Value in Nietzsche*. Washington, DC: University Press of America, 1982.

Articles

"Difference Makers: The Top Five Managers in the Major Leagues Today." sportsillustrated.cnn.com, May 23, 2006.

Donaldson, Thomas. "Morally Privileged Relationships." *Journal of Value Inquiry* 24 (1990).

Donovan, Richard. "The Fabulous Satchel Paige." *Collier's*, June 13, 1953.

Hales, Steven D., and Robert C. Welshon. "Truth, Paradox, and Nietzschean Perspectivism." *History of Philosophy Quarterly* 11 (1994).

_____."Satch Beards The House of David." *Collier's*, June 6, 1953.

"Joe Torre." *www.baseballlibrary.com*.

Khan, A., H.A. Warner, and W.A. Brown. "Symptom Reduction and Suicide Risk in Patients Treated with Placebo in Antidepressant Clinical Trials." *Archive of General Psychiatry* 57 (2000).

Paige, Leroy "Satchel." "His Sayings and Baseball Career Highlights, 1906–1982." *http://sports-betting-wagering.com*.

Roth, Robin. "Nietzsche's Metaperspectivism." *International Studies in Philosophy* 22 (1990).

Index